Shalom IN THE Home

Rabbi Shmuley Boteach

For you, Mom.
You are my hero. I pray that I may sacrifice as much on behalf of others
as you have, and that I might one day have the kindness of your heart.

And to Ronnie Krensel, my soul-friend and the man who gave every
particle of his being to make this series happen.

And to Debbie Myers, the matriarch of our show and a woman of
sublime dignity and wisdom, who gave our show depth.

Meredith Books
1716 Locust Street
Des Moines, Iowa 50309–3023
meredithbooks.com

Printed in the United States of America.

First Edition.
Library of Congress Control Number: 2006932662
ISBN: 978-0-696-23507-8

Discovery Book Development Team
David Abraham, General Manager, TLC
Debbie Adler Myers, Vice President Production, Discovery US Networks
Carol LeBlanc, Vice President, Licensing
Elizabeth Bakacs, Vice President, Creative Services
Caitlin Erb, Licensing Specialist

Illustrations on pages 14, 34, 98, 128, 150, 182, 234, 256 based on photography © Getty Images.
Illustrations on pages 14, 98, 206 based on photography © Veer Inc.

Table of Contents

Introduction   6

Chapter 1
Choosing Life The Morgan Family   14

Chapter 2
Adultery and the Crisis of the American Male The Romero Family   34

Chapter 3
Parenting Out of Fear The Maxwell Family   66

Chapter 4
Dysfunction as a Family Heirloom The Lubner Family   98

Chapter 5
The Passionless, Platonic American Marriage The Wexler Family   128

Chapter 6
Changing for Our Children The DiJoseph Family   150

Chapter 7
The Parents Against the Kids The Herron Family   182

Chapter 8
Bringing Passion Back to the Home The Warren Family   206

Chapter 9
Sharing the Burden The Gordon Family   234

Chapter 10
Achieving Self-Worth Through Our Children The Sterling Family   256

Conclusion   280

Shalom in the home, domestic tranquility, is the ultimate blessing.

Be of the disciples of Aaron, one who loves peace and pursues peace, who loves all humanity and brings them closer to God.

Mishna, Ethics of Our Fathers

Introduction

My parents divorced when I was a boy of eight. My father remained in Los Angeles while my mother moved us to Miami. Consequently, I spent a considerable amount of time on airplanes, traveling between one parent and the other. Other kids in my situation read magazines or played handheld video games while waiting in the airport; I spent hours watching families sitting together, trying to discern what elemental difference separated those couples who smiled and laughed with one another from those who, like mine, had been torn apart. What, I wondered, was the secret that kept a husband and wife together happily under the same roof for the duration of their lives?

From those long hours of thinking, my vision of myself was born. I saw myself as an adult who visited homes, rescuing marriages that could still be saved—the way my parents' marriage tragically could not. I saw myself helping children who had been hurt the way I had been hurt. I saw myself bringing together fractured families and giving other families what I most wanted: a peaceful, united, and loving home. I even gave myself a moniker: "The Marriage Missionary," which I later metamorphosed into "The Love Prophet."

Now all these years later, that childhood dream has come true via a blessed television project conceived by TLC television network. I have spent much of the past two years traveling around the United States with a camera crew and a state-of-the-art studio-trailer, living with distressed families to help them find togetherness and peace.

Families apply to be on the show. Once a family is chosen, our production company spends a few days with them, videoing virtually everything they do. I watch an edited version, which enables me to see what problems the family is confronting and how they're managing them.

Then I show up on the family's doorstep and stay with them for about a week. I spend pretty much all my waking hours with them, both in their homes and in interviews with them in the studio-trailer. We also do activities together designed to help the families to see the problems they're experiencing more clearly and to help them to heal.

Shalom in the Home has earned a place in the American heart and home as a program that sincerely aspires to help families in crisis. It addresses the foremost national emergency of our time: the utter disintegration and dispersal of the American family.

I offer each and every one of the families who appeared on the show in our first season my greatest thanks. They are all heroes. Not the heroes that troubadours sing of in marketplaces or to whom minstrels write epic poems. Theirs is not the heroism of the battlefield, bravery that will one day be captured in an equestrian statue or memorialized with a twenty-one gun salute. No, these family members are quiet heroes, unsung heroes, heroes without spotlights. Their bravery consists of being prepared to do what is necessary to heal themselves for the sake of their families—even if that means having their faults and foibles aired before a national audience in their effort to gain direction and inspiration. It takes a tremendous leap of faith to allow a stranger to see your most intimate moments. They did so for the purest of reasons: They wanted to make their families stronger, healthier, and happier.

I can only hope they know that, in addition to whatever help we were able to offer them, they have also done a public service by helping thousands of other families who are struggling with similar issues. As one of the show's viewers wrote me, "I could really relate to every single family you had on the show, and I learned something essential from every single one of them."

The people who appeared on the show—like most of us—are fundamentally good people. Like all of us, they want to do the best thing possible for their children. All they needed, as so many of us do, was a little help to find some shalom. If we have provided that help in some small measure, I am grateful for the opportunity to have done so.

Certainly I have learned more from these families than I can say, and I consider their friendships to be very real gifts. I remain in close contact with many of the families we featured in the first season of *Shalom in the Home*. They come to Friday night Sabbath meals in my home, they come to our family's celebrations, and many continue to approach me for advice about dealing with the trials and tribulations of family life.

The Importance of Peace

The ancient rabbis say that when God created the world in six days, it still lacked the most important ingredient of all: peace. When He rested on the seventh day from the whirlwind of activity, the world He had created was finally perfect.

A non-Jewish friend once asked me, "How do you say hello in Hebrew?"

"Shalom," I told him.

"And how do you say goodbye?"

"Shalom," I responded again.

He was confused. "How many things does 'shalom' mean? I thought it meant peace, not that it was a greeting or a salutation."

"In Hebrew," I told him, "peace is at the center of all words and all ideas. It surrounds us in our coming and in our going. It must accompany us wherever we go and in whatever we do."

Judaism places an incredible premium on peace, and nowhere is that emphasis stronger than in the home. As you may know, every

Friday night Jewish families light candles. The whole purpose of lighting Sabbath candles, one of the most important and meaningful of all weekly Jewish rituals, is to illuminate the home with warmth and light so that a loving ambience can govern the home on God's holy day.

Our homes are supposed to be a place of comfort rather than conflict, a haven from hostility, and a sanctuary from life's stings. In your spouse, you are meant to find passion rather than pain. Your kids are supposed to see you as a hero, someone whose attention they seek out and bask in, rather than someone they'll do anything to avoid.

Unfortunately, very few Americans feel this way about their homes. Instead of being a place to escape to, our homes have become places to escape from! Fun is something we seek instead over martinis with our friends, or on the golf course—not at the family dinner table.

This disconnect strains our relationships terribly. Our children feel that we don't listen to and don't understand them. We feel ineffectual and overwhelmed. Obviously this leads to a lot of conflict—whether that manifests itself in screaming and slammed doors or in monosyllabic answers to questions. When spending time together isn't restful, we achieve a sort of peace by isolating ourselves from one another. So Dad plays video games and surfs the Internet in his home office; Mom zones out in front of the TV; and the kids sit behind closed doors in their rooms, plugged into their music and sending electronic messages to their friends.

As far as passion is concerned, forget it. Teenagers lack so much stimulation in their home environments that they often can be kept at home only through bribery or threats. As for the parents, their passion is so dead that a platonic relationship is the norm in most American marriages. Indeed, about half of the ten couples in our first season had not had sex within the past year.

As Americans, we have all the trappings of "the good life"—and yet we lack the most important ingredient of all. Our prosperity, our military dominance, and our technologies and cultural advancements have not brought us the most valuable blessing of all: peace. After all, what good is a beautifully appointed home if it is not also filled with love and harmony? What good is a marriage if we bicker constantly?

What's the point of having children if every interaction with them is tainted by sullenness or shouting? Why do we bother having a family at all if we're all just going to slink off to plug into our various devices in order to avoid the pain of interacting?

This lack of shalom in our homes doesn't just ruin our own lives; it ripples out and reverberates throughout our culture. Unstable families are an unstable foundation upon which to base a society. When our homes are fraught with conflict—or worse, reduced to a series of linked isolation pods—we get none of the essential respite we need to rest and repair our battered spirits. And we bring that unrest back out with us into the world.

The great Oxford historian Arnold Toynbee showed, in his monumental *A Study of History,* that great civilizations are never defeated from the outside. Rather they decline from the inside. I find it amazing, in this uncertain age of terrorism and endless conflict, that we still cannot see that children who are raised in an environment of belligerence go out and create a world filled with fighting. It is children who never see peace at home who grow up and fill the world with endless violence and war. You cannot have a peaceful world without having peaceful families. The lion and the kid will not lie down together until husbands and wives first learn how to live together peaceably. The wolf will not dwell peacefully with the lamb until parents and children learn to sheathe their claws. As long as the American family is strong, America will be strong. But if the American family falls apart, do we really believe that there will be some other tie strong enough to keep us all together?

Shalom in the Home is all about teaching families how to find the fountain of peace from which flows the joy of family life. We have taught parents how to inspire their kids with conversation rather than harangue them with hollering. We have influenced husbands and wives to put down the cudgel and pick up Cupid's arrow. We have taught moms who medicate their ADD and ADHD kids that a far healthier medication is more attention and patience. We have educated children to forgive their parents' mistakes and to try not to judge them in the first place. We have tutored spouses in recapturing erotic desire and in mining the dormant spark of their once-passionate relationship. We have helped husbands and wives to remember why they fell in love in the first stages of their relationships, and we have helped them to remember why they wanted to have kids.

It has been my goal to do all these things without making my guests feel useless or stupid. How, after all, can you convince someone not to rage at their children when you're raging at them for doing it? How can you convince a dad to bring light into his home when you snuff out the flame of his spirit by making him feel like a failure? How can you make a mom inspire her kids when you depress her with an ugly vision of herself?

Instead I have tried to appeal to that which is heroic and noble in every one of us. It is my strongly held belief that people grow best when you help them discover not their underlying ugliness but their previously unheralded greatness. Helping people appreciate all of their neglected blessings gives them the motivation to change their behavior. I have tried to help the families we have worked with to rededicate themselves to building a peace-filled family life—not by humiliating them with their past mistakes but by alerting them to the glory of their future potential. When I had to be frank and candid, as I sometimes did, I spoke those words out of compassion and empathy, in the spirit of the ancient Jewish teaching that "words which emanate from the heart penetrate the heart."

I feel blessed to have had the opportunity to realize a childhood dream in the form of the show, and I feel that the opportunity to write this companion volume is yet another blessing. As you will see, each chapter is dedicated to one of the families we featured on the show. I personally welcomed the opportunity to share more of my own thoughts and feelings about the situations wherein we found ourselves, and I hope that you find these glimpses behind the curtain to be illuminating. But I also feel that this book gives me a unique opportunity to extend the potential helpfulness of the show to the viewers at home.

As the host of *Shalom in the Home,* I was, of course, involved in all that transpired on set and in the field. I was not, however, involved in the editing of the show and what appeared in its final form on the screen. In watching the finished episodes I saw many things I had not necessarily seen before. And what struck me on viewing the episodes again was how universal were so many of the problems we encountered.

Each family was special and unique, and yet all of them were struggling with issues that I have found haunting countless other homes. Issues like adultery, ineffective discipline, overscheduled children, a lack of passion in the home and bedroom, parents and children who feel at war with one another, children who are cold and distant from their parents, parents who are cold and distant from their children, children who have no desire to be with their parents, and parents who say publicly that they almost wish they had never had children.

More than anything else, we witnessed how family dysfunction was becoming an American heirloom, passed down from generation to generation. Angry parents were raising angry children. Moms who yelled raised children who yelled. And parents who fought with one another were bringing up children who fought.

As a father of eight children, I have struggled myself with many of these issues. And although in the show we dealt very specifically with these problems in the context of each individual family, I know that the solutions we proposed can work—and with the same degree of effectiveness—in yours.

Highlighting those universal themes—the root causes behind them, their typical manifestations, and solutions that really work—is the motivation behind this book. But mostly I hope that you take inspiration from these families—from their bravery and candor, and their dedication to making their families as strong and as joyful and as peaceful as they possibly can be. Their examples continue to inspire.

Choosing Life

When Carolyn Morgan first joined me in my studio-trailer outside her home in Orlando, Florida, the first thing that struck me was her tremendous solitude. I had come to expect two parents (some more together than others, of course, but always two) to sit down on the couch opposite me. Carolyn was alone. Unfortunately she was not that way by choice. She had survived a truly terrible tragedy: Her beloved husband, Chad, had been killed six years before on Valentine's Day as he drove them back from a romantic dinner.

By all accounts they had been a storybook couple. The attraction between them had been instant, and their happy marriage had never been happier than when they welcomed their two little girls, Mackensey (now 11 years old) and Megan (now 9 years old). Chad had loved being a parent. "It was like he was born again when he became a dad," Carolyn told me. Indeed, the two of them had spent their Valentine's Day dinner wondering what the future could possibly hold for them since they already had everything they had ever wanted. Even Chad's last act was one of love: As their car spun out of control, Carolyn believes that he turned the wheel so that his side of the car would absorb the impact, thereby saving her life.

It was a devastating story and one that touched the heartstrings of the nation when Carolyn appeared with me on the *Oprah Winfrey Show.* Carolyn had done a tremendous job of rallying after her husband's death. She had successfully taken over the business they had shared and stepped up to raise Megan and Mackensey. After Carolyn appeared on the *Oprah* show, many people who saw her wrote to tell me how touched they were by her heroism.

But Carolyn's energy and competence masked a fundamental truth: She had not gotten over her devastating loss. At her core there was a profoundly deep sadness, and because of the strength of her personality, that sadness had come to permeate every square inch of her home. Most of all it was a significant force in her relationship with the children, one with an increasing impact on their own growth and happiness. And at no time did that sadness gain greater prominence than around Valentine's Day, when the family once again came face-to-face with the heartbreaking anniversary of Chad's death.

The video Carolyn sent to me before the show touched me very deeply. In it she confides that the counseling provided to her by her friends and family and by professional grief counselors has failed. She confesses her deepest fear is that she isn't capable of change but destined to live the rest of her life mired in grief and depression. I couldn't claim to understand her anguish, but I felt tremendous sympathy for her. I felt it was up to me to show this woman that although fate had dealt her the very cruelest of blows—the catastrophic loss of a loved one—there was nonetheless a choice before her. I had to show her that by choosing life, she could take control of her destiny and choose a brighter future for herself and for her daughters.

A Beautiful Prison

At first glance Carolyn's home seemed like one to be envied. She and Chad owned an interior design business, and the stunning home they built together was a reflection of their exquisite taste. But a closer look showed some cracks in the impressive facade. Her daughters had been very young when their father had died, and Carolyn was dedicated to keeping his memory alive for them. To that end she had memorialized him around the house and put considerable effort into making sure that they maintained a relationship with her husband's family. These efforts, as with everything Carolyn did, were admirable. They were also, like everything she did, tinged with melancholy. Of course there's nothing wrong with surrounding yourself with precious memories of a loved one who has passed on, but the pictures that covered the walls and bookshelves in the Morgan home were revealing. While there were pictures of Chad laughing and playing around with the girls, these were small and hidden; instead, a large black-and-white picture of him looking handsome, heroic, and completely unreachable dominated Mackensey's bedroom. (I later discovered it was the picture that had been used at his wake.) It was the picture of a man who haunted, rather than inspired, his family.

The three of them would often curl up to watch poignant home videos of their family life before Chad's death. The conclusion that Carolyn would share with the girls after watching them was always, "There will never be another daddy like Daddy." It was a sentiment of eternal and irrevocable loss. No child ever fully recovers from the early loss of a parent, but some healing can take place—certainly enough to enable that child to go on, later in life, to create a happy and whole home of her own. But Megan and Mackensey were beginning to absorb their mother's melancholy, and I feared that it would permanently affect them. Although the girls seemed remarkably well adjusted despite their tragic loss, they were not happy children. "When Mommy cries about Daddy, we cry too," they told me. I didn't want to see Carolyn jeopardize her daughters' futures—but in order to give them hope—she would have to become a symbol of it herself.

And there was no question that she wasn't yet there. In fact when we set our video cameras up in the Morgans' house, we discovered some disturbing evidence of self-inflicted pain. Carolyn had held onto the sweater that she had been wearing the night Chad was killed, marked with his blood from where he had collapsed in her lap as she cried out for help and waited in desperation for an ambulance. The paramedics had to use force to pry Chad from Carolyn's arms in order to rush him to the hospital. "It's like a trip in my mind," she said about the sweater. "It takes me right back to that moment." It was a truly terrible artifact, steeped in violence and grief.

For me this bloodstained sweater became a very powerful symbol of how Carolyn had become mired in her grief. By keeping the sweater, by taking it out and looking at it, she was forcing herself to relive the worst thing that had ever happened to her—effectively traumatizing herself over and over again. Most telling, she kept it in her memory box—a box that was otherwise filled with happy, romantic memorabilia such as Chad's love letters to her and photographs of their family together. Keeping the sweater there meant that this relic of Chad's violent death became the dominant feature of her memory box, overshadowing all the evidence of her husband's joyful life.

What had happened to Carolyn and her young family was an unspeakable tragedy, pure and simple. A wonderful marriage, a beautiful partnership in business and life, had been cut short by forces completely out of her control. For six years she had allowed that tragedy to dominate her life, with the result that her life now didn't look so much like a life but like a living memorial. And her daughters were growing up in a dead man's shadow; he was a beloved man, and rightfully so, but dead all the same. As Carolyn realized, it was only a matter of time before the lack of light would begin to stunt their growth.

But there was hope. To me it was clear that this vibrant, dynamic, funny, insightful, and beautiful woman was not intended to spend the rest of her life in widow's weeds. And it was even clearer from the stories that Carolyn told me about Chad's generosity of spirit and love for life that he wouldn't have wanted her to remain in mourning. It was time for Carolyn to move on.

Letting Go

But changing was easier said than done.

Over the course of our early conversations, it became very apparent to both of us that Carolyn was very, very afraid. Her current emotional state was extremely painful for her, but she was holding on to it with

Ten percent of life is what happens; the other 90 percent is what you do about it.

white knuckles. Why? She didn't know. I believed that she was afraid to move on because she wasn't sure that it was the right thing to do.

Wasn't moving on a violation of sorts? If she had been the one who died that terrible night, would Chad have moved on, or would he have mourned their lost love for the length of his days? Wasn't that really the correct response? How could a woman claim to love her husband if she could date other men and even marry after he died? Was moving on not proof of the poverty of her love and of a limited and unsustainable commitment?

Carolyn may have understood on an intellectual level that moving on wouldn't mean forgetting about Chad or dishonoring his memory, but she didn't really *believe* it. Living as a tragic figure was Carolyn's way of continuing to honor his memory. Of course she couldn't reconcile that with living a normal, happy life with her children. How, in good conscience, could she be happy after this catastrophic loss? How could she laugh, sing, and goof around with her kids like every other young mother when the man she had loved so much had been so brutally taken from her? Didn't having fun somehow diminish what he had meant to her?

Carolyn wasn't just afraid of offending Chad's memory; she was afraid of offending his family. They had never been entirely enthusiastic about her, and she felt they had blamed her for the accident—for allowing Chad to drive a Corvette and to do so without a seat belt.

Staying single was part of the same strategy—proof, to herself, to Chad's family, and to the girls that she hadn't let go. If Chad was still in her life, however nominally, and still the object of her affections, how could she possibly entertain the idea of allowing another man into her heart and her arms? Remaining single was a way of showing her daughters that their father was irreplaceable.

Carolyn could see that her unhappiness was negatively affecting the girls, but Chad's perfection was her absolution. When she turned to her girls and said, "I don't think we'll ever find another Daddy like that one," what she was really saying was, "I know you want me to move on, to be more happy and less lonely, but I can't—there's nothing to move on *to*." What she was really doing was sending them a message of hopelessness.

I also think that Carolyn felt that letting go of Chad would leave her *even more bereft*. Grieving for her husband was her way of keeping a little piece of him in her life. Like that bloodstained sweater, it was a sad and unsatisfying piece, but it was a piece nonetheless. Carolyn had made her life a monument to Chad's loss—she filled the void he had left with her memorialization and with her loneliness. But she was trying to fill a void with another empty space, impossible by definition. This was the existential conundrum of Carolyn's existence. She owed it, both to her children and to herself, to try to rebuild her shattered life.

So we had a lot of work to do.

Bringing Comfort

The Talmud says the Messiah's name will be Menachem, a word that means "the comforter." (It is my first son's name.) The first Messiah's name was Moses, which means "to draw," because his mother drew him from the Nile River. Moses led the Jewish people out of Egypt, but he was not successful in leading them into the promised land. The final Redeemer's name will be "the comforter" because it means not just that he will heal the world but that he will bring us the ability to heal it by ourselves.

Most people think that the way to comfort another person is to be the Moses character—to draw something from our own reserves and give it to the person who is bereft. It is the philanthropist's approach: *You need money? I have money—here's some.* But the only philanthropic efforts that are truly effective are those that cause a fundamental change in the people they are designed to help. It is the old story: If you give a man a fish, you feed him for a day; if you teach a man to fish, you feed him for a lifetime. True comfort doesn't mean simply replacing what has been lost; it means effecting a fundamental change on the bereft, unearthing their own potential to heal themselves.

I wouldn't be able to replace Chad. I couldn't give Carolyn another husband. I could draw from my own reserves, like Moses, by bringing my own family and having fun with her, but that's not a permanent comfort; as soon as we left, whatever comfort we had been able to bring would wear off within hours. The point of *Shalom in the Home* isn't to create a dependency on me or on the show but to teach families how to function even when we're no longer there.

In short, I couldn't give Carolyn anything that she didn't already possess. All I could do was awaken in her the awareness that although she had sustained a terrible loss, all was not lost. For there to be a permanent change—in Carolyn and, indeed, in all of the families we worked with on *Shalom in the Home*—the change would have to come from within.

My mission was to get her to see herself more authentically—as a heroic figure, not a tragic one. And the only way to do that was to remind her of what she had—of what had not been lost. Thankfully, in Carolyn's case that was a great deal. Although Chad was taken from her too soon, she was tremendously lucky to have known love at that order of magnitude at all. As I told her, I counsel couples every single day who would give anything for a single day of a love like the one she and Chad were fortunate enough to share, and nothing could take away her happy memories of the time they spent together. Off camera I told Carolyn the story of David Hatuel, an Israeli whose pregnant wife and four daughters were killed in one of the most vicious terrorist acts in Israel's history. A gunman stopped the car and pressed the muzzle of the gun to her belly, killing the unborn child before wiping out the rest of the family.

I sat with Hatuel a little more than a week after the tragedy, and I asked him, "Don't you hate God?" I will never in my life forget what he told me: "Shmuley, I had twelve years with a woman I really loved. Most men never have that. I loved our daughters and enjoyed every moment I had with them. I am grateful to God for those things. That it didn't last longer is painful to me, but I will always have the memories of our time together." It was amazing to me to hear this man focus on what he had had, not what he had lost.

Chad had left Carolyn with two beautiful daughters, and it was here that I saw the greatest opportunity. In order to take the first step toward putting this traumatic incident behind her, Carolyn had to understand one crucial thing: Chad's memory didn't live on in that blood-soaked sweater in the closet. The memory of his *death* did, and that was nothing to commemorate. Chad's greatest legacy was right in front of us, eating cornflakes at the kitchen table. Carolyn needed to honor Chad's blood as it coursed through the veins of those two beautiful little girls, not the stuff dried into the matted fabric of the sweater upstairs.

There's a moving passage in the Bible where Moses, disappointed but not subdued over his inability to enter the promised land, tells the Israelite nation on the last day of his life, "I have set before you today life and death. And you *must* choose life." We are never meant to choose death; we are only supposed to choose life.

To be sure, sometimes death chooses us, as it had Carolyn, visiting when she least expected it. But even when death chooses us, it does not mean that we should choose it in return. This is a particularly Jewish message; many of our rituals and practices are oriented around separating life from death. Death is all that is cursed; life is all that is blessed and connected to God. Death is a humiliation to man, something to be abhorred.

You can see this repugnance in the face of death in many of the rituals and practices in the Jewish religion. For instance we call God "the living God." We refer to the Torah, our most sacred book, as "the living tree" or "the living spring." And we put a great deal of effort in separating the two. For instance, the idea of a Christian church with a graveyard out back is alien to us; in Judaism, cemeteries are always built outside the city walls. A husband and wife do not have marital relations during her menstrual period or in the seven days afterward, not because we only believe in sex for procreation but because it is not appropriate to celebrate life in that way when the body is incapable of hosting it. The separation of milk and meat is one of our most important dietary laws—milk is the elixir of life, and dead meat its antithesis. A Catholic priest attends to deathbeds; our priests are not allowed anywhere near them.

Choose life, the Jewish religion says—and that choice lies before us as well on a daily basis. Life and death are always set before us. Which will we choose? Will we choose the death of a relationship, in the form of a grudge? Or will we let bygones be bygones, allowing the relationship to flourish? Will we choose material possessions over spiritual succor?

In Carolyn's house there was insufficient separation between life and death. Death, unwelcome though it had been, had been given too much hospitality. It was honored every time Carolyn evoked Chad to her children in saddened tones. It was there in the monumental photographs that filled the house. And it was there in the bloody sweater.

Now she had to put the saddest aspects of Chad's tragic and sudden death to rest by honoring his memory in a more positive way—a celebration of the life he had lived. In this way his two young daughters might live their lives inspired by his memory, not cowed by his loss. And Carolyn herself might be able to choose life instead of living her life in the shadow of his death.

Joy to the Fishes in the Deep Blue Sea

As I have seen over and over again, sometimes the best thing in the world for a family in crisis, no matter how troubled or how deep the conflict or pain, is some good old-fashioned fun. In this case I felt that having fun would be an expression of life for Carolyn and her girls, a break from the dwelling in death they had done for the last six years. I wanted the Morgans to choose life—and so we started out with marine life at Florida's famed water park, SeaWorld.

There were only two stipulations, and the first one was a toughie. "No mentioning Daddy today," I told Carolyn. "You don't have to talk about him all the time; he's in all of your hearts already." The second rule, I hoped, would be a little easier. "Get out there and have some fun!"

Once again I focused my attention on Carolyn, because the girls had been very consistent on this: When their mother was happy, they were happy; when she felt sad, they cried. Indeed at SeaWorld she rose to the challenge admirably, and the children responded in kind. I listened in to their interactions on my headset as she led the children through their (sometimes wet and chilly) adventure, laughing at the expressive sea lions, marveling at enormous turtles, and feeding dolphins. I will tell you: It was amazing to see this family's tremendous capacity for joy expressed.

With Carolyn listening from the sidelines, I spoke candidly with Megan and Mackensey about how they really felt about Mommy moving on. Was Mommy happy today? I asked them. Yes, she was.

Is Mommy always happy? A resounding "no." Would you like Mommy to have someone in her life so that she's not lonely? Far from being alienated or upset by the idea, the girls promptly began enumerating the qualities they were looking for in a new daddy: He likes Mommy, likes us, likes cats but not dogs, and has lots of money to be used primarily to buy toys for Megan.

One thing was very interesting to me. The girls, unlike Carolyn, felt very sure that Chad would be happy to see her with someone who could relieve her loneliness. I had wanted Carolyn to know she had her daughters' benediction, but what she got sounded a bit more like marching orders: "Mommy, this is the time for you to go out and find another guy."

Carolyn described that day as a breakthrough for her, and I think it was: She was beginning to experience some relief from the burden she had been carrying around for six years. Certainly by the end of the day she looked visibly different—younger and more lighthearted than I had seen her yet.

Cleaning House

The next step was a first for me as a rabbi: a spiritual exorcism of the Morgan house. Chad's presence hung over the house, but not in the carefree way it had when he was alive. And the memorializing that found its expression in the solemn, static photographs that stared out from every wall found its furthest extreme in the bloodstained sweater in Carolyn's closet.

In death Chad was haunting the Morgan home. I believed that the family could move forward by making him a living spiritual presence who could inspire them. I wasn't criticizing Carolyn; I just wanted to present her with a different perspective. In 2006 I debated a number of prominent psychics on *Larry King Live*. It wasn't so much that I don't believe in what they do—although I don't. It's the attitude I don't agree with. You see, I don't believe that people end when they die. They are not abandoned by the people who love them; they live on forever in the things they stood for and did while they were on earth. We don't need to communicate with our loved ones through Ouija boards or mediums. I told Carolyn that I wanted us to go through all the rooms of the house to see if we could lighten the mood by changing how Chad was remembered. I made it clear that we weren't getting rid of the memories of their life together but of the grief associated with his death. By going through the house in this manner, I hoped to effect a transformation not just in the home but also in Carolyn's heart: from darkness into light.

And at the end of our conversation, I confronted Carolyn on what I felt would be the most difficult part of our exorcism. I told her that I thought it was time for her to give the sweater she had been wearing the night of the accident a proper burial—to finally put it—and all the dreadful sadness it represented—to rest. Keeping this bloody reminder was an act of self-destruction; there was nothing to be gained from reliving that horrific night! Carolyn had suffered enough—she had suffered *more* than enough. She would never be able to achieve any level of happiness while this symbol of pain was in her life; keeping it in her closet soaked the entire home in tragedy. Burying something precious symbolizes its association with eternity; it becomes part of all that is.

Together we went through the house and removed some of the more somber, solitary photographs of Chad; we pledged to replace them with more intimate, joyful ones. And finally we made our way to that closet. In an act of real courage, Carolyn agreed to bury the sweater under a ruby red grapefruit tree that had been planted by Chad's business associates to honor his memory. At her request I stayed with her for this very emotional moment. It was my hope that with this terrible artifact finally put to rest, the wound that it had reopened so many times could now begin to heal.

....
Widow Seeking Nice Guy . . .

None of us can truly be happy alone; we are meant to share our lives with someone else. "It is not good for man to be alone," God says in the Bible.

I have taken criticism for this position in the past. "I don't need a man," I've had women tell me. They do—but it's not from a position of weakness, as it may appear. Certainly, Carolyn didn't "need" a man to support her—she was doing an admirable job of running her successful business and a hyperefficient household and of raising two beautiful girls on her own. But she did need someone to share her life with.

Real loneliness is feeling that nobody needs your love. Real loneliness is feeling that you have a precious gift to give and there is no one to receive it. We gravitate to one another—to marriage, to families, to friends, even to villages and cities—because it feels good to share. Carolyn didn't "need" a man to take care of her; she needed to be a blessing in someone else's life. And with some of the pain and grief associated with her husband's death behind her, it was now time for this beautiful, energetic woman to begin her search for someone who could be an equal partner in her life.

In one of our first conversations, Carolyn had made an important point—she had said Chad was unique. That was true. He *was* irreplaceable. She would never, ever find another man like him, or have with another man what she had shared with him. But that did not mean that there was no other man out there with something—maybe even something very wonderful—to offer her.

I'm ambivalent about online dating, but I thought it might be perfect for Carolyn because she could do it from the safety of her own home, progressing as slowly or as rapidly as she wanted to. I wanted her to start to think of herself in dating terms again, and I thought that posting a personal ad would send an important signal (mostly to Carolyn!) that she was ready, willing, and able to meet someone. In one of the show's funnier moments, Carolyn doubled back and insisted that I force her into her office where the computer is and toward this next step in her life.

For me, it was a good metaphor not just for Carolyn but for all of the participants on *Shalom in the Home*. This is a risk-taking show, but I feel that we are within our rights to take the risks we do. By getting in touch with the show, by asking for our help, the families we meet with are tacitly asking us to push them out of the rut they find themselves in. Carolyn, for instance, had asked for help because she knew that living mired in grief was unhealthy, and she needed to be shown a way out of the labyrinth. She was ready to put her paralytic grief behind

There is enough uncontrollable pain in life without us unnecessarily adding self-inflicted wounds.

her, but she couldn't do it alone—she needed a gentle, well-meant push in the right direction.

So I pushed her to the computer and we sat together while she filled out an online dating questionnaire. Remarkably the picture that emerged was radically different than the ghost of the woman who had greeted my Airstream trailer a mere week earlier. *Warm?* Check. *Ambitious?* Check. *Extroverted?* Check. *High sexual interest?* Check. *Submissive?* Not so much. *Affectionate?* Check. *Organized?* Off the charts.

If nothing else, putting that personal ad together proved that Carolyn was finally beginning to see herself, not as a widow or the victim of a terrible tragedy, but as she truly is: a beautiful, formidable, confident, competent woman—a woman with a tremendous capacity for laughter and love.

A Day of Celebration

I knew that the biggest challenge for Carolyn was going to be Valentine's Day, the anniversary of Chad's death. The assignment I gave her sounded deceptively simple: I wanted her to find a way to enjoy herself.

I wanted Carolyn to know that she was in control of her life, so I deliberately removed myself from the premises, leaving her to her own formidable devices. *Shalom in the Home* is about independence. Carolyn knew what she had to do—and I hoped I had given her the tools to find the inspiration she needed to get over this hurdle. It was time for her to take over from me.

Before I left I gave her a suggestion. Perhaps instead of using Valentine's Day to remember the most terrible day of her life, she and the children could use the day to commemorate the joy and generosity of Chad's *life*. A person is not just a collection of bones and tissues—not even just a disembodied spirit. More than anything else, a person is the sum total of all the good things he or she did on this earth. Hitler was the sum total of all the evil he did; that's why his name remains a synonym for evil. Mother Teresa was the sum total of all the good she did; that is why her name is synonymous with good. In the Talmud it is noted that the Patriarch Joseph is not said to have "died"—the word used instead is *vayigva*—he was elevated. If he was buried, if his children mourned him, how could he not have died? The Talmud explains: His children had continued to live in his ways, so Jacob continued to live. We are not, as the popular expression goes, what we eat, we are what we *do*.

Chad wasn't just a man who had lived and died. He had been a remarkable man—a warm, loving member not just of his family but of a larger community. He loved animals. He loved his grandparents and loved to visit them. He loved the outdoors and loved to have fun. So I encouraged Carolyn and the girls to use Chad's life as an inspiration in their plans for the day. Their goal was to keep him alive, in a sense, by perpetuating the good things he had loved and valued while he was alive. In so doing, they could finally have a shot at a happy Valentine's Day, the one trumpeted on every foil-covered chocolate box.

The night before the anniversary, the children chose two favorite photographs of their father playing with them or hugging them to replace some of the more forbidding ones we had removed during our "exorcism" of the house. They hung these pictures in special places in their bedrooms, where every day they could see their father loving them and playing with them.

They focused on creating positive memories for other people. They would do good deeds in Chad's name—the things he would have done if he were alive. They observed Chad's love for his grandparents by stopping by a widowed neighbor's house with a valentine bouquet of beautiful flowers. They celebrated his love for animals and fun by taking another neighbor's dog for a romp. They flew a kite in the park and released helium-filled balloons filled with joyful messages to their father commemorating their love and remembrance of him. Finally after six years, this family was able to truly honor Chad's memory by celebrating his life and putting his brutal death to rest.

Life After the Show

The last shot of this episode is one of my favorites: In it, Carolyn does an astonishing backflip on a trampoline in her backyard. I like to think of that backflip as representing the progress that Carolyn made during the taping of this episode. She recognized what is required of her on the road ahead and recognized that taking those baby steps will require a tremendous leap of faith. As she has proven, however, that leap is one that she is more than capable of making with good humor and grace.

Recovering from grief is a long, slow process, but I am pleased to report that in the months since the show aired, Carolyn has indeed achieved some measure of peace. "Happiness comes a lot easier to me," she says. She also reported that she is taking baby steps toward a happier life and that *Shalom in the Home* showed her the value of taking them. And of course, the girls seemed happier too.

Learning to Choose Life

Although I can only pray that none of us will know the kind of tragedy in our lives that Carolyn Morgan has spent the last six years navigating, there are some lessons for all of us to learn from the Morgan family.

The first lesson is how to talk to our children about death. All children need to be reassured about death, specifically the death of their parents. This is obviously more apparent in cases like Megan's and Mackensey's where one parent has died suddenly, but the need is certainly not reserved to children who have lost a parent. In my experience all children experience some real anxiety about this issue at some point in their lives.

In this instance my counsel is specific. A child who asks you if you are going to die is not looking for an actuarial chart—she's looking for comfort; it is your job to provide it. Death is not the norm; life is. When my children ask me if I am going to die, I tell them, "Sorry, but you're stuck with me. I'm not going anywhere. Not now, not ever. I'm going to be here forever to bug you about cleaning your rooms and doing the right thing and eating every last stalk of broccoli on your plates. You're not getting rid of me that easily." If they persist, I continue to dismiss it with, "Why are you worried about this? This is a million years off—after the ice caps melt and the Red Sox, uh—never mind." This is no time for realism. The message to our children must be constant and unchanging: I will always be here to take care of you and to keep you safe.

But that's a lie, you're thinking. It's not! You're actually tapping into a higher truth. Life is eternal, and we do live on, even after death—not in spirit but in action and inspiration. George Washington and Abraham Lincoln are guiding this country right now, just as they did when they were alive. What you feel for your children, what you teach them, and what you mean to them will become a part of them.

But the biggest lesson that we can take from Carolyn Morgan's family is that we must always choose life. For Carolyn, of course, this choice was literal. Death had been forced upon her, and she had to decide whether to make it an honored guest in her home or to move on by honoring the more positive and inspirational aspects of her husband's life. But all of us are faced with the choice between life or death every day of our lives.

We face it in a less literal sense than Carolyn, thank God, but we face it all the same. There are so many deadly emotions—emotions that undermine the life force: selfishness, jealousy, guilt, envy, and spite. When we give in to these emotions instead of rising above them and choosing something more wholesome, we invite death into our hearts.

Let's say you get into an argument with someone you care about. Will you choose the death of that relationship, or even a diminishment of it, by holding a grudge against that person? Or will you choose life by letting bygones be bygones and allowing the relationship to move forward?

We all get paid for the work that we do; will you choose death by squandering your money on a toy or a garment or a gadget that will end up languishing at the back of a closet in a month? Or will you choose life by using that money to bring a smile to the face of someone in need?

Will you choose death by gossiping with a friend about a mutual acquaintance, getting down in the dirt and dissecting her choices with venom? Or will you rise above such behavior and choose life by changing the subject?

Every time we lose our temper with someone, choose unhealthy behavior like overeating or drinking too much, or treat our fellow humans with anything less than the dignity they deserve, we are making the choice to allow death into our hearts and heads and homes.

Letting go is one of the hardest things we have to do in life. Every day I see people who are prevented from seizing the moment they're in because of the grief they have internalized from a trauma in their past. Often it's an unhappy childhood or a painfully severed relationship. What, after all, is an unhappy childhood but forcing a child to grow up too fast? What is a divorce but the premature death of a marriage?

I hope that as you go forward in your own life you can remember that choosing a destructive feeling, like holding a grudge, is just a self-destructive, unsatisfying way of holding on to a little part of what you had, what you were promised, what you lost. Instead, as Carolyn Morgan did, choose to move forward by looking at the blessings you have and celebrating those blessings: Choose life.

Lessons for Life

We must always, *always* choose life—even when death chooses us.

Remember that your life is the sum of what you have done during the time you are given. Make sure that your choices and actions reflect the generosity and exuberance with which you would wish to be remembered.

Joy is one of the most crucial ingredients in a child's life, and making sure that it is present in the home is as important as imparting good values or exercising discipline. Even if something terrible has happened, we must keep joy at the center of our children's lives.

Even when we are parents, we are never *just* parents. We are people too. No one benefits more than our children when we make sure that our own emotional and personal needs are satisfied.

When we remember our loved ones and live by the values they instilled in us, we honor their memories and ensure that they live on forever.

Adultery and the Crisis of the American Male

Adultery is a subject to which I devoted an entire book: *Kosher Adultery*. When adultery strikes, it is catastrophic to a family. Such was the case with a once close-knit and loving Philadelphia family.

Luis Romero was a hardworking truck driver who loved his wife and four children. His wife adored him in turn. They didn't have a lot of money, but they had a lot of happiness, with the kids basking in the intimate family environment.

And then it all changed. Luis made an enormous mistake, a mistake that ripped his family apart when he took a mistress and cheated on Beatriz, his devoted wife of seventeen years. When Beatriz found out about the affair (from her 16-year-old daughter!), she left Luis, choosing to raise their three teenage girls and 7-year-old boy alone.

It was a tall order, and Beatriz quickly found herself overwhelmed. It might have been one thing if the kids had cooperated, but the reverberations of the breakup were still echoing through the family in some very disturbing ways. The Romero kids, especially the girls, brawled viciously all the time. I'll confess that the videos she sent me really shocked me. These young women not only fought verbally, using profane language, they fought physically with their fists. Despite Beatriz's best efforts, this family was rapidly fragmenting. So I drove to Philadelphia to see how I could help.

Is This a House or a Locker Room?

The first thing I noticed about the Romeros was the tremendous pain every one of the family members carried around with them. *Everyone* in this family, without exception, had been hurt by Luis' betrayal and by the subsequent breakup. I was reminded, once again, that the real pain of adultery isn't just in the damage it does to a marriage but to the whole family. Beatriz's heart had been broken, yes— but Luis' kids were also feeling betrayed, lied to, and abandoned. And they were starting to act out.

Everyone was hurt and everyone was *angry*. There was, of course, evidence of this in the fighting. The kids needed absolutely no instigation before turning on one another, and the intensity with which they fought went far beyond ordinary sibling conflict: "I hope you get hit by a f***ing truck. I hope you die." And that was before they went after one another with their fists! Instead of acting like a team, the Romero kids were engaged in civil warfare, beating one another with their hands and verbal abuse.

And then there was the issue of teen sexuality. Janice, the 16-year-old who had first discovered her father's infidelity, had started having sex with her 16-year-old boyfriend, James. Beatriz was not only morally appalled— she had banned dating until the girls were 18—but terrified that Janice would ruin her life by getting pregnant and having to drop out of school. Beatriz herself had gotten pregnant at 18, and she wanted her daughters to have the education and opportunities that she had missed out on.

Beatriz, meanwhile, was so furious with Luis that she couldn't stand to be in the room with him. In fact she no longer permitted him inside the house they had once shared. She would often roll her eyes when he spoke and seemed to go out of her way to show him contempt. Whereas she once saw him as the strong can-do man she had been in love with, she now saw him as a spineless mediocrity who had gone outside their marriage and lied about it. Luis, well aware of his wife's contemptuousness, looked like a dog crawling with his tail tucked between his legs whenever he was around her.

"I haven't forgiven my dad for what he did to my mother," daughter Jasmin said flatly. *Nobody* had—especially Luis, who felt completely demoralized by his own misjudgment. Although he visited with the children, he wasn't an active presence in their lives. He had effectively vacated his position as an authority figure and disciplinarian, as if he had no right to act in that capacity. Racked with shame, Luis seemed loving, yet weak and spineless, even in the presence of his own kids.

I had a great desire to be helpful to the Romeros. They were facing some of the most central ailments of the modern American family, all rolled into one. First, there was the issue of unfaithfulness and its utter destructiveness to marital commitment. Second, there was the issue of the single mother, forced to raise her children on her own after her husband's effective abandonment. Third, in the Romeros I saw an example of the shattered husband, plagued by low self-esteem, who is now forced to piece together the broken shards of his life after his family has moved on without him. And I also saw in this family an opportunity to address the all-too-early sexual expression of teenage girls who have no strong father figure in their lives making them feel special.

The Romeros were a loving family, but there was a big gaping wound right in the center where Luis should have been. These kids, especially the girls, needed a father, which meant two things. Not only would Beatriz have to let him back in, at least enough to fulfill that role—but Luis would have to once again step up to fill it.

But what would the filling of that gap be? Luis as father only, or Luis as a repentant husband who might win back his wife?

The conventional wisdom says that a husband who cheats on his wife is a lying scoundrel who deserves to be dumped. And Luis hadn't just had a fling but a full-blown yearlong affair. I agree that a lying, cheating, swindling husband who is a serial adulterer is best discarded, notwithstanding how painful and harmful the divorce may be. No woman should have to put up with a husband who makes her feel ordinary when the whole purpose of marriage is to be placed at the center of another person's life and to feel special. If Luis was going to hurt Beatriz by repeatedly running around with other women, then it was best to dump the bum.

But what if Luis was not the same man who had cheated on his wife? What if he were a new man? What if he so regretted the pain that he caused his wife that he was prepared to fully repent of it and utterly change his ways so that the new Luis bore no resemblance to the old one? If he could once again become the man whom Beatriz once fell in love with, and transform himself into a reliable and trustworthy gentleman, could the couple get back together again?

Well, that was a big question, and given how badly Beatriz had been hurt by Luis, it seemed unfair to even suggest she take him back. Except for one big thing. It seemed to me—and I knew all along that I could be wrong—that Beatriz still loved Luis. It was evident in the extreme contempt that she showed him, which showed me that he still had the power to hurt her. I have counseled many wives who have written off their husbands after similar indiscretions: When someone truly has moved on, there is a lot of pain but there isn't contempt. It seemed to me that Beatriz went out of her way to show Luis how disgusted she was, almost as a way of getting his attention.

Let me state here that one of the biggest questions I grapple with as a marital counselor is whether it is worthwhile to try to keep a family together and when it is best to simply let them break up. I do not believe that a couple should stay together just for the sake of the children. After all, we may be parents, but we are also people in our own right. A man and a woman deserve to have some happiness of their own in life, and if they are absolutely miserable in their marriage— even if their children are better off within it—they deserve to be let out. Marriage is not a prison cell or a life sentence.

My criterion for keeping a marriage *together* is this and this alone: that the couple still love each other, that they still have some measure of affection, even if it is buried under a mountain of pain. If there is even a small hint of love, then I will work my darnedest to unearth it. And I don't just mean that they still *feel* love for each other, because very often the love is so deeply buried under layers of pain that they may not even be aware that it exists. But sometimes a compassionate outsider can see—as I did with the Romeros—that there is a glowing ember of love under there, one that I can help the couple fan into a healthier blaze. If that ember of love is there, however dim, I believe that the marriage is absolutely worth saving, even if it has had a painful past.

If you love someone, having that person torn away from you for the rest of your life is indescribably painful—even if it's you doing the tearing. The way I see it, life is painful enough; there will always be plenty of things in life to cause us pain. Many of these are out of our control—sudden death, for instance. So why inflict further pain upon ourselves with something that can be avoided? If a couple still has feelings for one another, I would prefer to help them overcome the pain and stay together. It was clear to me that Luis still loved Beatriz and wanted to get back together with her. But did Beatriz still have feelings for Luis? And even if she did, could he be trusted?

Together Again

I met Beatriz and Luis together in the *Shalom in the Home* studio trailer—and they were *not* happy about it. It had been a while since they'd been forced to have any kind of discussion other than the strictly perfunctory, and the tension between them was palpable. But I was hoping it would be a little easier for them to take the gloves off in a neutral location, someplace comfortably outside of the home that they had once shared together.

I began by reviewing the bare bones of their history together: a 17-year marriage blessed with four beautiful kids, followed by Luis' betrayal and the subsequent separation and divorce. I called it a tragedy because I believe it was. I am the child of divorce and have counseled hundreds more like me. When I expressed my own sadness about the end of their marriage, something interesting happened: Both people on the couch across from me began to cry.

Then we watched videotape of the Romero kids interacting with one another. The footage looked like outtakes from a locker room or from a professional wrestling match. Luis was genuinely shocked, as I had been; he'd never seen his girls this way, savagely kicking and hitting each other and screaming, "Shut up. Shut up. You're a f***ing b**ch."

As it is, in our time we face a crisis in womanhood. Rather than witnessing the feminization of men—making them more domesticated and nurturing, we are instead witnessing the masculinization of women—which is making them aggressive and uncompromising. As I have written an entire book on this subject, *Hating Women: America's Hostile Campaign Against the Fairer Sex,* I will not now address the thesis here, save to say that in the Romero children we were witnessing the subversion of their natural femininity in favor of boyish locker-room behavior.

These were exquisite young women, you have to understand, but there was very little soft, nurturing, or graceful about their current behavior. In fact these girls had started to act like unruly high school toughs: foul-mouthed, physically aggressive, and hardened. And although it broke my heart to say it to the good-natured and gentle woman with the beautiful smile who was sitting across from me in the RV, they were learning this behavior from Beatriz.

Not, of course, that she was cursing like a sailor and hitting anyone who disagreed with her. On the contrary, it was immediately evident to me that Beatriz was one of those rare women with dignity in her very DNA. But Beatriz *had* hardened herself. When she was married to Luis, she had allowed herself to be vulnerable, as we all must do when we love and are loved. To fall in love is to expose to the object of love: our soft underbelly. Indeed this is the quintessential posture of love, to extend the extremities away from the torso, thereby exposing our heart and our body. It is the quintessential posture of trust. But Luis had taken terrible advantage of that vulnerability, and Beatriz was damned if she were going to let it happen again. By taking a mistress Luis had put a dagger into Beatriz's heart, and she was thereby transformed from a soft woman who showed her husband affection to a scorned woman who condescended to her man with contempt. And who could blame her? Luis had hurt her, and now Beatriz was going to show the world that she had toughened up.

Your spouse isn't the only victim of your infidelity. When you cheat, you cheat on your kids too.

I didn't blame her for that reaction, but I needed her to understand that her daughters were learning that same lesson at her knee. They were angry too, and they were looking to her to model a way of coping with it. Beatriz rolled her eyes at Luis, and Beatriz's children rolled their eyes at each other. While their expressions may have been a little different, the message was the same: "Don't mess with me, buddy, because I will give as good as I get." The result, of course, was unacceptable—not at all what the gentle, genteel Beatriz wanted for her daughters.

The first thing she had to do to heal her family was to make room again for her husband in her children's lives. No matter what had happened in their marriage, the Romeros still shared a common responsibility for their children. And no matter how rocky the relationship between the two of them might be now, they had to pull together and *parent* together for the sake of their kids. The kids needed to see that Mom and Dad could put their differences aside to present a unified front.

And Beatriz needed Luis there too! My brothers and sisters and I were raised by a single mother, so I know better than most what a woman is capable of doing on behalf of her children. Some of the viewers know my mother from her voice-over introduction to *Shalom in the Home;* what they may not know is what she sacrificed on behalf of her children. After seeing my mother's herculean efforts that put food on the table and still allowed her to be an active parent, I find nothing surprising about a mother who lifts an automobile to save her child. I will be grateful to my mother until my dying day. Even today I am in awe of her, seeing her as a woman of towering dedication and strength. But four kids, especially those as out of control as the Romero kids, were taxing all of Beatriz's resources. She needed Luis there to back her up and support her rules. And, perhaps most urgently, she needed Luis to lay down the law with her daughters' boyfriends.

This may sound old-fashioned, but I do believe that it is the father's job to lay down—and enforce—rules about whom and when and how his daughter can date. Men understand other men better than women do. Men understand men's motives and intentions—especially those concerning women!—better than women do. I have observed that though women are certainly capable of doing it, men tend to be more effective in this role.

I believed that Beatriz wasn't being successful in her role as disciplinarian because she, being a very feminine and nurturing soul, wasn't the right person for it. She preferred to kiss and cuddle her girls, not scream and yell and punish them. Beatriz needed Luis to be hard some of the time so she didn't have to be. The kids needed both a disciplinary and a nurturing presence in their lives to achieve balance.

So the Romeros' first assignment was to sit down together with their kids in order to lay down the law. They had to let their children know that *both of them* thought what was happening was unacceptable, and they were going to work together to put a stop to it.

And it *was* unacceptable. Kids fight—yes, even in a rabbi's house. But there is a humane way to fight and a more brutish way to fight. There are boundaries that you do not cross. You do not tell your little brother that you hope he gets hit by a bus. You do not scream words that would make a merchant mariner blush. You do not hit your sister with your fists or—to my eternal shock and horror—with a broom, as the Romero girls did on one occasion. As parents, Luis and Beatriz had to make this crystal clear: From now on there would be a zero-tolerance policy regarding hitting and screaming. And the Romero kids had to understand that if they crossed the line, they would pay a penalty—a penalty that their parents had agreed upon together beforehand, and one that they would strictly enforce.

A Man in Her Life

I thought Luis was going to crawl out of his skin during the next piece of footage, which showed Janice exchanging a juicy, open-mouthed kiss with her 16-year-old paramour, James. I asked him point-blank, "Luis, is it okay for a guy to have sex with your 16-year-old daughter?"

Sheepishly, he answered in the negative. "It's wrong," he said, which struck me as the mother of all understatements. *It's wrong?* You mean you're not horror-stricken? *It's wrong?* You don't want to grab your rifle and blow the kid away? Come on. This is your daughter, man. Some pimply, hormonal, 16-year-old youth is having sex with your daughter, robbing her of her innocence, leading her astray—and it's just *wrong*? "Wrong" is what you call parking in a handicap spot. "Wrong" is what you say when someone is saying something mean about someone else. But when some teenage boy has his hands all over your daughter—and in front of your 8-year-old son—go grab the rifle! So I'm being facetious. But my blood was boiling—and Janice wasn't even my daughter!

Clearly Beatriz was absolutely disgusted by what she saw. But Luis felt that because of his own transgression he had no right to express shock or moral outrage at his daughter's behavior. He felt that his own moral authority had been completely compromised, as a result of which he would have to accept silver-tongued James' hands crawling all over his daughter.

Of course this was preposterous thinking. Luis' huge mistake should have spurred him to greater action rather than inaction. Rather than saying, "Who am I to condemn my daughter or her boyfriend? They'll just see me as a hypocrite," he should have thought to himself, "I may have ruined my life, but I'm never going to allow my daughter to ruin hers." I set it as one of my goals to get Luis to stand up and be a stronger father—a dad who lays down the law, whatever his own personal shortcomings.

Moreover, once Luis started acting like a father, the situation with Janice would begin to right itself. What had happened in the Romero household was very simple—and unfortunately very typical. Janice needed a man to tell her that she was beautiful and special—every woman does, particularly very young women. But the man who *should* have been filling that role—her father—wasn't around, so she had found a substitute.

The substitute Janice had found was unfortunately a poor one. A 16-year-old needs many things a father can give her and almost nothing a boyfriend can. I am outspoken in my refusal to condone any form of teenage sexual activity. Nor do I believe in teenage dating. You are a child once in your life—childhood is but a brief period, and it should be blissfully free of adult pressures. Why should a child have

Even if you can't live together as husband and wife, you can still parent together as mother and father.

to worry about body image, about degrees of popularity among the opposite sex? Why should children not be allowed to just *be?* Does it make sense that we rob teens of their innate childhood naturalness in favor of artifice and pretense? I am not even speaking about the evils of teen pregnancy and sexually transmitted diseases. But taken as a whole, how can teen sexuality and dating too early be anything other than a distraction from the serious business of growing from being a child into an adult? And how can a child, with the emotions and the emotional maturity of a child, be expected to bear up under the emotional pressures of an adult relationship? A sexual relationship shouldn't be a stepping stone on the path to maturity; it should be its culmination and destination.

Janice, like so many of the young girls in our culture, had no secure source of validation from a man. Her father felt himself to be broken— who was he to give validation to anyone else? And his absence left her, as it leaves so many girls, wide-open targets for a kid like James. It is, tragically, a typical story in today's America. When I was meeting with the Romero girls, they sat before me with skirts that ended just below their backsides and tops that revealed a landscape of bra straps and cleavage. Remember, they were 16- and 14-year-old girls. I asked them what conclusions a man who didn't know them might draw about them simply from the way they dressed. They agreed with me that, given the revealing way that they dressed, men probably thought they had more to offer in the physical department than in the mental or emotional. It all came down to advertising. What goods, what wares were they advertising? Were they saying to men, "I want you to appreciate me for my mind, my personality, and my character," or was it, "Hey, get a load of my breasts and butt"? That wasn't what they really wanted to say—they'd simply never thought about it. They were just doing what everybody else was doing. But in the absence of a father, someone to put his foot down about belly shirts and skintight jeans, sexual availability was the message men were getting about them.

James was, in his own way, a victim here too. He shared with me the considerable dysfunction in his own home. For many young men like James, the "player" is the only model of manhood they have! But

I didn't think history was necessarily doomed to repeat itself, as long as Luis could step up and take a more primary role in his daughter's life—and perhaps even in James'.

Of course the problem was in Luis' own lack of conviction that he had anything to offer. To his mind how could he possibly speak to moral character when he had been so remiss himself? How could he tell his daughter and her boyfriend not to have sex when he had ripped apart his marriage doing exactly the same thing?

I'm always fascinated to find that a fear of hypocrisy is one of the first reasons parents give me for failing to adequately discipline their children. I don't understand why smoking pot in high school would make you feel that you can't talk to your child about drug use—who better than you knows the brain cells you killed, the laziness you succumbed to, and the risks you took? Because of his history, Luis felt that he couldn't counsel or instruct Janice, but I thought the events of the last few years were an object lesson in sexual prudence. There is a big difference between hypocrisy and inconsistency. You're a hypocrite when you say or do something that you don't believe in because of some external agenda—to please others, for instance. Inconsistency means saying something that you *do* believe, even if you don't always practice it. A politician may champion family values while secretly believing that he'd be stupid not to have affairs when so many women want to throw themselves at men with power—that's a hypocrite. He has contempt for the values he's preaching. But another politician may preach family values and sincerely believe in them and may still have an affair. Even though there is no excuse for his shameful and sinful behavior, it doesn't make him a hypocrite— merely inconsistent, like so many of us.

Luis was an adulterer and a cheat. But that did not mean he could not rectify his behavior and become an honorable man—there is always repentance. Second, he was not a hypocrite; he had stumbled out of weakness, succumbing to the cheap thrill and artificial ego boost of feeling desirable to a stranger. No matter what, he was still a father. His past, no matter how sordid, did not absolve him of his obligations in the present. And I thought that by taking a stand for what is true and moral, he could start to get his little girls to once again see him as a hero, because losing the respect of his children had been one of the most terrible casualties of Luis' affair.

Luis could no longer let James do his job for him. He had to make Janice feel special, he had to protect her, and he had to put a stop to any false imitation. His abdication of responsibility came at a terrible price—nothing less than his daughter's honor and future were at stake.

Still in Love?

I have to say that by this point it was clear to me that there was quite a bit of unfinished business between the Romeros. I've sat with a lot of fractured couples, and in the process, I've learned a thing or two about how to tell when a relationship is really over. It was as clear as day to me, as I noted earlier, that there was still a lot of love and deep feeling between the Romeros.

"Leave these people alone!" you might be thinking. "They've gotten closure—a divorce—they've moved on!" But I couldn't see any proof at all that they had moved on. For one thing Beatriz was still racked with grief about Luis' affair. "I was crazy in love with him. He meant the world to me, he and the kids. He shattered that. I didn't want to be by myself; I didn't mess it up. I was happy in my own home. I was happy the way it used to be." It was devastating to see the immediacy and the intensity of her grief.

Luis knew that he had broken Beatriz's heart, and he said he would do anything to put his family back together. To see his family reunited and to earn Beatriz's forgiveness, he said, were the things he wanted more than anything else in the world. But there was a disconnect. When I pressed him, I discovered that he was still periodically speaking with—and seeing!—the woman he had been having the affair with. So although he said that he was willing to do anything, his actions spoke louder, and they said, "I'm not doing much at all."

At that point I really went to town on Luis, and not, as I said to him, because I was judging him, but because I wanted to wake him up. At Luis' core there was a strong man, a passionate man, a moral man. But

When a teenage girl doesn't have a father around to tell her she's beautiful and special, she usually seeks validation elsewhere.

he had become demoralized—he had demoralized himself. And now he was passively letting everything he valued run through his fingers. "You're the father; then *be* a father," I said to him. "You want to be the husband; then *be* a husband." In short it was time for Luis to step up and be the man he could be, and I was going to help.

Some people wrote to me to complain that I had bullied Luis, that I was too harsh. "Okay, he cheated," they said. "But why throw it in his face?"

My thinking was this: If there were any chance of convincing Beatriz to take Luis back—or even just to give him a chance—then I had to show Beatriz that I did not trivialize what Luis had done. In order to get her on board with even the idea of reconciliation, she had to trust me, and in order to gain that trust I had to show her that I understood the magnitude of his offense. I couldn't risk speaking in any way that she might interpret as reflecting a "boys will be boys" attitude. When Luis insinuated that he had had an affair because Beatriz was being cold and ignoring him—an excuse used by so many errant husbands, my response had to be strongly unsympathetic. And to be honest, it didn't require great acting skills on my part, although I did feel very sympathetic to Luis.

Yes, *sympathetic*. Because I felt that Luis was caught in the same snare that captures many American men. It may seem curious to viewers that this turned out to be a show about masculinity. Certainly there was nothing effeminate or girly about Luis—quite the opposite, to be honest. And in fact some might say that it was Luis' "masculinity" that had gotten the whole family into this mess in the first place. But I believe that whatever had compelled Luis to cheat on his wife wasn't masculinity in overdrive but a *crisis* in masculinity. This is symptomatic of a disease that runs throughout our society, attacking the American male.

Although Luis worked hard at a good job, he had felt undervalued. This is not exceptional—many American men reach a stage in their 30s and 40s where they feel as if they're big failures. Their once-high expectations for themselves and their futures have been crushed. They see their friends doing better than they are, and they feel like losers.

Luis drove a truck in a culture that rewards celebrity and excess, not the simple value of working hard to put food on the family's table. Let's face it: Our culture does not celebrate the man who gives up temptation and comes home to his wife; it celebrates the corporate CEO who trades his third or fourth trophy wife in just minutes before the prenup escalator kicks in. Heroism is measured not by our ability to conquer ourselves but by our ability to conquer the world.

So Luis looked around himself and felt like a big zero. And of course his wife couldn't help. Although she was a beautiful woman, it's the old Groucho Marx joke about not wanting to belong to any club that would have someone like you. Beatriz had already chosen him—and he felt like a loser, so what did she know? If you think you're a big nothing, then any woman dumb enough to marry you is a double nothing. It took another woman—outside affirmation, if you will—to make Luis feel special. And that's exactly what happened. Luis went with his friends one night to a bar, feeling like garbage, met a stranger who made him feel desirable, and succumbed to the cheap ego boost that an affair provides. Little did he know that the ego boost was artificial. Not only would it wear off, but when its catastrophic repercussions were felt in the form of losing his wife and children, he would feel, *and become*, a big zero—his worst fear.

Now, Luis may have felt more like a rock star when he was with that other woman, but the reality was precisely the opposite. A truly great—and a truly secure—man does not cheat on his wife. The great man is characterized not by indulgence but by sacrifice. He is known not for his selfishness but for his self*less*ness; not for egomania but dedication and devotion to others. Plenty of men have made money in this world. What's the big deal? A far smaller number have led lives of outstanding moral virtue and devotion to others. *They* are the ones to be celebrated. The man who reads a bedtime story to his children—though no movie will ever be made about it and no picture will appear on the cover of *Time* magazine—is the truly great man.

As a good wife will, Beatriz had seen right through the ruse. She had loved Luis for his commitment to his family and for his melting brown eyes. His work ethic and fidelity were sexy to her—evidence of his masculinity, not his deficiencies. But he had thrown away that commitment to their family, and those handsome eyes now evasively shifted away from hers out of guilt and shame. Their marriage hadn't ended because she had fallen out of love with him; it had ended because she had lost all respect for him.

Now Luis wasn't playing a more active role in the family's life because he didn't feel like he deserved to; he was letting Beatriz chase him away. He fundamentally believed that she was right about his worthlessness. But his failure to take a stand was only compounding her convictions about him. Instead of standing up for himself, he was acting like the spineless worm she had accused him of being. What then was left for her to fall (back) in love with?

Indeed it quickly became apparent to me that Beatriz's primary problem with Luis was not that he had hurt her. Studies show that when a husband cheats, the marriage survives two-thirds of the time. It makes sense to me: If a woman truly loves her husband, then even if he has caused her enormous pain, she will probably seek to get beyond the pain in order not to lose the man she loves. But Luis' affair had done rather more damage than simply inflicting pain; it had made him seem weak in Beatriz's eyes. She could no longer see Luis as the strong, dependable, stalwart man that she once respected. Now he was just a spineless pleasure seeker who put his own interests before that of his wife and kids.

It felt to me like the Romero marriage could be repaired, but Luis had work to do even if getting back together with Beatriz wasn't a possibility. Even if these two were going to lead their separate lives, Luis had to win back Beatriz's respect, the respect of his girls—and, not least, his self-respect.

Short Jews Can't Dunk—Or Can They?

I asked Beatriz to bend her "No Luis in the house" rule so that the whole family could sit down together, but the result wasn't particularly productive. Luis and Beatriz bickered ineffectively about the right way to handle Janice's inappropriate relationship while the kids looked uncomfortable. I was disheartened to see Luis undermining his ex-wife's authority when she was putting her foot down. It's one thing to shirk your responsibility as a father and let your daughter be taken advantage of, but it's quite another to pull the rug out from under your daughter's mother as she puts up a futile battle to save her child from sharks.

So I decided, once again, to get this family onto neutral turf.

I took them to a basketball court at a nearby community center. And I asked them to break up into teams. Not surprisingly, Jasmin and Janice ended up supporting Mom, just as they did in life, while Desiree and J.R., the two younger children, took Dad's side. A pretty heated game of basketball ensued—and was it my imagination, or did Beatriz and Luis almost look like they were having fun?

After the game, I sat with the family on the hardwood, and I told them about my own family's experience with divorce. I shared with the Romero children the only silver lining I have been able to find from that childhood trauma: When my parents split up, my brothers and sisters and I became closer than ever. When I was a boy I dreamed of bringing my parents back together again. When that didn't happen I turned to my brothers and sisters for comfort, and they became, to this very day, my best friends. Only they were there to witness my childhood and the brokenness it entailed. Only they shared the same pain, and only they could truly understand what I had endured.

The same was true for the Romero children. Only they could appreciate what all had undergone together. And once they realized that, they would stop fighting each other and start loving each other. I encouraged them not to waste time in battle but to take refuge in the comfort and strength that they could glean from one another, simply by showing the love they had in their hearts.

You've heard the expression "There's no 'I' in team"? Well, there can't afford to be more than one team in a family. When there is contention between family members, the others have to take sides, and that can do a lot of damage. Let's say, just to give an example, that Dad was a poor math student in school. So now he helps Johnny sneak around behind Mom's no-baseball-until-homework-is-done rule. Innocent enough, right? But it's not. Not only does it severely undermine Mom's ability to discipline Johnny in the future, but it also creates a false bond—a bond based on lying to the one person they both should always honor with the truth—Mom. What kind of basis is that for a relationship?

So it was with the Romeros. I could understand why the older girls were angry on their mother's behalf, and I could understand why the younger kids felt sorry for their father who was now all alone. But we had to break up the cliques in this family. The kids had to see their mother and father working together again—even if it was just to score a couple of points in a pickup game. So when we hit the floor again, I changed the roster: the kids on one team, Mom and Dad on the other. It did all of us good to see Beatriz and Luis working together. And again, the two of them looked like they were having more fun than friction.

Puppy Love?

Teen sexuality is an issue I counsel and write about a great deal. Kids in their young and middle teens having sex should shock us to our core, and it kills me that we are so complacent about it. But all the conversations that parents are encouraged to have with their kids are usually ineffective or even counterproductive. In essence, the sex talk you're encouraged to have with your kids is about them not getting pregnant or contracting a sexually transmitted disease. In short, it's all about fear, and I believe that's why it doesn't work: Fear can never inspire.

The real conversation we should have with our kids is about the dignity of the human person and the magic of love. Our goal should be to make our teenage girls understand that to deliver yourself to someone who hasn't earned you is to fundamentally devalue yourself. A girl who dresses and behaves as if she is bereft of dignity attracts a player. But a girl who carries herself like a lady attracts a gentleman. Likewise, the boy who takes advantage of teen girls, manipulating them into things that are harmful to them and which they will regret, denies himself the gift of honor. We have to give our teenagers a sparkling vision of what they could be and inspire them to fulfill it.

Emotions that aren't demonstrated may as well not even exist. It's not enough to feel love. You have to show it.

With this in mind, I invited the three Romero girls to join me for a conversation in the RV. Although I was concerned about all of them, I wanted to focus on Janice and her relationship with James. She agreed with her sisters that having sex with James had been the wrong thing to do: "I should have waited, like my mom told me to."

But she got a little harder to pin down when I asked her exactly why Beatriz was so down on the relationship. "He has a bad temper, and he yells at his mom," she hedged. Her sisters called her on it immediately. James also yelled at Janice, and instead of standing up for herself and insisting that he stop, she had taken to blaming herself.

When I heard that James yelled at Janice, all the alarm bells went off. A terrible pattern of disrespect toward women was emerging. Luis had disrespected his wife by cheating on her. Then in his absence his daughter sought out affection from a boyfriend who was mistreating her. Those few moments were some of the tensest filming we did in the entire season. As Janice broke down and began to cry, the full tragedy of this family hit me. If we didn't do something, negative patterns would become ingrained in this family for another generation, and who knew how many more generations it would take before it would end.

I told the Romero girls that after getting to know them and living with them for a couple of days, I felt as though I had to protect them like my own daughters. And I told Janice that letting James yell at her indicated a lack of self-respect. Confronting James myself would have negated the point of the exercise: *Janice* was the one who had to lay down the law. So I asked her to sit down with him to let him know that he must not again—ever, for any reason—raise his voice to her or speak to her disrespectfully. And I asked Beatriz down to the RV so that we could watch that conversation together on the monitor, coaching over the headset if need be.

The scene was uncomfortable for all of us to watch. Beatriz's emotions flitted across her face: bemusement at the flirtatious, infatuated teenager her tough-edged daughter could become; love and concern as Janice broke down in tears, unable to really ask James for the respect she wanted and deserved; and then glowering anger as the smooth-talking, "show me that sexy smile" James twisted Janice around his little finger again.

In my eyes James became the living caricature of the teen lothario, silver-tongued and oh-so-smooth. To watch James was to watch a master player at work; at 16 he was already able to manipulate a teen girl like she was a puppet on a string. Guys like this are what teen girls are up against all across the land. When Janice would rebuke him, "Shmuley said that you shouldn't yell at me—ever!" he would respond, "Baby, baby. I don't want to yell at you. It's just that you do things that upset me. You know you shouldn't do those things, baby. I'm yelling at you because you deserve it; behave and I won't have to." A couple more years of this kind of manipulation and Janice might, God forbid, become one of those women who remain in abusive relationships because they have been conditioned to believe that the abuse is their fault.

I should mention that I harbored no animosity toward James; I criticize him as a stereotype, rather than as a specific person. In fact I got along very well with him, had a few long conversations with him, and for several months after the shoot, he sent me greetings through various conduits. When I tried to inspire him to be a gentleman, he listened with intensity and honesty. He shared with me his own broken childhood and past, and it was clear that he had no role model of his own. But for the moment I had to get the Romeros to lay down the law. Yes, Janice's job was to stand up for herself. But she was only 16, and a child needs the guidance and protection of her parents.

"I'm Here Now."

We hadn't had much luck the last time that Luis and Beatriz sat down to discuss the best way to handle Janice and James, so I took matters into my own hands. If the relationship between these children were going to continue, someone—and by someone I meant Luis—had to sit down and have a conversation with James. Before we left the trailer, I impressed upon Luis how important it was for him to act like—and to *be*—an authority figure. James needed to understand that dating Janice now meant dealing with Luis.

I sat Luis down and said to him, "No 16-year-old player is going to have sex with your daughter, because you're the father and you simply won't allow it." Luis nodded his head in full agreement.

And he rose to this occasion as I'd hoped he would. Gone was the ineffectual parent, the guilt-ridden jellyman slinking around with his tail between his legs. In his place was a fierce, no-nonsense father laying down the law in order to protect his daughter. This is not a negotiation, he told James. I'm telling you the way it's going to be. No yelling; you don't make my daughter cry. And no more sex with my daughter. If you really respected her, you would have waited until she was older and you were married. Going forward, you listen to Beatriz: *She* tells you, not Janice, whether or not you can come over. And Beatriz jumped in, telling James that if he wanted to see Janice, he'd have to call and arrange it through her—or Luis.

It was a big step for the whole family. Janice, James, and Beatriz saw a side of Luis that had too long been buried underneath guilt and self-recrimination. Janice's own conversation with James may not have gotten the job done—any more questions about why 16-year-olds shouldn't be conducting adult relationships? But there was no question in my mind that James was going to comport himself differently now that he knew Luis was back in town.

Second Chances

It hadn't slipped my notice that Beatriz included Luis when she was spelling out the future for James. It was a big step forward for someone who, a week ago, hadn't even been letting him into the house they had once shared. That little detail told me something important: When Luis acted like a man—something more than the lying dog she felt nothing but contempt for—Beatriz *treated* him like a man.

I noticed something else: Beatriz always knew where Luis was in a room. When he got up off the couch to leave after their conversation with Janice and James, she noticed—and looked unhappy, as if she'd been able to forget for a short time that they weren't parenting their little girl together.

So that night I sat with Beatriz and asked her some tough questions about her feelings for Luis. She said she was confused. I said that the answer to two questions would unravel her confusion: "First, can you trust him? Second, can you love him again?" She didn't know. I asked her permission to have a conversation about a possible reconciliation with Luis, telling her honestly that she didn't have to make a decision and that she could always reverse any decision she did make. But I made plain what I knew to be true—that Luis was still crazy about her. I asked her simply to agree to keep an open mind.

When I talked to Luis about his feelings for Beatriz, he wept. He loved her, he loved their family, and he wanted everything to go back to the way it had been. He wanted to try to put the pieces of their family life back together, but he was afraid that Beatriz was going to reject him. Of course I could understand his fear: It's terribly painful to be rejected, and Beatriz hadn't exactly been giving him the green light so far. But if risking that rejection was the only way to find out if he could have the thing he wanted more than anything in the whole wide world, wasn't it worth taking that chance?

I told him what I consider to be the secret of life: You can do anything you want to do. He had won her hand once. What would happen if he devoted his best efforts to winning her back? If he were serious, he would have to get rid of the other woman in his life.

Divorce is only a necessity if you can't fix a bad situation. After my conversations with the Romeros, I felt very strongly that their marriage, although legally dead, might be resurrected. Where others— including the Romeros—saw only cold ground and the mulch of the 17 years they'd shared, I saw some fresh green shoots.

But these two were going to need some help if they were going to revive the relationship. Luis was going to have to woo his ex-wife and engage in some good old-fashioned chivalric courtship. I hoped Beatriz would stand by her promise to keep an open mind. If she did, I believed that she would see a brand-new Luis—or rather the Luis she had fallen in love with originally.

I did warn Luis that the going might be tough. His mistake had indeed been a grave one, and any fool could see that Beatriz had *a lot* of anger to burn through before she could get to a better place. I told him that positive feedback from her might be a long time in coming; while, in ordinary circumstances, he might have had the right to expect a word of thanks or a compliment, he might have to labor in obscurity for a while. Furthermore there was absolutely no guarantee that his efforts would pay off in reconciliation. Hopefully they would, but he could not get frustrated and discouraged if success was not immediate.

For the Romeros' next assignment I went searching for a task that would highlight the best in Luis—and I came up with something that directly benefited Luis' ex-wife and his children. The basement in the Romero house looked like Baghdad after "shock and awe." It had been ruined by flooding, and the only things in there were rubble and debris. So their next project, under Luis' direction, would be to remove the debris and waterproof the room so that Beatriz and the kids would have more space in the house.

It was the perfect project for a number of reasons. Not only would it give this big family a little more room to spread out, but it would also showcase the very best of Luis. It would allow Beatriz to see her ex-husband as a competent, decisive man. And it would show her the new leaf he was turning over: one devoted to her happiness without regard for his own. He didn't even *live* in the house anymore, so it was a purely selfless act of devotion.

As they hauled trash and smashed ancient tile, I was left with the tough job of supervising from my studio-trailer with my feet up on the couch, consulting with the various family members via headset. It was pretty exhausting, but I found the strength to encourage Luis to use the project as an opportunity to reconnect with his kids. He did a good job, and the kids were happy. There was no fighting, no screaming, no violence, and no profanity.

At one point I suggested to Luis that he go upstairs and get a cold drink for Beatriz, who was working very hard ripping up some old concrete. I couldn't believe the interaction between the two of them when he got back. First of all she was visibly surprised that he'd thought of her—imagine a wife expressing shock at the simplest of thoughtful gestures. As they drank they were as awkward with one

*Here's the secret of life:
You can do whatever
you want. Our lives
will never be judged
by what we intend to
happen, or even by our
characters—they will be
judged by the choices we
have made. And we are
always free to choose
whatever we wish.*

another as teenagers. They could barely look each other in the eyes, and Luis kept that plastic cup up to his lips like he'd just crossed the Sahara. When I suggested to Beatriz that she warmly thank Luis for the drink, she laughed nervously like a teenager and made a big production out of doing it. It would have been easier for her to thank the guy behind the counter at the corner deli for a soda than it was for her to thank the man who had shared her life for seventeen years.

The awkwardness between them meant that we were starting behind the eight-ball. But there was a silver lining too. More than any other thing, boredom and familiarity are marriage-killers. Beatriz and Luis were—after a sequence of very unfortunate events—new to one another again. They were nervous around each other again, the way they had been when they were first courting. A lot of couples who had long since stopped looking up from their newspapers at breakfast would do anything to regain some of the nervous anticipation and tension that made Luis too antsy to meet his ex-wife's eyes. Hopefully they'd be able to convert some of that tension into fuel for their newly blossoming relationship.

Putting a Family Back Together

Later that night I commandeered a seat in the Romero living room to talk to the kids about their day. "Did you guys have fun today?" I asked. I have a couple of teenage daughters myself, and I have a pretty good idea what that general population would say about a day spent hauling filthy, broken concrete up a set of basement steps. But I also knew that the Romero girls had gotten something out of the day besides chipped nails and sore shoulders, so I wasn't surprised when they told me they'd had fun.

Luis had ruined his family's happiness through his selfishness. But in that debris-filled basement, he had helped his family to take one step toward regaining happiness through his selflessness. And he continued to take steps in that direction after the *Shalom* trailer left the street outside the Romero house. He and Beatriz began dating. For a good few weeks it was very promising. They drew closer, and the embers of love were being stoked. I received reports from members of my crew who visited them that Beatriz was warming to Luis. I was encouraged.

But unfortunately the reconciliation between them petered out, and at some level, I blame myself.

At the end of the show, I asked Luis whom he could talk to—a friend, a priest, a counselor—in order to make sure that he didn't lose forward progress. He said he'd call me. I laughed, but I think I missed a red flag at the root of why we were not ultimately successful with this family.

What went wrong? In this case I created a dependency, not an independency. About all I can do in a week with a family is to go in, use insight to point out the problems, identify the underlying issues that give rise to destructive patterns, impart behavioral and character-based solutions, and motivate them to make the changes. That's probably twenty percent of what I do. The other eighty percent is the inspiration to implement the advice I've given them. The main thing we try to do on *Shalom in the Home* is inspire families with a vision of their own blissful togetherness. To get anyone—my colleagues, my children, the families I work with—to listen to me, I have to take them to the mountaintop, inspiring them to discover their own inner heroes, and thereby impelling them to become the best they can be. People know right from wrong. Deep down they know what they have to do, but most of the time, they simply lack the inspiration to do it.

When I am successful, they begin to see themselves as I see them—as heroes. Within each of us there is a hero. But each of us is a hero of the spirit, a person capable of infinite quantities of love. The change comes from within ourselves, and these people recognize me for what I am: a facilitator. They find other sources of inspiration to get over life's hurdles.

Luis, unfortunately, continued to see me as a magic bullet. While I was there, he could see himself as a hero and he knew what he had to do. I lifted him up above his past, and in the comfort of a new present he was no longer shamed by his actions. But while I could give him a new present, only he could create a new future. But he couldn't summon the fortitude and stamina to keep the ball in the air once I left. Luis needed an alternate source of inspiration, but he did not find it. I wish I could have stayed around to provide it, but he would have to find someone local to fill the function, and he did not—with terrible consequences. I do believe that he could have won Beatriz back. It would have taken a relentless and selfless campaign, and he failed to reach within himself for the inspiration to mount that campaign or for the stamina to sustain it.

Beatriz had a hard time accepting the new old Luis. She found herself angry, dwelling on his past mistakes, unable to respond to his overtures. And when she did not respond quickly enough to Luis' overtures, Luis again became despondent and reached back into his past relationships for comfort. If he had continued being chivalrous, I believe that he would have overcome her coldness. And to a great extent, that cold front she showed him was really a test to discern the sincerity and extent of his commitment. Instead he got angry and became frustrated. When she didn't respond, he stopped making the effort, and when she provoked him, he called his former mistress for a movie date. Nothing happened between them, but for Beatriz, it was the last straw.

I am sorry that we weren't able to effect a complete reconciliation in this family. But I know that we helped the Romeros to *parent* better together, even if it's the only thing they ended up doing together. Luis now sees a great deal more of his children and is a more present father for them. The warfare that used to characterize the Romero children, while not completely a thing of the past, has been greatly diminished.

And the amorous James? Well, he tried to be a gentleman—or so he said—for a brief period, until Janice found out that he had a cyber girlfriend and she summoned the courage to dump James for his duplicity. She had reverted to being a young woman of high standards.

Lessons for Life

Adultery destroys families, not just marriages.

Even when a family has been pulled apart irreconcilably, parents must find common ground so they can continue to parent together.

Fighting between siblings is inevitable, but there is a good way and a bad way to fight. Let your kids know that physical violence and profanity will not be tolerated under any circumstances.

Teenage sexual activity doesn't just expose children to pregnancy or sexually transmitted disease. It robs them of their precious childhood and their innocence.

—※—

Don't be afraid to have unpopular and restrictive rules about your children's interaction with the opposite sex; they'll thank you for it later.

—※—

Lost romance can always be rediscovered because the secret to renewing love lies not in what we feel but in what we do. Actions control and create emotions, rather than the reverse. And if we begin treating people lovingly, we will ultimately begin to feel love for them.

Parenting Out of Fear

Indulged children are a big problem today—and with real consequences. Beyond the problems presented to the child by being spoiled and unruly, it has major repercussions for the family as well. That's primarily why I took a trip to New York City's Chinatown to see if I could help Lynnsue and Craig Maxwell with bedtime for their 3-year-old son, Zachary.

Zachary was the cutest kid imaginable: sweet and handsome, precocious and playful. But boy was he spoiled! Every night the Maxwells had to do full-on battle just to get Zachary down to sleep. This 3-year-old dictated when, where, and even *whether* he went to bed. Without fail he ended up in Mommy and Daddy's room. The unpleasant ritual took several tear-filled hours and ended with all parties collapsing in exhaustion—Zachary in bed with Mom, and Dad on the couch. "Obviously it cuts down on intimacy," Craig said dryly. The adults weren't getting any alone time, and Zachary wasn't getting the sleep he needed to learn and grow. In fact the Maxwells had to drag him out of bed in the morning as if he were a teenager.

I am a well-known opponent of children sleeping in their parents' bed. A couple's bedroom should be Fort Knox. It is a love chamber, a private space—not a family sitting room. The repercussions when married couples have their children sleep with them are nothing short of catastrophic. The parents can never be intimate, and after a while they stop relating to reach other as husband and wife, becoming roommates who happen to have children in common.

This is what was happening with Craig and Lynnsue. Their intimate life had diminished to near nonexistent. Lynnsue put it best when she said that the couple formerly known as Craig and Lynnsue has essentially ceased to exist.

But sleeping issues weren't the only problems I found when I got to the Maxwells' house. This was a dictatorship based on fear—with a child on the throne.

Laying Down the Camera—and Some Rules!

The Maxwells were a lovely couple: attractive, dedicated, and smart. But they had made some poor parenting choices, decisions that gave their child the power to rule the roost. Here was a household whose timing and momentum was being dictated by a 3-year-old. The current situation was not only making the parents' lives unpleasant, but it was beginning to negatively affect their son.

After looking at the video we shot of the family, I had isolated two problems. The first one was simple enough: There were no rules in the Maxwell house. Zachary did *what* he wanted, *when* he wanted. Sometimes he even endangered himself, as when he ran ahead of his parents off the sidewalk and into the busy streets of Manhattan. So these parents needed help to impose some basic behavioral dos-and-don'ts and help in learning an effective way to enforce them. Above all else, Zachary had to learn to listen to and obey his parents; he needed to learn boundaries.

The second problem I saw was a little trickier to address, particularly because I first had to bring the Maxwells around to seeing it as a problem. Craig had a website on which he meticulously documented Zachary's every move, from his first dirty diaper the day he came home from the hospital to the waffle he was eating the morning I arrived. The website had attracted a lot of traffic—about 200,000 visitors a year—but that success came at quite a price. Craig estimated that he spent about one hundred hours a month filming and editing the footage (which works out to more than three hours a day). In essence he was relating to his son not directly but through the prism of a camera.

Now, I spend a considerable amount of time and money on archival footage of my children—most parents do. And of course it's not a waste; the whole family gets a tremendous amount of pleasure out of looking at those photographs and videos. And just like Craig, I don't want to lose precious moments with my children—I want those moments to be eternal. But I had to train myself to understand that the eternity of such moments is not created by capturing them on film. The memories are eternal because they are in our hearts. I always have a distaste for those weddings and bar mitzvahs where capturing it on video is the primary focus, and you have the bride and groom giving all kinds of fake smiles and acting for the camera instead of just being themselves and enjoying their wedding. And the cameraman is pushing around guests, with a terrific sense of entitlement, in order to get the best shots.

All this is sad because it reflects a loss mentality. Here we are at the biggest celebrations of our lives, and rather than enjoying and living in the moment we are focused on not losing the moment. It is far better to proceed into such experiences with a gain mentality, where we feel that our lives are being immeasurably enriched by wondrous moments rather than focusing on how such moments are fleeting. They are not. They stay with us forever. Though pictures can capture images, they cannot capture emotions. When we get married or when a child is born, it is the emotion of the moment that is supreme and that can be captured only in the heart. I can still close my eyes and feel the emotion of holding my babies in my arms when they were first born. And I can close my eyes and experience the elation of my wedding. We dare not lose these experiences by having them through the cold distance of a lens rather than participating directly.

Was it really conducive to family life when the father was spending a hundred hours a month behind a camera or at a computer? This was getting in the way of Craig's normal parental involvement with Zachary. I suspected that Zachary's behavior might improve if he had a little more face-time with Dad, time that wasn't mediated by the camera lens. The boy might stop acting like a Hollywood diva, with spoiled-celebrity-like tantrums to match, if he stopped being treated like one.

I wanted to share some of these thoughts with Craig and Lynnsue and see how they would react.

Good Cop, Bad Cop

I invited Lynnsue and Craig into my trailer so we could talk and watch the highlight reel I'd compiled for them. "Bedtime for Zachary" did provide a very good example of what was going wrong in the Maxwells' attempts to enforce discipline.

In the clip Lynnsue tells her son that she's going to give him to the count of five to get into his bedroom or she will give him a time-out. That's good—it's appropriate for a child to know the consequences he'll be facing if he doesn't comply with a reasonable request. But in the video, Zachary ignores his mother completely as if she weren't even talking.

Okay, fine—time to get into the time-out chair, right? Not in the Maxwell house. Lynnsue sees that Zachary is ignoring her, but instead of letting the time run out, she stops counting and starts waffling: "Zachary. Zachary! Did you hear what I said? If I get to five . . ." By my count she was up to 40 by the time her cajoling began to have any effect, when Zachary begins to move into the bedroom as if it had been his idea all along.

There are a few absolutely unbendable rules of discipline. The first is that if you give your children an ultimatum, you have to stick to it. One of the most important rules of parenting is that you should never make a promise that you don't intend to keep, and you should never issue a threat that you don't intend to carry out. If you tell your child there is a punishment for misbehaving, then no matter how much it hurts you as a parent, you have to carry it out.

*When we make a
promise or deliver
a warning to our
children, we must
carry it out. And when
we parent, we must
show a unified front.
We cannot undermine
each other, especially
when we discipline.*

And then, as if Lynnsue weren't doing a good enough job of subverting her own attempt at discipline, just before she hits "five," Craig neatly steps in and delivers the coup de grace: "Zachary, do you want to lie down with Daddy?"

Zachary never had to worry! Apparently Mommy and Daddy were going to work to subvert each other to make sure that the dreaded time-out never happened.

We saw similar sequences over and over again on the tapes. There were no rules in the Maxwell house to begin with—and any shot that either of the adults made at disciplining Zachary ran a very good chance of being sabotaged by the other parent. Instead of deciding together on an appropriate course of action and supporting each other to make it happen, they took opposite roles. If one was the enforcer, the other was the rescuer. The Maxwells were playing "good cop, bad cop" with their son; unfortunately, the way they were undermining each other made them look more like the Keystone Kops. Meanwhile, Zachary was getting away with murder.

What Are You Afraid Of?

Craig confessed that part of the bedtime problem was the ambivalence he felt about Zachary going to bed at all. "He'll go to bed, and I'll be bored," he said. I found this statement pretty surprising. Most of the parents I know very much look forward to the hour or two of peace and adult conversation that happens between their children's bedtimes and their own. What did it say about the Maxwells' marriage that they didn't?

And what about making love? Sex is not a luxury of marriage; it is the very soul of marriage. You are not brother and sister, but husband and wife. Not best friends, but lovers. Not roommates, but soul mates. But here was Craig, married to a beautiful woman, saying that when his 3-year-old son went to bed at night, he was bored. How was his wife to understand that?

But the more I heard from Craig, the clearer it became that his reluctance to let Zachary go to bed was part of something bigger.

Craig's whole mode of parenting seemed to be driven by a very real fear of loss—and I believed this same fear was behind his compulsion to record Zachary's every move for posterity.

Of course every parent reels with a combination of pride and disbelief at the "firsts." It's impossible to believe that the tiny, helpless baby you once held in your arms can now walk without help, win a three-legged race, or drive a car. And sometimes it can be quite poignant to know that a child will never be the age she is *right now* ever again, particularly if you are enjoying yourselves. But it is natural for children to grow up, and there is tremendous joy to be taken from watching your child advance and develop. Why did Craig seem to be approaching this from a place of desperation and grief, immortalizing every step so that it wouldn't be lost, instead of having a ball with his beloved son?

Craig was parenting from fear. He wasn't enjoying the moment; instead he was scrambling to preserve it because he feared losing the moment. He would not discipline his son for fear of losing his son. If he was mean to Zachary, he feared that Zachary would love him less or cease loving him altogether.

It seemed as though Craig were haunted by the possibility that their relationship wouldn't continue, that some estrangement or tragedy would rob him of Zachary, and all he'd have to console himself with would be hours and hours of digital footage.

This might be the result of Craig's relationship with his own father. Perhaps he was not as close to his father as he would like to have been, and he feared that history repeating itself in his relationship with Zachary. Although Craig disagreed, my assessment immediately struck a chord with Lynnsue, and I pressed the point home: Craig was parenting out of fear and he was causing himself a lot of unnecessary pain.

He was also hurting Zachary. Craig's fear was leading him to preserve the memories of his son's childhood—and it was happening at the expense of their real-life relationship. I feel so strongly that fear is one of life's most toxic emotions that I dedicated an entire book to the topic. Fear misleads us, manipulates us, diminishes us, and ultimately destroys us. When we use it as our compass, it delivers us without fail to a place of weakness and spiritual poverty. And as a parenting strategy, it is destructive without parallel: It poisons one of life's most joyful experiences and warps some of our most important relationships. Most important, fear is a terrible legacy for us to pass along to our children.

There are many parents whose greatest fear is that their children will one day stop loving them. So out of a sense of insecurity they indulge their kids and give them everything they want. Little do they realize that this eventually becomes a self-fulfilling prophecy as the child grows up, blaming the parents for never teaching them satiety or boundaries. Moreover, the parents who parent out of fear and out of insecurity will most likely pass on their insecurities to their children.

Not that I'm passing judgment. I am just as afraid as the next parent of my children not wanting to love me. I hate having to punish my children. I see how it makes them withdraw from me, becoming bitter or angry. And at times like that, I feel like giving in and removing the punishment. It's then that I have to remind myself that the discomfort is temporary. If you parent your children responsibly, if you impart to them a sense of right and wrong from a position of strength, they will forever be grateful. Ah, they might sulk now as teenagers. But when they grow older, when it really matters, they will seek a lifelong relationship with you because they will feel indebted to you.

Children are not stupid. They know the difference between good parents and bad parents. They can smell a parent's weakness from a mile away. And while they may resent you standing your ground and not giving in to them, ultimately they will respect you for it, even if it takes some time. But parenting out of fear will ultimately earn the contempt of a child. Children want discipline. Deep down they hate chaos. They need structure and routine if they are to flourish.

And as it turned out, Craig wasn't being totally honest with us—or with himself. In fact there was more going on than a simple capturing of those elusive first moments. Together we watched tape of him "directing" Zachary to feign sleep—he even cracked a joke about how he still hadn't gotten his sleeping shot. It was disturbing to see: Although Zachary didn't seem all that interested in playing

Putting another person before your spouse—even if that other person is your own flesh and blood— is the cardinal sin of marriage.

the role, Craig persisted, giving his son notes and advice to tweak his performance, just as a movie director does with an actor.

Now there's nothing wrong with the occasional canned shot—my kids can "hold up the leaning tower of Pisa" with the best of them, and I bet yours can too—but this was a whole different animal. Craig wasn't *capturing* Zachary's childhood; he was *directing* it.

This was deeply problematic. The whole beauty of being a child is the ability to be completely natural. It is we adults who live lives that are contrived and artificial. It is we who laugh at jokes that aren't funny in order to impress a boss or who will have sex with someone we don't love for an ulterior motive. But kids are completely natural, completely themselves. They say what they think, without censorship, and do not yet feel a need to bend to external pressures. Our job as parents is to help them preserve that natural state for as long as possible.

I feared that the impact this interference made was not innocent at all. When you take a picture of your daughter standing proudly in front of her first finger paintings, you're telling her, "You did something great, and I'm proud of you and want to remember this moment forever." But when you tell her that you'll take the picture after she adds a little cadmium yellow to the upper left corner—and while she's at it, could she artfully dab a little paint on her cheek for verisimilitude?—you're telling her something very different: that what she's done naturally and without your interference isn't good enough for prime time.

When a 3-year-old gets the message from his father that his natural childlike behavior isn't good enough, he's going to stop acting like a child. And we were seeing some of that already with Zachary. Of course we were seeing it in his resistance to follow any kind of parental direction. But there were other troubling markers, such as the way he would choose games on his computer over toys.

Healing an Old Wound

As we have seen many times on *Shalom in the Home,* it is a natural tendency to parent the way we ourselves were parented, continuing a legacy of dysfunction. So if your father was a yeller, you'll turn into a yeller with your own children, unless you're careful. But there is another, opposite tendency to watch out for as well. When something truly traumatic has happened in our childhoods, there is sometimes an opposite reaction. Everything we do as parents is dedicated to making sure that our children never feel the same pain we felt as children. I suspected that something like this was behind another one of the major obstacles to discipline in the Maxwell household.

In the tapes we watched, Lynnsue seemed constitutionally incapable of letting Zachary cry for even a minute without rushing to offer comfort. As soon as there was a peep of discomfort out of Zach, Lynnsue was there to make it better—even if it meant running herself and her marriage ragged in the process. I knew something about Lynnsue's own childhood that I suspected was feeding this behavior: She herself had been cruelly abandoned by her biological parents. The story itself was truly shocking: They had left her in Korea as a days-old infant on a public bus.

Lynnsue, understandably, had deep-seated abandonment issues that she might not have even been aware of. Indeed when I asked her what effect she thought her biological parents' abandoning her might have had, her response was that she felt it might not have affected her very deeply. But of course it had—and we were seeing the effects in a number of ways.

While the best parents do their utmost to make sure that they do not repeat the mistakes of their own childhoods, in this case it seemed that Lynnsue was taking the advice to an extreme. Discomfort and separation are a part of life. They are lessons that we all have to learn, and ones best learned in the context of a loving family. All parents find it painful to hear their children cry, but there are times when a child's complete comfort cannot be paramount. In this instance Zachary was not learning how to be independent of his mother or how to marshal his other resources to comfort himself. When Lynnsue panicked when she heard him cry, he saw her reaction and thought, "Being alone *must* be as terrible as I think it is, or else why would Mommy be upset about it too?"

I thought it might be better in the long run if Lynnsue's behavior conveyed a different message: "Daddy and I love you very much and we're always here if you need us, but it's time for you to sleep in your bed and for Mommy and Daddy to sleep in ours. If you get lonely before you fall asleep, why don't you try looking at the pictures in this book with your doggie?"

Consciously Lynnsue knew that there is a very big difference between abandoning a defenseless infant on a public bus and teaching a very secure 3-year-old child to soothe himself to sleep while his loving parents wait just outside the door. Unconsciously she wasn't so sure. Of course Lynnsue wasn't abandoning Zachary when she disciplined him, but because of her own life experiences, it felt as if she was.

It worked the other way too. Lynnsue was also afraid, not just of being an abandoning parent but of once again being abandoned herself—this time by Zachary. Although she manifested it differently than Craig did, Lynnsue was also afraid that imposing discipline on Zachary would cause him to sever his relationship with her later in life. Better, she figured, to give in to him whenever he cried.

I think these insights helped Lynnsue; throughout the remainder of the time we spent with the Maxwells, I saw that she found it much easier to stand firm.

Removing the Wedge

I also felt that it was my responsibility to raise a red flag on an issue I thought the Maxwells were ignoring, at their peril. Zachary's sovereign rule over the household was doing a number on their relationship!

This handsome couple, sweethearts since college, no longer even shared a bed. Where a healthy, vibrant, intimate love life should have been there was instead a sleepy, bossy 3-year-old. In a healthy marriage, that relationship comes first. In an unhealthy one, it is the children that come first. And this was rapidly becoming a marriage more about friendship than intimacy.

Zachary's extended bedtime drama and Craig's work on his website meant that the couple had virtually no adult time together. "The couple formerly known as Craig and Lynnsue no longer exists," Lynnsue told us. That's a pretty hefty thing for a wife to be admitting! I was amazed that their own alarm bells didn't go off when they heard themselves make statements like that.

And whether they liked to admit it or not, they were starting to show the strain. They admitted, for instance, that on the few occasions where they had left Zachary with a sitter and just the two of them had gone out for the evening, the conversation between them had been awkward. After twelve years had these people really run out of things to talk about? Or were they just in need of some practice?

Harsh as it may sound, this is where divorce begins. Couples gradually drift apart as something comes between them. It could be work, it could be TV, it could be another woman, or it could be the kids. The couple starts spending less and less time together, even though they love each other. And then they wake up one day and they've fallen out of love. I could see that Craig and Lynnsue loved each other very deeply. But unless they could find some shared experiences as a couple that weren't only about their son, they risked allowing their love to atrophy.

Jewish *kabbalistic* sources speak of two kinds of hell: one of fire and the other of ice. Divorce is a kind of hell, and true to the analogy, there are two kinds: a divorce of fire and a divorce of ice. The divorce of fire is where you fight so much that you simply cannot get along: Every minute spent together is painful, and you'll kill each other if you stay together. The divorce of ice, on the other hand, is where you get along just fine, but it's freezing cold in the house. There is no warmth, nor passion, nor love. Your marriage dies a slow, arctic death as your former romance is gradually incapacitated by hypothermia.

Those couples who experience the divorce of fire usually see it coming. But the divorce of ice is much more sudden. You think everything is fine. You don't fight a lot. You feel you love each other and your marriage is comfortable. But then one day you wake up and it hits you that the two of you have grown completely apart. Aside from kids there is basically nothing keeping you together. Your life is boring, predictable, and monotonous. Strangers seem to appreciate you and show you greater desirability than your own spouse. In these cases divorce simply confirms an existing reality: The two of you lead completely separate lives already, with only offspring and a mortgage in common.

That's the direction that Craig and Lynnsue were headed. They were still deeply in love with each other. But Zachary was the primary focal point, and their lives began to revolve around him. That meant that as time progressed, aside from Zachary they had increasingly little in common.

The Bible says very beautifully, "Therefore shall a man leave his father and mother. He shall cleave unto his wife, and they shall become one flesh." (Genesis 2:24) The physical manifestation of a man's and woman's love for each other occurs when they become one flesh through the life they have created. Their child represents the physical manifestation of their love. How tragic, therefore, that for so many couples, having children does not bring them together but drives them further apart. Children should solidify rather than obstruct the marital relationship—and that can't happen if parents draw no boundaries with their kids.

Lynnsue hastened to reassure me. "I never fear an affair," she told me. But I jumped in immediately and said, "Oh, you better fear that." The Maxwells, in my opinion, were prime candidates for a crisis like an affair. Healthy, passionate people will find an outlet for their healthy passions. If they don't find it in their marriage, they will eventually turn elsewhere. With no talk and even less sex, how long would it be before one of the partners in this couple began going outside their marriage for what they could not seem to get within it? Don't get me wrong. Craig and Lynnsue were moral people and deeply committed to each other. But passion is not a luxury, but a necessity. And if we don't feel alive in our marriages there is no telling where we'll turn to find something that makes us feel passionate and appreciated.

In short, the Maxwells' ineffective parenting wasn't serving anybody. It was exhausting them, putting undue strain on their relationship, and it was ruining Zachary. It was time to lay down the camera—and to lay down some rules.

Craig, Meet Lynnsue

Our first assignment for Craig and Lynnsue was to send them out for a "get to know you—again" dinner, just the two of them. The only rule: no talking about Zachary. While they were out, they'd be leaving Zachary with an ace babysitter: Rabbi Shmuley (complete with a secret weapon—my own 4-year-old son, Yosef).

The show's cameras followed the couple on their date, and as Craig had said, the conversation between the two was indeed awkward. Lynnsue bravely broached the subject of the website and whether the constant interaction with Zachary through the lens of the video camera were interfering with their human interactions. Craig, however, dismissed her concerns; there was still some resistance to breakthrough there.

At home things were a little awkward too. Over and over again, Zachary chose to play with the computer rather than choosing toys or human interaction. It took real effort to tear him away from the computer and into a simple ballgame with Yosef and me, but I persisted, using my legendary charm and powers of persuasion. I was eventually rewarded with a glimpse of the funny, fun-loving little boy hiding inside the Hollywood diva.

When they got home, it was time for part two of Craig and Lynnsue's romantic revival: taking back their bed. Suffice it to say, it was not a success. Once again the Maxwells were sabotaging themselves. They lacked commitment to the plan from the outset, something that communicated itself loud and clear to Zachary. As we had all predicted he would be, Zachary was indeed upset by the change in routine. I had told them that they were looking at a few nights of unpleasantness—a small price to pay for being able to once again sleep next to your spouse! But as Craig and Lynnsue had tried to put Zachary to sleep, he first cried his guts out and then threw up. Craig, in particular, was very upset by Zachary's reaction and did not want to stay the course.

I could feel the tension building between me and Craig. He didn't seem to like me, to put it mildly. He thought my diagnosis of the trouble in their family was completely off and that I was foisting something on him that would be bad for his son. It got worse. A surveillance video of a conversation he'd had with Lynnsue indicated that he was highly irritated with the amount of time I was spending talking about their marriage. He had brought me in to fix the problems with his kid, not to invent problems between him and Lynnsue. He wanted me to limit my attention to Zach's sleeping problems—although, as he made perfectly clear in a conversation the next morning, he wasn't prepared to listen to my advice on that either.

"The cold-turkey approach isn't going to work for us," he told me. He agreed with me about the importance of rules but believed that Zachary needed "to feel like he has some kind of control over those rules too." So there you had it: Zachary got upset, and Mom and Dad threw in the towel. Even at the tender age of 3, Zachary knew exactly how to control his parents.

I didn't want to alienate Craig; I could tell that he was really angry with me, and I feared that if I pushed him further he'd ask me to leave. In Craig's mind I was not a parenting expert whom he had called upon to assist with his out-of-control child; we were equals. I had my parenting method; he had his. Who was I to tell him what to do?

Fair enough. I wasn't pulling any kind of rank on Craig, as if I had some heavenly parenting insight that he lacked. I don't see myself as smarter or wiser than the next person. And I do not claim that I am more correct than the next person. Rather my own expertise comes from raising eight children. And the proof, as they say, is in the pudding. If I were wrong and Craig were right, then why was a 3-year-old running a household where there were two capable parents?

I liked Craig and Lynnsue a lot and felt especially awed by how much Craig loved his son—this was one great father. Still I was truly shocked at the idea that you'd ask a 3-year-old to participate in his own parenting. Come on. That's ridiculous. That was a recipe for disaster. Since when do children know what's best for them? Isn't it our job as parents to teach our children to eat their vegetables, to brush their teeth, to look both ways before crossing the street, and to say please and thank you? What would the world look like if children made the rules?

Not only is children collaborating on their own parenting a terrible idea, *but kids know it.* Kids want boundaries. As far as I'm concerned, letting a 3-year-old know that he's making his own rules is like a flight attendant letting you know that you can get off a plane any time you want simply by opening the door in midair. Loosey-goosey boundaries aren't comforting to a child—they're terrifying!

I remember when my first daughter, Mushki, was born; I was surprised to see how tightly the British midwife swaddled her. I joked to my wife (who was really not in a joking mood at that point) that Mushki felt like a football, so tightly was she wrapped. The midwife explained to me that it's comforting for a newborn to feel tightly embraced; what might feel restrictive to an adult feels secure to a child. I have thought many times since that this is a terrific metaphor for the boundaries we need to set for our children.

Is asking our kids to make their own rules "freedom"—or is it throwing them to the wolves? How do you feel when you're asked to do something in an area where you have no skills or experience? I, for one, am happy never to hear the pilot say, "It's cool if the guy in seat 7A wants to fly the plane for a while." Forget about it! Let's stick with our core competencies: I'll fix the families; you fly the plane. Parents need to enforce broccoli and manners so that kids can do what they're good at: being kids. There will be plenty of time for them to be parents later.

Craig and Lynnsue had a couple of years of bad choices to undo, and there would be some unpleasantness associated with that. But the driver behind many of those poor choices was this fallacy that Zachary was a full, voting member in his own parenting council, and I was concerned that unless the Maxwells addressed this discrepancy, their poor choices would continue.

Day at the Ranch

Knowing that I needed to do something to diffuse the tension between me and Craig, I decided that it was time to break up all this intensity with a little fun. We decided to treat Zachary to his first-ever horseback riding lesson. The choice wasn't an idle one, however. Could I demonstrate to the Maxwells how having more control over Zachary's behavior would improve all of their lives?

And could I show Craig that interacting with his son directly would reward him more than capturing his image ever could? Now what parent wouldn't want to document his son's first pony ride? It's a special moment. But I knew that Craig's tendency would be to film the whole thing, and I was hoping that we could encourage him to share his time between documenting Zach and actually interacting with him.

The day got off to a rocky start. The academy that we were visiting had strict rules about riding without a helmet, but Zachary, stubborn as a mule, refused to put one on. No amount of begging, bribes, or threats would change his mind. I watched in astonishment as Craig tried to cajole his 3-year-old into putting on an essential piece of safety equipment. Amazingly Craig refused to forcefully tell his son that he *had* to put on the helmet or he could not ride—period!

It was very instructive for me. I hadn't realized the depth of Craig's aversion to exerting parental control. Craig really felt that *any* act of parental coercion was barbaric. To his mind he had no right to tell Zachary to do anything but needed to cajole his son's consent. Of course this presupposed that Zachary was old enough and mature enough to both understand what was good for him and to understand right from wrong. This scenario entered the realm of the truly absurd when, to my amazement, Craig got the academy to bend its regulations and allow Zachary to ride without a helmet!

Man alive! It was an excellent example of how not disciplining Zachary wasn't doing anyone any good, including Zach. Wouldn't it have been way more fun for him to be playing cowboy instead of wasting precious time on a tantrum? And was it really "the best thing" for his parents to put him *in actual danger*—just because they would not force him to do something he didn't want to do?

Four adults, 45 minutes, and one emergency dispensation later, Zachary and his trusty mount, Huggie Bear, were on their way. Lynnsue was having a blast; she was directly involved in what was going on, asking Zachary questions, pointing things out to him, running alongside. Craig, as predicted, stuck himself behind a camera.

In the hope that I could show Craig what a barrier the camera was between him and Zachary, I set up an experiment. First I had Craig do an on-camera interview with Zachary while he was perched atop Huggie Bear. True to form, Zachary went into celebrity mode,

There's no equality in the parent-child relationship. Parents are the bosses because they know better.

hamming it up for the camera. Then I asked Craig to put the camera down so he could communicate directly with his son instead of through the camera.

The result was astonishing. As soon as Zach had the opportunity to connect with his father in a more natural way, he held out his arms for a hug, sliding right off the horse's back and into his father's arms. As soon as the digital barricade between them was eliminated, not even the chance to be a cowboy—every little boy's dream!—could compete with the simple pleasure of his father's embrace.

Craig had been parenting out of fear. When he looked at his 3-year-old, he saw a teenager and a young adult rather than a little boy—and he was afraid of losing his little boy. Zach, he feared, would grow up so quickly that he would miss the whole thing, so he felt he had to record everything. Likewise he believed that if he got tough with Zach, his son would stop loving him. So Craig negotiated everything. And by inadvertently projecting the fear he felt, Craig was creating impediments between him and his son. Once Craig put the fear away, the love poured out and Zachary responded.

You see, when you remove fear, you make room for love. Fear and love are directly antithetical: The more of the former, the less of the latter. The quintessential posture of love is one of expansion, of opening, and of extension: what we call a hug. Love is trusting; when we hug someone, we expose our soft underbelly. Fear, by contrast, is precisely the opposite: The quintessential posture of fear is to curl up into a ball, shutting others out. Fear does not trust, so of course it cannot love.

I took over Craig's video camera and encouraged him to go and enjoy every moment of this wonderful "first."

The Rage

That night my suspicion that Craig's website was a wedge driving the family apart rather than uniting it was given further substantiation. Craig spent the evening loading and editing footage of Zachary's pony ride on his computer while the real live boy sat eating dinner by himself in front of the television. What kind of family unity was this?

The next morning I resolved to speak candidly with Lynnsue and Craig about the website and the role it played in their family life. Far from believing that the website's role was destructive, Craig and Lynnsue felt that it could effectively be used as a parenting tool. For instance, they told me, they would sometimes film a tantrum and then show it to Zachary while they were talking about it.

Needless to say, I had some problems with the idea of using the website as an educational tool. My first problem with this strategy was that it wasn't, as even Craig had to admit, very effective. Zachary still had tantrums—a lot of them. It didn't seem like watching himself having a fit on video was really getting through to him. In fact it seemed to be having the opposite reaction: Like a real actor, Zachary was learning to distance himself from the roles he played onscreen. For instance, I learned that he would sometimes refer to himself in the third person while he was watching the videos, as in "Zachary doesn't look very happy."

I was more convinced than ever that the camera was supplanting normal parenting, not reinforcing it. And I was never more convinced than when I saw a particularly damaging piece of footage called "The Rage," one of the most watched on the website.

Before we watched it together, Lynnsue related the back story. The beginning was familiar enough to anyone with a young child. Zach had been throwing his toy trains; his parents told him that if he continued, they would take the trains away. He threw another train, so they packed them up and took them away. For once the Maxwells had made good on one of their threats!

Zachary, naturally, became upset—the way a 3-year-old will when you take away his trains, even if he has been warned. That's okay; in fact, this is precisely the kind of everyday parenting moment that enables us to teach our children the big lessons of life, like the fact that actions (throwing trains) have consequences (losing access to those trains).

But a garden-variety temper tantrum turned into something very different when Zachary saw that Craig was filming it. In short, he completely freaked out. And to be perfectly honest, I found the resulting footage to be almost unwatchable.

Over the next few minutes Zachary whips himself into an absolute frenzy of rage. Trains forgotten, he screams, "No, Daddy!" as his tiny bare legs scramble on the hardwood floor in an effort to get his father to cease filming him. This goes on for about fifteen minutes. Soon Zach is throwing things at his father to get him to stop taping. The footage is pretty brutal, and the viewer is confused about what Craig is seeking to achieve through filming it. By the end Zachary is exhausted, and the viewer feels like he's stood by and witnessed a form of torture. Craig, behind the camera, just keeps on filming.

Much of the discomfort I felt watching the video was because watching it felt like the violation of the privacy of a person. We all, of course, believe in the fundamental rights of every human being, with the right to privacy being foremost among them. Well, children have a right to privacy as well, and this rage video seemed to violate that right. It is one thing to post pictures of your children's smiling faces at Six Flags on a publicly available website. It's quite another when you post their ugliest moments, such as a horrific temper tantrum. Kids, like adults, deserve to have their dirty laundry remain private. Zachary Maxwell might "just" be a 3-year-old in a diaper, but that does not make him any less of a person. In "The Rage," he is very clearly asking his father for privacy. It seemed terribly ironic to me that Craig, who believed so strongly that Zachary should have a say, would ignore him on this matter.

That's not to say that I don't understand—I do. As parents, it can be easy to forget that our children have an inalienable right to privacy just as we do, because we have a level of intimacy with our children that's impossible to imagine with anyone else. We know how they like their sandwiches cut, what childhood illnesses they've had and when, whether their shoes are getting too tight in the toes, and when they need a nap. On any given day most parents know exactly what their child has eaten—and, too often, how it looked when it came out the other end. It's not a relationship with a lot of boundaries built in, but just because we cannot always give our children privacy doesn't give us the right to strip them of their dignity. In fact as with so many other aspects of parenting, we must be especially vigilant about protecting

*Our children need
us to be present with
them in some of life's
most private moments.
Because we cannot give
them privacy, we must
do what we can to
help them preserve
their dignity.*

this right, precisely because a child doesn't have the wherewithal to secure it for himself.

I should mention that I did not judge Craig harshly for posting the tantrum. I knew he meant well. He wanted to show, I assume, the full gamut of his son's experiences, and the fact that Zachary sometimes blew a gasket was one of those experiences. Indeed as a TV host I wrestle with the issue of children's privacy in a very personal way. My children participate in the program, and I often bring some of the troubled families we encounter to our home to be filmed. But it seems self-evident to me that even as my children participate in aspects of my public life, I would never want to expose their faults in a way that would embarrass them.

And Craig wasn't just failing to protect Zachary from prying eyes—he was failing to protect him from himself and his own emotions! In the moment captured on tape, Zachary was literally driving himself crazy with anger and frustration and rage. Craig explained that he felt it was necessary to let Zachary "work through" those emotions. First of all, being filmed (and frustration at failing to get his father's personal attention and compassion) was a big part of what was driving Zach's tantrum. So it was a little inaccurate for Craig to suggest that he was just standing by.

But even if the tantrum were just about the train set, Craig still had a responsibility to step in when it became clear that Zachary wasn't just venting frustration but was working himself up into a truly worrying state of agitation. It's not good for *anyone* to experience emotions at that high a level, especially for a protracted length of time, and especially not for a vulnerable child! Imagine how frightened and alone Zachary must have felt at that moment. Taking the trains away was only part of the lesson; Zachary also needed his parents to show him how to manage the frustration and anger he felt at the punishment he was receiving.

I don't believe we should ever allow our children to experience rage at a fever pitch. We have to get them to calm down quickly or they can scald themselves in a way that can be permanently harmful.

We can never forget that young children need our guidance in navigating the choppy waters of their complex emotions. A child doing a new puzzle will become frustrated very quickly. In that instance her parents' job isn't just to show her how she can make it easier for herself by starting with the corner pieces and getting clues from the picture on the front of the box. Those may be important skills, but our *real* work is in helping her to understand that she'll have more fun and get further if she can take a deep breath (and a break, if she needs to) instead of throwing the pieces on the floor.

Earlier I had felt that Craig was "overdirecting" Zach's childhood. But watching this "Rage" video made me feel that he wasn't offering enough direction at all. But every time I attempted to bring this to Craig's attention, he shut me down. Craig had a lot of time and energy tied up in his website, and it was turning into a real sticking point. Before we left the Maxwells, I needed to find a way to get through to him.

Breakthrough on the Roof

Craig might have been beginning to trust me a bit more, but he still viewed me as an intruder. So I sat down with my producer and director in an effort to figure out how I could get through to him. How could I outflank his defenses?

It seemed to me that the main reason Craig was shutting me out was he felt I was disrespecting him. Here he was, a very decent man and devoted father, being told by this arrogant expert that his parenting tactics were harming his precious little boy.

I had to show him that precisely the opposite was true. I wasn't judging Craig as a father; in fact, I thought he was a *great* father. He was inspirational as a dad who was totally devoted to his son. His commitment to his son was not just admirable, but exemplary. I would much rather be in a position of telling someone to hold back on filming his son's first pony ride than to have to tell him through his secretary that it had happened at all. Craig's heart was absolutely in the right place.

But Craig did feel that I was judging him. He hadn't been prepared for us to talk about his marriage as much as we had—indeed, he hadn't been expecting us to talk about *him* at all.

I wanted Craig to see himself as I saw him. I wanted him to see himself as a great father, not one who had to immortalize every moment of his son's life on camera as a defense against an inevitable break with him. I wanted Craig to see himself as a great man, one whose greatness came from the intimacy of his marriage and the closeness of his family, not from the number of anonymous strangers who clicked on his website for five minutes of random amusement.

So many of us cause ourselves such terrible pain by allowing externals to determine how we feel about ourselves. We look at magazines and feel worthless because our bodies aren't as toned and tanned as the airbrushed celebrities on their pages. We determine our own intrinsic value by comparing our paychecks, our houses, our cars, or our children with the neighbors. We feel that we're nothing unless the world is interested in what we have to say, impressed by our degrees and title, and laughing at our jokes.

But when we allow externals to determine who we are, we put all the power in other people's hands. If you're only valuable because you're vice president, then what happens when your company outsources your department? We must unhitch our sense of our own value from the vagaries of the outside world. We must learn to develop our special gifts, and we must share those with the world. Only then will we have a true sense of our own value. Craig was a great father with a great kid, and my mission was to make him see that he didn't need anything more than that to feel great about himself.

What was the best venue to communicate that message? I decided it was amid the skyscrapers of New York City. My producer arranged for the two of us to go to the top of his building in Manhattan. Behind us stood the Empire State Building and other New York landmarks.

Craig had no idea why I was inviting him onto the roof. When he arrived, I looked at him and said, "You see everything around you? It's part of a big and ancient lie. The lie goes like this: The big things really matter, and the little things don't.

"Now most people live this lie. They put all the big things like earning money and prestige—building skyscrapers, in other words—ahead of the 'little' things, like reading their children a bedtime story

Responsible parenting involves teaching our children appropriate actions and appropriate emotions. Anger is the most destructive of all emotions, and we must do our best to help our children gain control over, and end, a tantrum.

and helping them with homework, because those little things don't bring them prestige.

"Somehow *you* saw through that lie. You saw that what really matters are the things that pass for little but are really big. You don't spend your time attempting to make a billion dollars. You spend your time focused on your son when he's playing ball and making pictures. These little moments are so precious to you that you even film them and obsess over them. That's how much you love them.

"That's why we came to your house, that's why we chose you—because the essential material was already there. You were already a great father and a great man who knew the truth. *The substance was already there.* All I want to do here is refocus and rechannel some of your efforts so that you're not motivated by a sense of loss, but by a sense of love."

I spoke these words in the spirit of the ancient Jewish teaching that "words which emanate from the heart penetrate the heart." I was not saying anything disingenuous but sincerely conveying to Craig that, while I disagreed with his inability to enforce discipline, I was genuinely moved and inspired by his infinite love for and devotion to his son.

"Watching you has made me a better father; from you I am reminded to cherish every little thing my children do," I said to him. The whole time I spoke, Craig was completely silent. I could see that he was taking my words to heart and that he now understood that I was not judging him—indeed, that I had much to learn from him.

I felt finally that he understood that he was an inspiration rather than a failure as a father and that all he had to do was parent from strength rather than from fear. We hugged each other and walked away with a new relationship.

A Pleasant Stroll

It was the end of the week, and I was pleased with what I was seeing so far. Craig was spending less time with the digitized Zach and more time with the real person. The Maxwells had laid down some basic rules about sleeping and eating, and Zachary seemed to have absorbed them!

Our final assignment was, as usual, simple on the surface: Lynnsue and Craig were to take a casual stroll around the neighborhood with their son, with me on the headset offering suggestions and feedback. But this was really an exercise in seeing how well the Maxwells could make and enforce rules and how firmly the parents could stand together against Zachary's inevitable resistance.

It's important for everyone to remember—parents and children alike—that the majority of the rules we have for our kids are *to keep them safe*. Manners are one thing: Nobody's going to die from chewing with his mouth open. But obedience is essential, precisely because parents need to know that they can give their children an appropriate amount of independence while still keeping them safe. Zachary on the street was a prime example of how dangerous it is to fail to enforce rules. In fact this segment contained one of the most harrowing moments of the show: Zachary got ahead of his parents, and, true to form, ignored them when they yelled "Stop!" But this wasn't playtime or bedtime when disobedience was a mere inconvenience—they were on the bustling streets of Chinatown. I actually thought I was going to have a heart attack as Zachary darted away from his parents and halfway across the street, traffic whizzing by, horns blaring.

Craig (relieved, I suspect, that nothing terrible had happened) had a bizarre reaction: Once he'd finally caught up to Zachary, he actually praised his son for stopping! Never mind that it had been too little, too late. Lynnsue's reaction was more appropriate. She got right down to Zachary's level, grabbed his arm, looked him in the eye, and reprimanded him in her sternest voice. I was pleased to see this progress, praised Lynnsue, and felt more confident than I had all week that the Maxwells were beginning to understand the gravity of the situation.

Disciplining our children is not a luxury but a necessity. Failure to do so is to be contemptuous both of our children and of our obligations to them. Withholding discipline in the name of loving our children is, in practical terms, to despise our children and to cause them grievous harm. Discipline is just another form of love. The ancient Jewish mystics of the Kabbalah remarked that there are two kinds of love: the love of the right arm, which is compassion and generosity; and the love of the left hand, which is severe and disciplinary. With only one arm of love we cripple our children. With both we make them whole, teaching them acceptance as well as boundaries.

Later Craig and Lynnsue successfully distracted Zachary away from a table full of toy cars, but it gave me an idea. Whenever possible, I feel that it's important to encourage children to think of others and to teach them how good it feels to do something nice for someone else. We must teach our children to be selfless. So through the headset, I encouraged Craig to help Zachary pick out a present for his mother from a table of inexpensive trinkets. He picked a pink "I Love New York" heart—very nice! But when it came time to present the gift, instead of handing it to her, Zachary threw it on the floor.

It was, plain and simple, a form of manipulation—and it was how Zachary had gotten the upper hand in the Maxwell home. He knew that if he indicated that he was unhappy, his parents would immediately do something to make it better. His parents had to stand firm, even in the face of his unhappiness and anger. Certain things—like behaving in a safe, manageable way on the busy streets of Manhattan—are nonnegotiable. On the way home, Zachary did kick up a little bit of a fuss. But his parents both stuck by the rules they had laid down. They didn't capitulate by carrying him or offering bribes. And it worked: Zachary walked home by his parents' side. Not without resistance, but he did as he had been asked to do.

The best was yet to come. You can hear the pride and relief in Craig's voice-over to the footage of another, very welcome "first": Zachary *finally* sleeping in his own bed. And I was very pleased to see that Craig and Lynnsue were using the time after Zach went to bed to share vitally important "grown-up" moments together over dinner and a bottle of wine. And a few weeks after the Maxwell episode aired, Craig changed his website to a semiprivate one, granting access only to those who have a password. In my opinion, that was a positive development.

As the Maxwells had discovered, it is essential to give our children boundaries and to enforce those boundaries in a fair, evenhanded, but unyielding way. Far from restricting them, our rules give them a safe space in which to learn and grow. I wish the Maxwells all of God's blessings.

Lessons for Life

Rules are an essential part of parenting. Children do not benefit from a life without boundaries—no matter how compellingly they might make the argument otherwise.

Never back down on a promise—or on an ultimatum—to a child. Instead consider what you are saying carefully before you say it, and then don't hesitate to follow through.

We cannot subvert another parent's disciplinary efforts. Talk to your partner beforehand about the rules you'd like to implement and have an action plan in place for appropriate rewards and punishments you're both comfortable enforcing. Doing otherwise sends mixed messages to our children and undermines our partner's authority.

Get your child out of your marital bed! Your bed is a place for you and your spouse to be intimate, whether that means sex or just sleep. It is not a playpen.

Take photographs and videos, by all means—you'll love looking at them later. But make sure that your relationship with your child isn't taking place through a lens.

Know that parenting from a place of anxiety or fear—whatever the cause—is toxic and detrimental to the relationship and to the child. Parent out of love rather than fear.

Dysfunction as a Family Heirloom

The episode that we filmed in the Lubner household was one of the most difficult of *Shalom in the Home*'s first season. Each of the family members was unusually sensitive and volatile. Emotions ran high during the filming of the episode and escalated afterward. In the end, however, the struggle was worthwhile. We helped their young daughter considerably, and left the parents' marriage—after a long period of real crisis—in significantly better shape than how we found it. Indeed the major transformation that was brought about in the Lubner home took place after the show was over, in counseling that I continued to provide Todd and Lisa. Even then I wasn't sure that I was making any progress. And suddenly, when I least expected it, we had a major breakthrough.

For me the Lubner episode was an object lesson both in the show's power and in its inherent limitations. In just a week we made a serious difference in this home. But—as with all the families we work with, and yours as well—the Lubners would have to change from within to make those changes permanent. And it would take all of them, working together, to make their family whole.

Get Thee Behind Me

We were called in to my home state of New Jersey to help Todd and Lisa Lubner with Hannah, their 9-year-old "devil child." "There's no end to the torment," Lisa told us. From their description I was expecting something akin to the Linda Blair character in the movie *The Exorcist*— and what I saw was pretty bad: scene after scene of this beautiful little girl leveling cuttingly hurtful remarks at her mother, as well as some full-blown screaming temper tantrums, including a few where Hannah hit her mother, although not very hard.

Over and over we saw evidence of an incredible reserve of rage, and I couldn't help but ask myself, "What in God's name brings a 9-year-old girl to this kind of a boiling point? What was tormenting Hannah Lubner? Why was she so angry at her parents, and especially at her mother? Why did her mother accept her abuse? Most important, what could be done immediately to reduce the toxicity level of the Lubner household?"

When a child is displaying that kind of untrammeled anger, you have no choice but to look at the people she is closest to: her parents. And when I did, I saw three very serious problems in the Lubner household.

The first was Lisa's failure to discipline Hannah—a failure that seemed to grow out of her inability to engage with life on the outside. In every piece of film we had of her, Lisa seemed to want to numb herself to her environment even when she was on the receiving end of some pretty shocking abuse. She sat in front of the TV and watched many hours in an almost zombielike state.

Asking why Lisa had retreated to this catatonic state led me to the second big problem in the Lubners' home: Her husband, Todd, seemed very angry. Todd never threw giant temper tantrums. But he spoke in such a harsh and coarse tone that his family members bristled. His efforts to discipline Hannah may not have been ignored like Lisa's were, but they could hardly be considered successful. He often yelled at Hannah and left her deflated and sometimes crying.

Todd also spoke to his wife an a manner that was not conducive to teaching his daughter to respect her mother. "Get up and do something," Todd roared at Lisa when Hannah treated her disrespectfully in one of the clips we had. "Your way hasn't worked for nine years!" The tragedy of the interaction is that it all takes place in front of their daughter. In fact it seemed that Hannah was learning all of her (non) frustration-management skills from her father. In one unintentionally ironic moment on the tape we had, Todd leaned over and screamed, "You stop screaming in people's faces this very second!"—*right into his daughter's face.*

I want to make it clear that I did not judge Todd as a bad husband or father. In fact from the very beginning I respected Todd and was able to bond with him, and he and I grew especially close after the show was taped. I am certainly not one to judge anyone who is challenged by anger: This has been one of my own foremost character shortcomings. So although I had begun to discern that Todd's anger was the principal cause of dysfunction inside the Lubner household, I wasn't there to judge him. I was there simply to bring his anger to his attention and, if possible, to give him strategies to control it.

Where the Lubners saw a devil child, I saw one who was left much too much to her own devices because of the terrible conflict in her parents' marriage. This was the third problem: The Lubners were just too distracted by their own problems to be parents. At night they retreated from each other—Lisa to her television-aided stupor, Todd to sulking and Internet surfing in another room—leaving small Hannah by herself, eating dinner all alone. To be sure, this wasn't always the case, but it happened enough to create a real crisis. Hannah's diabolical behavior was becoming less mysterious to me by the minute: The tantrums were attention-getting devices. This little girl had to resort to behaving like a demon in order to get attention from her parents. If Lisa sat down to watch TV, which she did all too much, Hannah would push her mother aside and say that she was sitting in her place. What Hannah was really saying was "I'm tired of you watching TV and ignoring me."

So I had my work cut out for me. I needed to snap Lisa out of her walking coma, get Todd to control his own temper, and encourage the two of them to act like parents so that their little hellion could once again be a child.

"You Both Treat Me Terribly"

I was interested to see how the Lubners would react to the clips we showed them. Seeing yourself on tape, as I now know, can be an unsettling experience, and it's one of the reasons the show is successful at effecting change: We're able to give the families we work with the gift of self-awareness. Most of the time we're so trapped in habit, so immersed in our normal routines, we don't really even realize what we're doing. Seeing our behavior onscreen makes us, for a moment, objective observers of our own lives. You might not think of yourself as a nag, but when you look at a reel that shows you nagging your kids from morning 'til night, you can't ignore the truth! It can be surprising, uncomfortable, embarrassing, and even painful to see those habitual behaviors laid bare, but recognition is usually a very powerful agent for change. Once you really see what you're doing, you can teach yourself a more productive strategy.

Not so with the Lubners. As soon as we started to roll the tape, Todd began to criticize Lisa in exactly the way that he was criticizing her onscreen. In fact the tape seemed only to confirm to Todd how much in the wrong his wife was. As we watched the tape of Hannah refusing to obey her mother, Todd rounded on Lisa, "Why do you let her treat you like that?" just as he was berating her onscreen. "Get up and do something!" Onscreen we saw Lisa begin to laugh uncertainly as Hannah's screaming gives way to pummeling her mother with a pillow. "It's a joke to her," Todd said, and Lisa in the trailer began to laugh uncertainly. "It's still a joke to her," he said with disgust.

It fell to me to clarify the situation: Todd was unable to see that Lisa's laughter—like her catatonic state when at home—was a by-product of the humiliation caused by the way he was treating her. Her nervous laughter was yet another coping mechanism.

I recognized what Lisa was doing instantly—in part because I have seen a version of it in so many other American homes. When a husband is unhappy and in part takes it out on his wife, she has only three options: She can convince him to change his behavior, she can leave, or she can try to find a way to cope with the stress and loneliness of living with a marriage that is not always happy. Too many times the American

In relationships, actions speak louder than words. Be careful how you treat one another in front of your children. They're watching, and they're copying!

wife finds the consolation that she should be getting from her husband at the bottom of a pint of ice cream and the companionship that she should be getting from her marriage from a television that's always on.

There was no question that we had to address Lisa's failure to discipline Hannah—and that we had to give Lisa some commonsense strategies to help her get the upper hand. But almost more important, we had to understand why she had so willingly relinquished it in the first place. As the old saying goes, every doormat reads "Welcome." I didn't want to make Lisa feel even worse about herself than she already did, but I sensed that her emotional blankness was an issue that we would have to confront—if not for her sake then for Hannah's. Lisa's torpor wasn't just robbing her of her own life; it was robbing Hannah of the one thing she needed more than anything else in the world: a fully engaged mother.

In fact the ostensible instigation for the fight we were watching in the trailer was Hannah trying to take her mother's customary television-watching perch on the couch. Lisa relinquished the seat, but Hannah was not appeased. Why not? In my opinion, she wasn't really trying to get the seat at all but to get her mother *out* of it. Hannah wasn't fighting about a spot on the stupid couch but making an (unsuccessful) bid for her mother's attention by trying to break the connection between her mother and the television. Thwarted in this she began screaming and ultimately escalated to pummeling her mother with a pillow.

Of course Hannah didn't get anywhere—her mother had already checked out. Hannah could beat at the physical body on the couch as much as she wanted to; there was no one home to respond. Lisa, in an attempt to defend herself (or at the very least to hide) from Todd's constant criticism, had retreated from the real world into her own interior one, leaving nothing for Hannah to engage with—no matter how violent Hannah's efforts.

This is very common, and not just with spouses; I see it often in children whose parents are hypercritical as well. When blows are physical, people curl up into a ball to protect themselves; they do the same thing in a way when the blows are verbal and emotional.

People who find themselves constantly beaten down by criticism will eventually numb themselves to everything as a defense mechanism; if you've trained yourself not to feel, then how can anyone hurt you? But of course you can't go through life anesthetized against *every* feeling.

The problem was compounding itself right in front of me. In fact as I was seeing in the trailer, Todd's attempts to bully his wife out of her stupor were just making the problem worse. I could understand why he felt so angry at Lisa; her passivity in the face of Hannah's abuse was shocking for me too until I understood what was going on. But Lisa didn't need more rage and verbal abuse—she needed support and encouragement. She needed someone to buttress her efforts with Hannah, not undermine them. But when Todd criticized and abused her, she retreated further and further into her private world—making him angrier and angrier. It was a vicious cycle that could only change if Todd tempered his aggression. To do that he would first have to become aware of how scarred he was himself—something I felt he avoided out of fear at what he might find. The more he raged, the further Lisa pulled her head into her shell, and the more enraged he got. It was a cycle that would have to end.

Now I have been in the room with *a lot* of fighting couples—it's an occupational hazard when you're in my line of work. It's never particularly fun, and my crew and I have been through a lot of it. But as I have said, I found that I could relate very strongly with Todd. I too struggle with anger. I too have said too many mean things to a wife I love very much. I felt very compassionate toward Todd; it seemed glaringly obvious to me that his anger was the result of a great pain, a pain that came from the very center of his soul. If anything, his great sin was not his anger but that he had so assiduously avoided self-reflection.

When I told Todd that he needed to rein in his temper, he explained that he thought he was showing Hannah that she couldn't treat him the way she treated her mother. "With all due respect," I said, "all you're showing her is that her mother is a punching bag that she can beat up on." Todd may have been complaining about his daughter's behavior, but in relationships, actions speak louder than words. We can never,

ever forget this, particularly when we have children, because children respond to what we do, not to what we say. What Hannah was *seeing* was the way he screamed criticisms at her mother—a behavior that she then went on to mirror.

Lisa herself pointed out the similarities in their behavior. "You're worse than her—you both treat me terribly," she told Todd, to his disbelief. But he couldn't hear her. "Is that the only thing you got from that clip?" he asked her, returning again to her failure to exercise discipline.

It was up to me to lay the ground rules for this couple: It is categorically and unconditionally unacceptable for a husband to speak disrespectfully to his wife or to humiliate her in any way—*especially* in front of a daughter. There could be no ifs, ands, or buts about it.

Husbands tell me all the time that they regret yelling at their wives. Don't regret it, I say—*don't do it*. We human beings are capable of rising above every provocation, every irritation, because between every cause and the effect, there is a split second of choice, and in that moment of choice lies our humanity. Animals do not have that split second; they respond immediately and directly to a provocation. But we are defined by our ability to choose how we respond to what happens to us. As I have said many times on the show, life is only 10 percent what happens to you, and 90 percent how you react to it.

For the Lubners to take even the smallest step toward tranquility in their home, Todd would have to rein in his temper. As I told him, "If you want to teach your daughter the lesson of self-control, you have to exhibit it yourself." It was a difficult conversation; Todd felt that I was partial and was taking Lisa's side. He couldn't see what he was doing to his family—or to himself.

But although Todd's anger may have been at the root of many of the Lubners' problems with Hannah, he wasn't the only culprit. Lisa's inability to step up and discipline her daughter was destroying the family as well. Todd made the legitimate point that Lisa wanted to be her daughter's best friend rather than her mother. She was afraid of alienating her daughter by being strict. As often happens in unhealthy marriages, for Lisa, her principal source of affection in life was her

It is categorically unacceptable for someone to speak disrespectfully, sarcastically, or humiliatingly to another person— especially to your spouse or in front of a child. Rise above provocations to respond acceptably.

daughter rather than her husband, and she feared Hannah's feeling distanced from her. So she became her daughter's buddy rather than her parent.

Lisa admitted to me that she knew it wasn't right for Hannah to treat her so disrespectfully. She admitted that it upset her. And she had to concede that she knew it wasn't the right thing for Hannah. Lisa's solution? "To love her more."

I didn't disagree—but I felt very strongly that Lisa needed to redefine her understanding of the word "love." As parents we must understand that we show our children love with both hands. An ancient kabbalistic concept says our right hand is the generous, giving side—the kind that waits patiently in the freezing cold while hockey practice wraps up, kisses a skinned elbow, and then serves hot chocolate. The left hand is the hand of discipline. This is the hand that yanks our child back from the curb's edge and admonishes him severely about crossing the street without looking. The left hand is a sterner hand, *but it is no less loving for being so.*

I had to make Lisa understand that sparing Hannah from discipline wasn't an act of mercy but a real abdication of her responsibility toward her daughter. What service was she really doing her daughter by allowing Hannah to continue to carry on in this way? By permitting her temper tantrums, what kind of life was Lisa setting Hannah up for? How was Hannah supposed to learn how to treat the teachers, mentors, neighbors, and bosses she would encounter in her adult life if she couldn't show a base modicum of respect for her own parents while still a child? What kind of man could be expected to marry and stay with someone who screamed like a banshee at the slightest provocation? And how did this crippling bode for Hannah's future children?

Clearly not everyone Hannah would encounter in life would put up with her tantrums the way her mother did; in fact most people would choose to give up on or avoid her instead. So this little girl's temper was going to be a real liability in her life. She needed to find some constructive outlets for her frustrations—and before the week was out. I would make it clear to Lisa that it was a mother's job to help Hannah do just that.

A Return to Eden

"I'm not the outdoorsy type." That's what Lisa said when I told the Lubners that we'd be taking them on an overnight camping trip.

No kidding. But my choice of venue for the first Lubner family exercise was carefully considered. What I wanted for them was a return to Eden, a place of pristine purity and clarity, a time before they had been so terribly hurt, and before they became so hurtful to one another.

As I have written in other places, the Garden of Eden isn't a place as much as it is a state of mind—the state of mind of childhood. For me childhood is a time of innocence and unselfconsciousness, the hallmarks of true freedom. As we grow up we become world-weary; we get cheated and do some cheating ourselves, and our innocence is lost. But I believe that every single one of us is given the opportunity to get back to the garden—and that the key to the gate is through the eyes of a child. Through our children we can recapture true joy and an unselfconscious love for life. Our kids can teach us everything we need to know to get back to Eden, if only we will let them.

But there was another lesson I wanted the Lubners to learn: Adam was in Eden until God made Eve; then he was in *paradise*. We don't need all the material possessions on which we have a dependency. When our family is there we have everything we need to withstand life's pressures. The man who has a wife who loves him is invincible. Paradise is wherever our loved ones are—and love is what transforms an ordinary garden into Eden.

Practically speaking, I felt that the Lubners needed to spend time together. Specifically, Hannah needed to feel that she was the focus of her parents' undivided attention. It didn't hurt that taking the family to the wilderness would also unplug them from *Desperate Housewives* and the Internet. And maybe, while we were at it, we could lighten the mood of this family and get the Lubners to have a little fun too.

Easier said than done! Their first task was to use a map to find the campsite and food we had stashed for them and to pitch a tent to sleep in. I gave them tips—emotional ones, not navigational—via walkie-talkie. The point of the exercise was to see whether they could put their bickering and material possessions aside and work together as a team for the greater good of the family. As I reminded them, family time is not about the destination but about the journey.

Everything started out fine. There was minor complaining and bickering, but nothing too major. In fact when Hannah challenged her father's authority ("Who made you the boss?"), he softened in a lovely way and asked for her help instead of freaking out. But they didn't get far. Todd began to show some frustration with the instructions for putting up the tent, which admittedly seemed as difficult to assemble as a nuclear submarine, and Lisa asked him to calm down. Immediately Todd faced off with her, forcing an argument. Before long they were at it again, with Hannah in the background jumping up and down and screaming, "No fighting!"

At any rate it was a good example of how little shalom there was in the Lubner home. Instead of neutralizing one another's frustrations, the Lubners did the exact opposite—they exacerbated them. I see this over and over again in the families I counsel. Our families and homes should provide us with some respite from the competitive jockeying and lack of security outside. No wonder we're so agitated and exhausted when our families and homes are yet another battlefield!

Headset discarded, I waded into the fray and called a time-out in order to remind the Lubners of the point of the exercise. This wasn't about the tent! They weren't there to earn a merit badge. They were there to learn how to manage their disappointments and irritations so that they could work together as a family. "Read the instructions again in a calm way and they will reveal themselves to you," I said. And, as I had predicted, with a little help the family was able to pull together long enough to put up the tent. In fact Lisa turned out to have a natural knack for camping!

The Lubners were indeed a family who struggled with frustration, but I don't know many families who could have gotten that tent up without a spat. Our instant-gratification culture has made us so intolerant of any delay or setback! It is sobering to trace Lewis and Clark's route and to realize that the second-by-second satisfactions of microwaves and movies-on-demand and our PDAs have essentially phased out the kind of fortitude, stamina, and personal strength

We love our children with two hands. With one we coddle and comfort them; with the other we establish borders and restraints. To give them only one hand of love is to cripple them as they move through life.

a journey like that requires. Look, I'm not a particularly patient person. But it is, let's face it, one of the most important qualities for a parent to possess.

I left the Lubners toasting marshmallows in front of a blazing fire. Now I wasn't kidding myself about what we had accomplished. This tent pitching was just one measly exercise, over one measly afternoon. But the Lubners had seen that they could transcend frustration, trust one another, and work together. All I could hope was that this knowledge would empower them to use those skills again in the future.

Up in Smoke

The next morning seemed promising. For all the complaining and bickering, the Lubners had actually had a pretty good time. Hannah in particular was having fun; she had slept well and seemed invigorated by the experiment. So we set out to do some basic trust exercises to show the Lubners that family cooperation is the best way to surmount the obstacles that life throws at you.

Once again it started out okay. In fact after a morning of guiding a blindfolded family member and after using fallen logs as balance beams, the family was having one of the cuddliest moments I could remember seeing them have, with Hannah's arms draped around her mother's neck.

I took the opportunity to talk to Lisa about her nightly television habit. Now, television is a very powerful tool. But if abused, it can also be addictive and all-consuming. Watching television together as a family cannot serve as an authentic substitute for real family activities or togetherness. And in the case of Lisa Lubner, it had taken the place at the center of her evening that her daughter should have occupied.

"I think Hannah should decide how much TV Mommy gets to watch," I said—and Hannah gave her mom an (overly) generous three hours a night. After some discussion I got Lisa to agree to restrict her television viewing to *after* Hannah's bedtime ("because you need Mommy") and even then to just a single hour maximum ("because then Daddy needs Mommy").

It seemed that we were making some real steps forward—but then Lisa took aim and fired a dart. She said, "I'll make a deal: I'll give up my television if Todd gives up his screaming." And all hell broke loose. With one ill-advised comment, all the progress we'd made out there in the woods went up in smoke. This family was like bone-dry kindling—the slightest spark started a conflagration that took hours to get under control! Todd stormed off in a rage with Lisa at his heels, alternately apologizing and defending herself. And once again poor little Hannah was alone, a victim of the conflict between her parents.

There may be married couples who don't fight, but I've never met them. Spats are going happen—it's how you cope with them that determines the kind of relationship you'll have. Truly successful couples are like surgeons—they know where to cut in order to do the least collateral damage. When successful couples fight, they know how to air their grievances while still limiting the overall hurt they cause. But with the Lubners, every fight was a nuclear detonation, destroying everything in its path.

In this case both of the Lubners contributed to the explosion. Lisa attacked Todd just when we were beginning to make progress; Todd was explosively defensive. Although Todd certainly had the right to feel irritated by Lisa's needling, he didn't need to be quite so hypersensitive. As we had seen, Todd really had the ability to set the tone for the family. (The needling was retaliation for his yelling anyway.) And Lisa needed to learn to pick—and time—her battles. The family had been having a nice time, sharing one of the few intimate moments of togetherness I'd seen them enjoy. Why had she chosen that particular time to unnecessarily criticize Todd?

Even as I counseled them I could see that Todd and Lisa were still caught up in scoring points and winning arguments. No successful relationship—with our children, our spouses, our own parents, our business associates—can be achieved if we're more preoccupied with who's "right" than with nurturing the relationship. And if we insist on living in the past—in the negative feelings, the grudges, and the history of our conflict, we can never move into the future.

So I ended this particular fiasco by reintroducing the Lubners to one another in the hope that they could put their difficulties behind them and begin anew: "This is your husband, and he wants a better marriage." "This is your wife, and she loves you."

Bridge of Life

It was during our next exercise that Todd and Lisa got a chance to see what the problems in their marriage had done to their daughter's sense of herself. The task was to use a low rope bridge to cross over a murky swamp—both a balancing exercise and a confidence challenge.

Lisa crossed it like a star. Hannah got halfway across and panicked: "I can't do this." Her parents stood at either end of the bridge offering encouragement and suggestions, but Hannah wasn't having it. Instead she jumped off the bridge in the middle and disappeared into the trees. And once again I was running through the woods after one of the Lubners.

As I trotted through the foliage after Hannah's retreating back, I was reminded of the tagline from the Stephen Spielberg movie *Minority Report*, "Everybody runs." It was certainly true in the Lubner home! Todd needed almost no excuse to retreat in a rage, and Lisa had checked out long ago—now Hannah was carrying on the legacy. Was I ever going to be able to explain to these people that you can't outrun your pain?

When I finally caught up with her, Hannah told me that she'd looked like a fool because "kids can do more stuff than their parents." Really? If children could do everything their parents could do, why would they need parents? In my experience it is parents who teach kids—whether it is how to read or how to drive. Children aren't born knowing how to do things; they need to be shown, they need to be encouraged, and they need *someone* to do those things. What we saw on that bridge was the depth of Hannah's discomfort *with being a kid*.

You can't be a kid if there's no one to parent you, and that's what was happening to Hannah Lubner; Lisa was too withdrawn and Todd was too angry. There was no room for Hannah to show a child's vulnerability without exposing the absurd situation she was in: She was a 9-year-old adult, a child raising herself. She was holding her childhood together

Married couples need to know love, and sometimes they need to know how to fight. Before you start something, ask yourself three questions:

1. Is this worth fighting about?

2. Is this worth fighting about now?

3. Am I saying this in the most constructive way, or am I just trying to get the other person's goat?

And, once engaged, remember the first rule of combat: Do as little damage as possible.

as best as she could, but that bridge crossing depended on her invulnerability. How could she admit that she needed help without drawing focus to the fact that there's no one there to give it?

Hannah was fundamentally uncomfortable expressing need, even on those rare occasions when there *was* someone there to encourage and help her. That's why the bridge incident threw her for such a loop: She was forced to confront her dependence. On that bridge she couldn't hide that she was just a kid—someone who needed help.

Much of Hannah's relationship with her parents involved causing them pain in order to get their attention. In a sense her declared independence was yet another weapon in her arsenal against her parents. Nothing arouses warm parental emotions more than feeling that small hand in yours, with someone dependent on you to be the brave one, the one who knows how to solve the problem. So what better way to injure your parents than to refuse their help, to tell them you don't need anything that they can give?

"There's nothing wrong with telling Mommy and Daddy that you need help," I told Hannah. And then the whole family and I went back to the bridge, where we cheered Hannah as she crossed the bridge: a happy ending to a very turbulent day.

One Last Shot

Our time in the woods was finished, and my producer and director were ready to pack up and go home. "We have an episode," they told me. "We've helped the family move forward; we've done the right thing by them. We're done."

At one level I could see their point. Certainly there had been a marked change in Lisa's behavior. She had really heard what I had to say, and she had shown a real willingness to make fundamental (and potentially painful) changes for the benefit of her marriage and her daughter. She was ready to cut down on TV watching and to be Hannah's mother again and not just her friend. I was really impressed by the new energy I saw in her and by her commitment to change. She wanted to do the right thing, even if it meant accepting some implicit (if gently given) criticism of some of the things she had been doing before we came.

So I believed that we had woken Lisa up from her daze, giving Hannah the most important thing in a child's life: a mother. But I could see that we had not even scratched the surface of Todd's anger, which had a debilitating effect on the Lubner home. I had known that I couldn't solve *all* of the Lubners' issues in just a few days, but I also knew that we wouldn't be anywhere near done until I had made another attempt to get through to Todd. Unlike Lisa, he had deflected most of my advice. It was clear that he still believed that Lisa and Hannah were the root causes of the problems in the family and saw himself as the victim.

I couldn't give up on him. In fact I agreed with his assessment of himself as a victim. He was not Lisa's and Hannah's victim perhaps, but he certainly was someone who had suffered tremendously. The kind of anger Todd so frequently displayed always comes from a tremendous wellspring of pain. I felt that beneath Todd's bluster was a man who desperately wanted someone to get through to him. The question was: how?

Perhaps if I could be more honest about my own shortcomings I could bring Todd's defenses down and really get him to listen. So in one last-ditch effort to try to address Todd's anger issues, I asked him to come with me down to our Airstream studio trailer.

The Hot Seat

As you've probably noticed by now, I don't exactly shy away from uncomfortable topics, but this conversation—even by my standards— was extremely challenging. The tension in the trailer was palpable; I felt like a boxer, weaving and bobbing, doing anything I could to avoid a direct confrontation. It wasn't that I was scared, but I needed to find a way to get through to Todd without raising his defenses. I decided to tell him the truth, keeping in mind "Words which emanate from the heart penetrate the heart." My honest desire was to help Todd to become the man that, deep down, *he* wanted to be—to grant him happiness and inner peace through a feeling of satisfaction with who he was as a man.

I believed that Todd was repeating the destructive patterns he had witnessed in his own home when growing up, and Hannah was continuing the tradition. And I knew that it would just go on and on—the way a legacy of dysfunction always does—unless we nipped it in the bud by getting Todd to change himself.

If nothing else, before we left the Lubner home, I wanted Todd to see two things. First, although he could not change the devastating events of his own childhood, he could put them behind him. In fact by becoming a better, more patient, more loving parent, he could reintroduce himself to love, playfulness, innocence, and hope. As God evicted Adam and Eve from the garden, He told them that they could always come back through the cherubim—the angels with babies' faces. I believe that every one of us has the opportunity to get back to Eden through our children. Todd too could return. But in order to do so he would have to allow Hannah to be a child instead of making her more adultlike through his anger. What was happening now was an inversion and a corruption of the process.

Second, and perhaps even more important, I wanted Todd to understand that he could single-handedly stop the cycle of destruction that had undermined his own childhood. Nothing could really give Todd back his own childhood. But Hannah still had hers, and Todd held its future in his own two hands.

I knew that Todd's father had left his family when Todd was just 9 years old—Hannah's age. His father had cut off all contact for many years. Todd's father had written a letter to Todd's mother, on Todd's 18th birthday, making it known that he would no longer be responsible in any way for Todd's financial or personal well-being. In short it was a story of painful abandonment.

Of course the effects of desertion weren't limited to Todd's own childhood. Todd was still reacting to the pain of that rejection. As an adult he reacted by preempting further rejection. He lashed out at those he loved, hurting them before they could hurt him. Todd didn't see himself as lovable; he didn't believe that Lisa and Hannah could really love him. In his mind they wanted him to leave—but before they could say so, he'd threaten to leave them—just as his father had left his family.

I could clearly see how he was perpetuating this destructive pattern; now I just had to show Todd. So in anticipation of the meeting, I had asked my production staff to compile a reel of clips. In each of them—and there were a few—Todd was threatening to leave Lisa and Hannah, just as his father had left him. "If my family is unhappy being my family, then I'll leave," he said. In one sad incident, in a fit of temper he asked Hannah—a 9-year-old girl!—if she wanted him to leave the family. When she said she does, he told her, "Fine. I won't come home from work tomorrow night." He set her up to reject him, the same way his father had discarded him when he was a child. But because she is a child herself, all he is really doing is threatening her with the same injury he experienced when he was 9 years old— abandonment by a father. Without meaning to, Todd was becoming everything he knew to be wrong.

When I showed him the clips, Todd was very angry at me. He felt that I had ambushed him, and perhaps I had. But it was the only way I could think of to get him to confront the truth of his situation and his actions. He wasn't yet ready to hear what I had to say, and his wrath at me for confronting him with it was highly discomforting. It was clear that I had not gotten through to Todd and had created even further distance between us. Indeed I wasn't all right for hours afterward. I felt terrible and despondent—as if my own heart had been broken.

No matter what happened to you in your childhood, you can choose to respond differently than your parents did, giving your children a different experience. Every one of us has this power—it is the most hopeful thing I know. But I did not break through to Todd that day; I had not convinced him of his own power to effect change. The cycle would continue.

Dinner with Hannah

Well, the show had to go on, metaphorically and literally, and I wasn't about to quit now.

Part of being a family is spending time together. And it had been a long time since the Lubners had done the things that most normal families do together as a matter of course, little things like eating dinner together. So the Lubners' next assignment was nothing more complicated than a normal night at home: dinner, some bedtime stories, Mommy and Daddy tucking their little girl into bed and kissing her good night.

Simple enough, right?

I'm outspoken on the importance of the family dinner, and believe me, the Lubners aren't alone in overlooking this absolutely essential ritual. According to a July 2005 *Wall Street Journal* article, fewer than one-third of all children sit down to eat dinner with both parents on any given night. And yet *Time* magazine reported on a variety of studies showing that "the more often families eat together, the less likely kids are to smoke, drink, do drugs, get depressed, develop eating disorders, and consider suicide, and the more likely they are to do well in school, delay having sex, eat their vegetables, learn big words, and know which fork to use."

Family dinners give us a chance to be together of course. But they also give us a chance to share information—about a pop quiz, or a chance encounter with a neighbor—that makes up the casual but important stuff that weaves the fabric of our days. You'd be amazed at how much more easily conversation comes with your children when you know more about the details of their everyday lives. Everyone listens, so everyone feels important. The focus is both on each individual and on the family as a collective unit.

When we only sit down to eat with one another on holidays, or with the television blaring in the background, we miss a real opportunity to relate to our children in a relaxed, peaceful way. Of course religious Jewish people can be guaranteed at least one sit-down dinner a week—uninterrupted by television, phone calls, or other distractions—when we sit down for the Sabbath celebration on Friday night. But even nonreligious people can bring this tradition into their homes; just unplug the phone, turn off the television, and give the most important people in your life 45 minutes of undivided attention while you eat. Not so difficult!

Parents must be parents so that kids can be kids. When kids have to parent themselves, they grow up all too quickly, skipping some of the essential stages of development and life.

Experts say that the more we do this, the better it gets: We eat better food, we have better conversations, we relate better to each other. We need to get back to the basic rudiments, the basic structure of family life, and the family dinner is the perfect place to start.

I delivered food to the Lubners' door (this is a full-service operation!) and retreated to my high-tech Airstream studio to watch the proceedings. Hannah started acting up right away, pushing her parents' buttons and testing their authority. I had suspected she would; the challenge was to see if Todd and Lisa could hold their ground. It was a special challenge for them because they already felt on such shaky ground with their daughter. It's much more difficult to discipline our children when we're fearful about our relationship with them and feel like we're not close to them. When the relationship is rocky, we fear that we'll alienate them permanently.

Right at the outset I noticed that Hannah had a little toy near her at the table. Through her headset I asked Lisa to ask her to put it away, eliminating the distraction during dinner. Hannah conceded by putting the toy in her lap, and when Lisa pressed the issue of getting the toy off the table, she threw it onto the kitchen floor. Lisa held her ground and asked her to get up and put it away, and Hannah eventually complied.

It will take a little while—and a lot more of these family dinners!— for Hannah to realize that she doesn't need to behave badly to get her parents' attention. But it was a first step, and I can't emphasize enough how important it is to take those first steps to getting your kid on the right track: All you have to do is start with the basics.

The conversation was a little stilted, but in general I was pleased with what I was seeing onscreen. But Hannah persisted in her misbehavior—and it was unbelievable how manipulative she was about it and how accurately her barbs landed. I remember watching the scene on our monitors in our trailer and how it saddened me. There is nothing more painful for a father and mother than to feel unloved or put down by their own child, and Hannah was doing exactly that to Todd. The Bible commands us to honor our parents, but it was a lesson that Hannah clearly had not learned. As Todd is telling her something she doesn't want to hear—that he and Lisa are going to put her to bed after dinner—Hannah interrupts him to criticize his table manners in the most hurtful way possible. Todd is wounded and the scene threatens to escalate. But to his credit, and with a little coaching from me through his earpiece, he holds the line, refraining from losing his temper or using sarcasm to put her in her place.

Yes, Hannah's behavior was disturbing. But if Todd wanted to teach Hannah the lesson of self-control, then he had to exhibit it himself. He could not allow Hannah to get under his skin—one of the ways this little girl had traditionally won the upper hand with her parents. Instead he calmly and firmly informed his daughter that she was not to speak to anyone hurtfully, least of all her father. It was a small step, but progress all the same.

Similarly Lisa held her ground upstairs when Hannah talked back about going to sleep. For the first time since we met this family, we saw Lisa effectively assert her authority over her daughter, enforcing the bedtime. Anyway in my version of events it was time for Mommy and Daddy to have some grown-up time together, to reconnect and to work on their relationship. Hannah did get out of bed, of course, over and over again. But Todd and Lisa calmly put her back and closed the door.

The only way to get our kids to listen to us is to show them that we're serious. If that means blowing an entire night putting your kid back to bed every time she gets out just to demonstrate your resolve, that's what you have to do. Ask Todd and Lisa.

The Morning After

As I have said, for me the Lubners served as an important reminder of both the power and the limitations of a show like *Shalom*.

The limitations, at least, were apparent: I had no illusions when we left the Lubners that we had brought them a holistic sense of tranquility. To be sure, Hannah was much better off, and on several fronts. First, we had given her parents some very practical advice about how to handle her behavior, which worked well in the long run. Second, we had given her back her mother by helping Lisa come back to life from her zombielike trance. To this day Hannah is a completely different child, almost unrecognizable from the spoiled brat we initially met. She has been to my home many times and has stayed overnight with my daughters, who adore her. She is now a sweet, helpful, and respectful girl; the transformation is astounding.

But for all that, we had not brought peace to Todd and Lisa. In fact I was concerned that we had endangered it by waking Lisa up. She had gone within herself so that she didn't have to come to terms with Todd's criticism and anger. Now that she had poked her head out from under her shell, how would she react? And, as I suspected, once awake this sleeping beauty did not like what she saw when she looked at her relationship with her husband. Now that she was putting her foot down about Hannah's abusive behavior, what was she going to do about Todd's?

This was a scenario where we had to risk a marriage in order to save a child. I invited the Lubners to a party at my house to celebrate the birth of my son; Todd was traveling so Lisa came with Hannah. In front of all my guests, Lisa confronted me, asking me why I had left them alone with all their problems. It was a very uncomfortable moment, and once again I could only choose honesty: I told her that I thought further intervention would have put them at the risk of divorce. She agreed with me.

I still believe that it was a risk that had to be taken. Divorce is a terrible thing: As the child of a divorce, I will do everything within my power to prevent one. Yet people in unhappy relationships cannot possibly expect their spouses to change if they consistently send the message that they are prepared to put up with unacceptable behavior. In fact after we left, the Lubner marriage got much worse. A few months after filming the show, Lisa and Todd agreed to divorce. They made it all the way to the stage of consulting lawyers. All along I was counseling them both on the phone, trying to get them to change their minds and commit to their marriage.

Both remained entrenched. Todd was respectful to me but politely accused me of setting him up, of ruining his marriage, of taking his wife's side in their disputes, and he accused Lisa of not loving him. I have said that I felt a very real kinship with Todd. But I could not

It is essential, no matter how tired or stressed we are, that we rise above those feelings to let our children know that we have an infinite reserve of energy to be used for love and discipline on their behalf. We can never be too tired or too distracted to serve as parents.

persuade him to take responsibility for his own contributions to the marriage's deterioration.

So when we met I asked him to put aside the anger, not for anyone else's sake, but for his own. I wanted him to get in touch with the part of him that I could see plain as day: the hero within him. His heroic self was too long buried underneath all that unfortunate hurt and pain. I appealed to that part of him that housed his innermost desire to be what he truly is—a special human being, the part of him that wanted his daughter to see him as a great man.

In the end it was Todd who changed himself. He decided that he did not have to divorce. He would learn to control his frustration and not vent it in the presence of his daughter. He decided of his own volition that he did not have to alienate the people closest to him. He could win Lisa back; she did love him, but that love was buried under a thick layer of scar tissue, made up of all the anger and pain he had caused her over the years. If he could begin to treat her lovingly again, those layers would dissolve, and she would be able to rediscover what had made him so special to her all those years before.

Now they have begun to make some of the fundamental changes they so resisted while we were filming. Todd still becomes irritated, but when he does, he takes a walk outside instead of venting. Lisa is amazed at his restraint and flattered by the knowledge that he's made these changes for her. Their marriage is infinitely better. When Lisa was diagnosed with breast cancer, Todd was an exemplary husband, offering unequaled love and support. And Lisa, thank God, is now doing much better and healing well from her illness.

I believe America will be really surprised and impressed by the level of transformation the Lubners have been able to effect. We got more mail about this episode than about any of the others we filmed. I suspect that the strong reaction was due to the fact that this couple struck a very real chord with many of our viewers. After all, I suspect that many of us struggle with these same problems, if in a slightly less extreme form. Who among us hasn't retreated into a private world—aided by technologies like television, the Internet, and cellular connections to our friends—rather than confront the realities about a relationship? Who among us hasn't felt that it is easier to turn our anger outward than to closely examine what's causing us so much pain in the first place? Who among us hasn't used someone else's poor behavior as a license to behave badly ourselves?

Waking Lisa up was the right thing to do for Hannah: A young girl needs a mother to love and discipline her and to teach her how she needs to be treated in a grown-up relationship. It was also the right thing to do for Lisa. She is a person and she had to live and feel like all of us, no matter how uncomfortable that might sometimes make her. As I have said elsewhere in this book, we must choose life, with all of its myriad pleasures—and transient discomforts.

Lessons for Life

Treat your spouse not just as you would like to be treated but as you would like *your child* to treat you. Never forget that your children are watching what you do and learning from it.

Discipline and love aren't mutually exclusive—in fact, discipline is just another side of love! Helping your child to determine appropriate and inappropriate behaviors and responses to frustration is a crucial part of parenting. You cannot do that without using reasonable and appropriate disciplinary measures.

Spend time together! Family dinners (without television or other distractions) at least four times a week should be nonnegotiable.

If you're going to watch television, make it something edifying, something wholesome, and something that the whole family can watch together. But don't allow TV to dominate family time. Consider board and card games, walks, reading, and other wholesome activities.

The Passionless, Platonic American Marriage

In the winter I traveled to Hershey, Pennsylvania, to meet Ali and Tijen Wexler. The deep snow that accompanied my visit was the perfect metaphor for their marriage. Once upon a time Ali and Tijen had fallen in love and gotten married. But since then a substantial freeze had set in, and they needed some help to thaw it out.

Ali and Tijen have two children: their 7-year-old daughter, Dilara, and their infant son, Tanner. The Wexlers' marriage had once been a passionate connection between two people of radically different backgrounds. Now, just a few years in, the couple had lost the spark of connection and were slowly drifting apart.

Every night was the same: Tijen immersed herself in the children, while Ali sat in complete isolation, a stranger in his own home. The passion was completely gone from their union. In fact it seemed as if the Wexlers came together only to squabble about domestic details; they couldn't even get the passion together for a big blowout fight! But 7-year-old Dilara was frightened and upset at the constant sniping taking place between her parents, as if she intuited that theirs was a faulty connection. And her parents were equally frightened to discover that Dilara speculated about a divorce. "It's heartbreaking that she even knows that word!" her mother sobbed.

I fought to get the Wexlers on the show at all. Our producers weren't convinced. It seemed like a pretty humdrum story to them—the Wexlers were just bickering, and the kids seemed okay. I said, "Are you kidding? This—the loss of passion, the end of sex, the death of intimacy—is the biggest problem of all in American marriages Marriages don't end because people argue—as long as their desire for each other is stronger than the differences, then they can always get past the fight. Marriages die when couples lose the natural gravitational pull toward one another that we call attraction."

The couple still loved each other—that much was clear. But the attraction between them was buried under mounds of laundry and child care schedules. A roadblock between them had forced them to take separate paths, and we would have to figure out how to surmount it before the Wexlers could find shalom.

Two Worlds

I was fascinated by the story of Ali and Tijen's courtship. The couple had met while working in the cruise industry, and they had traveled the world together. This really was a case of opposites attracting. Ali was adopted by Jewish parents and grew up in Philadelphia, while Tijen was a Muslim who grew up in Turkey. Ali's family consisted of his parents and a sister, also adopted. Tijen came from a large, close-knit family. Ali was quiet and solitary; Tijen was passionate and outgoing.

But they were immensely drawn to one another, and both had made big sacrifices to be together: Ali had converted to Islam, even changing his first name from Carl. Tijen had moved to the United States, leaving her country, friends, and family behind. Their enormous differences had added to their initial attraction, but now those differences were just an excuse to fight—and fight they did, to their daughter's dismay.

The fighting was what we were called in to fix. But when we started to watch their tapes, I found that it was what the Wexlers *weren't* talking about that really alarmed me.

Attraction trumps compatibility. A man who doesn't like jogging will take it up to get closer to a woman he likes; he will become compatible with her because of the attraction. But no amount of compatibility can create attraction. And by attraction we refer not merely to the physical but to the polar opposites of masculine and feminine.

First of all it felt almost as if the Wexlers were using their schedules to avoid one another: Ali worked two jobs while Tijen worked evenings and Saturdays. Any spare time was dedicated to being with the children or attending to the cooking, cleaning, laundry, shopping, or one of the other household chores that loom so large when you have two small children. They had not had a night out, just the two of them, since the birth of their son—almost a full year! And then there was the elephant in the room: For the last year, since Tanner's birth, Tijen had slept with her infant son, *not* with her husband. Ali had long ago fled to the guest room, while his baby took in his place in the matrimonial bed.

It would be tempting to see the problems in this marriage as the result of a clash of cultures, but in the Wexlers' case I suspected a far more common and less exotic culprit: For the Wexlers, domestic drudgery had replaced the romantic passion in this relationship; apathy had replaced a thirst for adventure. Where were the glamorous, globe-trotting, sexy people that had fallen in love with one another? Buried under unsorted laundry and arguments about who had last taken the garbage out. They had gone from being lovers to being partners. The clash between the Wexlers' cultures had once been the source of their passion—it was their newfound domestic compatibility that was causing the rift! And unless something changed, 7-year-old Dilara was right: The marriage would die of neglect.

One thing I try to do on *Shalom in the Home* is to cut through some of the conventional thinking that endangers modern families. One of these myths is the belief that compatibility is more important than attraction. Nonsense! What better argument do I have for this than the fact that the majority of the population is heterosexual? If people really wanted compatibility, they would choose a member of the same sex so they would automatically have more in common with one another than men and women do. Compatibility makes for best friends, and you don't get married to have a best friend! *Attraction* makes lovers.

We're all attracted to the unfamiliar and the unknown, just as the Wexlers were. Their differences might have been more exaggerated than most—he was Jewish, she was Muslim; he was American, she was Turkish—but those differences acted like lighter fluid on their attraction to one another. It was when compatibility set in that the fire started to fizzle. They got married and had children together. Like all parents, this united them in a common goal: doing what was best for the children. Suddenly these two people from different worlds shared a foremost interest. They were now compatible! But this compatibility threw a wet towel over their mutual attraction: The more alike they became, the less interested they became in one another.

Strangers in Their Own Home

There's no question that raising a family is hard work—but not every couple loses the spark. There was a lot of love between these two; what was dragging them down? It's not my job to delve deeply into the psychology of the individual family members. But in this case I sensed I needed some more information about Ali's past before we could begin to unpack what was going wrong in this family. Like it or not, many of us parent as we ourselves were parented, and I knew that Ali's childhood had not left him with the happiest of memories.

It is natural for adoptive children to struggle; it can be very painful to know that the people who gave you life also chose to give you away. In many cases that wound is healed by knowing that your adoptive parents chose you, raised you, and loved you as their own. Ali had had a different experience. He had spent his childhood feeling abandoned by his adoptive father, a man he felt had been largely absent— emotionally, financially, and otherwise. This had hurt him terribly as a child, and he had been unable to put his feelings of bitterness behind him as an adult. He had not spoken to his adoptive father in years; in fact he refused to call the man who had raised him "Dad."

This feeling of abandonment and isolation translated into enormous trust issues in his marriage with Tijen. It was these issues that we would have to address, from different angles, over the next week. Although Ali was clearly a man searching for a home, he was not all that well equipped to open up and share his heart, now that he had found one. "He doesn't let me in," Tijen told us. Ali's tremendous need to isolate himself in order to prove that he didn't need anything from anybody put a tremendous, impassable barrier between him and his wife. As Tijen was discovering, there is nothing more hurtful for a spouse than to feel shut out. Ali's internal loneliness wasn't just causing him pain; it was making his wife lonely as well.

Wounded and angered by Ali's rejection, Tijen had thrown herself into showing that she could give just as good as she got. If Ali was going to exclude her from his inner life, she was going to exclude him from their family life. We watched a very telling tape of Tijen coming home from work. She exploded through the door, full of cuddles and coos for the children, while ignoring Ali completely. Her husband did not even merit the courtesy of a simple "hello." It was if he was not even there.

And in some ways he was *not* there. Over the course of the evening Ali sat on the couch or at the kitchen table with almost no expression at all on his face. His family life was taking place five feet away, and yet he made no move to join in. His natural sense of isolation, always present, was compounded by the fact that he was being excluded by his family. Tijen, meanwhile, was bestowing her considerable love, energy, and affection where it was appreciated: on their children. If you want to ignore your husband, what better excuse is there than the children you share? Children are the ultimate in busywork: There are always noses to be wiped, diapers to be changed, and meals to be prepared and cleaned up. Best of all, the children *need* you and will admit as much—unlike Ali.

But Tijen's passive-aggressive return salvos were backfiring on her. Isolating Ali made him feel even more lonely. Also, pushing him away from participating in their family life was making Tijen feel angry and overwhelmed, like she was parenting and running the household by herself. Unfortunately, by acting like a ghost in his own home, holding himself separate from their family life, Ali was unwittingly repeating the pattern of isolation and alienation that had characterized his own unhappy childhood. In short, this couple was trapped in a compounding game of abandonment one-upmanship. So of course the evening ended with the couple retiring to their separate rooms—Tijen with baby Tanner to the master bedroom, Ali alone. Whew!

Your marriage is not a facet of your life; it is your life. It is not a detail of your happiness but its source and greatest blessing.

Back to Basics

In some ways it pays to tackle the easiest problems first. And one of the problems that I saw very clearly in the Wexler household was that Tijen had chosen her role as mother over her role as Ali's wife. I had expected some resistance, but Tijen stepped right up and admitted that she considered her primary role in the home to be that of mother, not that of wife. "Children come first," she said over and over. In this case Tijen's role as mother was probably a more satisfying one—at least her children were responsive to her! But the couple's romance was suffering in this relationship as a result. There was plenty for Tanner and Dilara to like about the new Tijen, but not much left for Ali. And it was a situation that had to change if Tijen was interested in salvaging her marriage.

Life with small children is exhausting; as the father of eight, I can understand that brushing your hair and putting on makeup so that you feel and look sexy don't seem essential the way feeding a hungry baby does. And in an age of limited marital intimacy, many wives identify strongly with their kids because they get the emotional closeness from their children that their husbands deny them. But we cannot and must not choose our role as parents over our roles as husband and wife. A healthy marriage is the foundation upon which a healthy family is built.

The widely held misconception that good parenting means that children should come first in the marriage isn't just bad for the marriage—it's bad for the kids. When we allow our parental roles to overwhelm our responsibilities toward our spouse, we allow our children to be a wedge that drives us apart instead of the glue that brings us together. Talk about perversions! Children are created out of the physical manifestation of our love for one another; they should not have to shoulder the blame of knowing that they're driving us apart.

And where will our children learn what to look for in a spouse if the model of marriage in their own home is one of shared domestic drudgery? When you dream of walking your daughter down the aisle, do you dream of giving her away to someone who knows her most intimate soul and who will always treat her like a princess, plumbing the depths of their mutual passion for all the blissful years they spend together? Or do you dream of her finding someone who will fold his own boxer shorts? Ali said about his arguments with Tijen, "I don't want my children to think that that's the way relationships go."

In fact the greatest gift we can give our children is to have a truly romantic, passionate union with our spouse. *This* is how we will teach our children one of life's most important lessons: to believe in love. Your children will eventually move out of your house in search of their own romantic relationships, ones that confirm their own uniqueness. When they do, it will be hugely important that they have seen love— true love—with their own eyes so it's not just a Walt Disney fantasy for them. If you love your spouse—and demonstrate that love—your children will believe in love as an empirical truth, and they will have no excuse not to achieve it. This is why the children of divorce have such astronomical divorce rates themselves: They don't fundamentally believe that it can work, and they don't know how to make it work.

Putting children before passion in a marriage is fatal for the union, but it's also fatal for the individuals in that union. Even Tijen protested to me, "I used to be fashionable; I used to be in shape!" There is no greater or more rewarding work than motherhood, but it must be one aspect of a woman's overall being—not her whole persona.

It's absolutely essential for every one of us to feel desirable and attractive some of the time, the way we do when our spouse finds us desirable and has the opportunity to show us. But it's hard to feel foxy with mashed banana on your oversize T-shirt! This wasn't just about Tijen's appearance—but her view of *herself*; in her own eyes she had ceased to be a woman when she became a mom. Tijen needed to get back in touch with her sense of herself as a woman that she had before the babies—not just for Ali's sake or the sake of the marriage, but for herself.

Ali shared some of this responsibility. I strongly believe that when a woman begins to "let herself go," as offensive as that phrase might be, it is almost always the fault of an inattentive or distracted husband. When a woman's looks no longer matter to her, it's usually because she thinks she's married to someone who doesn't notice her anyway. I have often said that the healthiest diet for a woman is one made up of her husband's compliments. When a woman is told by the man she loves that she looks beautiful, it gives her incentive to live up to the compliment. If he's too busy watching the game, why shouldn't she eat her way through the kitchen?

The first thing the Wexlers needed to do to mend their family was to sit down with Dilara, to let her know that they understood how frightened and unhappy they had made her by their fighting. They needed to apologize to her and to eliminate any thought in her head that their marriage was not going to survive. They apologized, individually and together, and I was gratified to see how well it went. For the first time in a long time they were working together as parents to give Dilara the security she needed.

But Dilara's well-being wasn't the only issue. The parents needed to take care of one another too, and that meant they needed to attend to their marriage. A first principle of marriage, a basic so fundamental I could barely believe it needed to be emphasized, is a man and a woman sharing a bed. This couple needed to get baby Tanner out of their marital bed and Ali back into it.

It's true that getting sex back onto the Wexlers' agenda was part of my thinking. The functional termination of a couple's sex life (especially that of a young couple) is a functional termination of the marriage itself. The marital bedroom isn't a dormitory! Coming together to make love is an important reaffirmation of our commitment to one another; in those moments we become bone of one bone, flesh of one flesh. And it brings a tremendous flood of positive feelings toward our spouse, which are nice to have in reserve! But sex wasn't the whole picture. We cannot discount how disturbing it is to our children when they see that we have begun to sleep apart. Seeing their parents wake up together in the same bed gives kids a real sense of security, even if they have no idea what it means.

And after all, just sleeping with someone there in the same bed is one of the great comforts and intimacies of marriage; we are never as vulnerable as when we are asleep. This couple needed to open up to each other, and the bedroom was a good place to start. We had plenty of time to worry about getting them to be more available to one another while they were both conscious.

A-Milking We Will Go

The Wexler family also needed to break out of their stultifying routine. They needed to rediscover the sense of adventure that had brought them together, and they needed to learn that marriage and family life can be fun!

Everyone thinks that excitement is always to be found somewhere else—never where we are, in our own towns, our own families, our own homes. What terrible self-loathing this implies! Why must the grass always be greener somewhere else? Perhaps if we spent a little more time watering and tending our own grass, it would become the verdant carpet that we so envy in our neighbor's backyard.

You don't have to travel to exotic locales to find excitement—but you do have to break out of your stultifying routine once in awhile. With this in mind, I arranged for the Wexlers to go for a tour of a nearby dairy farm. It was something a little different, and I would be whispering sweet nothings into the Wexlers' ears via headset.

Even though the day was frigidly cold, the family had a great time running around the dairy and milking the cows. I encouraged Tijen to work against Ali's natural tendency to isolate himself by constantly involving him, asking him for help, complimenting him, and encouraging him to participate—and by encouraging Dilara to connect with her father. And Tijen laughed when I reminded her that—unlike our four-legged friends—she was more than just something to produce milk; she was a person in her own right.

In one of the show's touching moments, I prompted Tijen to show Ali a little affection, and she obliged by giving him a squeeze and a peck. The surprise—and pleasure—on Ali's face made me laugh out loud; it looked like there might be hope for the Wexlers' rekindled romance after all.

Catch Me (I'm Falling)

Now that we had reminded this family that married people are supposed to sleep together and have fun with one another, it was time for us to tackle a bigger problem: Ali's trust issues that were causing him to isolate himself from his own young family. Perhaps more important, it was time for this couple to see the tremendous impact that their own interactions—both negative *and* positive—had on Dilara.

I took them not ten minutes from their house to a gym equipped with a climbing wall. Our trust experiment was simple: Tijen would belay Ali as he climbed, putting tension on a rope that would keep him aloft even if he lost his hold on the wall. He would, quite literally, be putting his life in her hands. And what better metaphor for life is there than a vertical face, and knowing that you can't make the climb without the help and support of people who love you?

Once again I coached them through the earpieces, encouraging Ali to show his need for Tijen with the occasional "Have you got me?" and for Tijen to shore up Ali's confidence in her with constant reassurance and encouragement. "I will never let you go; I'll never let you fall," she said—and she didn't. She was all the safety net he needed.

After Ali had successfully climbed the wall, I invited them to look at how their daughter had reacted to the sight of them working together. When we had first come in and confronted the vertical face, Dilara had been anxious and afraid. But seeing her parents working together, depending on one another, had transformed her. When Mommy and Daddy were strong and working together, her fear evaporated. By the time Ali rappelled down the wall to rejoin us, Dilara was clamoring for her turn. I watched with satisfaction as her parents—the two of them once again working as a team—coached their daughter to the summit.

We get married so that we will never have to climb alone. But marriage is not for the faint of heart; it is for the courageous. It can be difficult to take the leap of faith required, and it is even more difficult when there are substantial trust issues involved. But in a good marriage that risk pays off handsomely in a reliable and meaningful safety net. If your marriage is solid and loving, your spouse is always there for you. Your boss may humiliate you, your stock portfolio may fall, and your waist may thicken. Nonetheless, at the end of the day you know that there is someone at home who sees the hero in you, someone who will comfort you and bolster you when you've been buffeted by life's rougher winds. And that, my friends, is shalom.

Passive-aggressive posturing is a popular way to "get back" at people who have hurt you, because it feels like you're giving them back what they're shelling out. But it almost always backfires, leaving both parties feeling wronged and lonely. It's better, frankly, to have a fight that actually clears the air—and even better to reach out in a way that inspires your spouse to give you what you need.

Forcing the Issue

I was pleased and relieved to see that the family was making good progress. But I suspected that all of our work was just a Band-Aid unless we dealt with the issues underlying Ali's inability to let his wife into the deepest and most intimate corridors of his heart.

Being locked out of Ali's innermost life had caused Tijen terrific pain in the relationship—every day, every interaction felt to her like a rejection. My own heart felt like it was going to break when she sat in my trailer and wept, "What do I do wrong that he can't trust me?" I suspected that the root cause of Ali's inability to trust had nothing at all to do with Tijen but stemmed from unresolved issues with his adoptive father.

Tijen must have had similar suspicions because she had long been advocating for Ali to heal the rift. Unfortunately Ali had refused to consider it. There had been very little contact between him and his father for twenty years. When he spoke of his father, Ali was very judgmental, calling him cold, unresponsive, and unaffectionate. I cautioned him, reminding him that our first and foremost responsibility as children is to honor our parents, not to judge them. "You have no idea what your father went through, what issues of his own he had to face," I told him. And I reminded him of the old Talmudic teaching that how we treat our parents is how our children will eventually treat us.

So few of us ever really deal with the emotions we feel toward our parents. We can try to bury these emotions, but eventually they surface—usually in a very negative way—in our relationships with our spouses. What is the number one cause of the male midlife crisis? The death of a parent. Imagine how many sports cars and stupid affairs we could avoid if we'd simply have the conversations we need to have with our parents while they're still alive?

I wanted to save Ali from all that. I wasn't sure if healing were possible, but I knew that Ali needed to take a step toward closure. He needed to clear the air by respectfully but truthfully telling his father how he felt. But if we left it up to Ali, there would be no possibility for reconciliation. So Ronnie, the show's producer, and Marcus, our director, and I took a tremendous risk: We called Ali's father, Alan, in

Philadelphia and invited him to the Wexler home. In fact I have to give Marcus the credit because even I thought the venture too risky and too potentially troublesome. We told Alan it once again was time for him to have a relationship with his son, and we felt that his son's future rested on salvaging some part of their relationship.

Alan agreed to come immediately. Parents almost always want a better relationship with their children, especially later in life. There is nothing—nothing—more painful than to feel rejected by your own children. Parents will do almost anything to avoid that. Unfortunately by that point the child has grown used to the parent's absence and feels, "You weren't there for me when I was little, and now I don't need you." That was what had happened in this family. But that's the kind of passive-aggressive response that leaves both parties even lonelier and angrier than they were to begin with.

I will tell you that the scene where I told Ali that we had invited his father to his house without his permission was one of the most uncomfortable moments I endured filming this season's shows. I had no idea how he'd react, although I guessed that he wouldn't be pleased. We were taking a big chance by springing this on him. But what was the alternative? To ignore the problem and let a father and son go on for a lifetime with almost no contact? Was that not a huge tragedy and one that had to be rectified?

The cameras didn't quite capture Ali's rage, but I can tell you that it was pretty intense. I was so unsettled by the scene that I went back to the Airstream to lie down after we'd filmed it, shaky and unable to support my own weight.

Ali was angry. He told me that he didn't feel ready to take this step and felt that I had overstepped my boundaries. I apologized; of course he was right! No therapist in the world would countenance what we had done. It *was* a terrible case of overreaching. We had taken a very real risk, but my instincts had told me that Ali was ready. He had called us because he wanted to achieve shalom, and we weren't doing him a service by putting Band-Aids on the gaping hole in his life. I felt sure that getting these two men face to face was the key to forward progress for this family. And if not now, *when*?

Ali had to choose between maintaining his pride or having a father right up until his father entered the house. I had no idea which one he would select. Tijen came to my aid, telling Ali, "I'm happy we're doing this. I couldn't do it by myself. I think you've done really well, and truly, I think you wanted this. You want to deal with your issues, and there it is. You have one chance to get rid of all your anger."

The scene between Ali and his father was emotional, one of the most memorable moments of our first season. Although because of time constraints very little of that meeting made it into the show, father and son were together for more than two hours. I was concerned that Ali would respond to our "ambush" by shutting down and shutting out the experience, but he showed himself to be a person of tremendous courage and reengaged his father as soon as they were seated.

I told Alan that I had brought them together so Ali could share some of his feelings. Our intention, I explained, was not to be hurtful but to clear the air between them in the interests of a better relationship—or any relationship at all—between them in the future. I told Alan how I had once hurt one of my own children by failing to turn up at a school function when I had promised I would be there; so I went to her and apologized. Sometimes in life we let our children down. We don't mean to, but we do. And when we do, we have to go before them and do the right thing by asking their forgiveness. By the same token I believe that the meaning of the biblical commandment to honor your father and mother expresses itself in its highest form when we act benevolently toward our parents, especially by not judging them. I asked Ali to afford his father that respect by hearing him out.

Ali talked of his feelings of loneliness and isolation in childhood, of feeling that his father hadn't been there for him. He talked of how little encouragement he had received and how alone that had made him feel. For his part, Alan told Ali—for the very first time—of his own feelings of isolation and abandonment in childhood. No one had shown him enough support or affection either. Once when he was just 4 years old, he had been left alone for hours while his parents went out to a luncheon. He had done the best he could with the example he had, and he wished that the example had been better. Alan also shared some

Every parent must be two things: a parent and a person. As a parent you are a link in an ongoing chain of existence, which means that you must subordinate your interests to something higher. But parents are still people in their own right, and as such you must also work to realize your own dreams and ambitions. A good parent balances these two roles without sacrificing one to the other.

of his own hurt with Ali about their relationship. He told his son that he had always felt distressed by how closed-off Ali was to him, and he told him how wounded he was that Ali had stopped calling him "Dad," calling him by his first name instead.

Both men expressed a willingness to open up some of those doors. "It's not too late," Ali said. "I do love you. I was disappointed with you as a father, but we can be closer. I have one father until I die, and it's you." Ali agreed to once again call Alan "Dad." They had dinner together, chatting intimately like a father and son should. It was remarkable: a much more complete reconciliation than I had hoped for, ending with a hug (and a cheer from Tijen).

Magic Hands

The next assignment for the couple was taken straight from my book *Kosher Adultery*. With the arrival of their children, the Wexlers had misplaced the romance in their relationship, but if this couple thought the passion in their relationship was gone for good, they were in for a surprise!

The loss of eroticism is one of the most common problems I am confronted with when I counsel couples; solving this problem was the motivation behind two of my books, *Kosher Sex* and *Kosher Adultery*. Husbands think they aren't attracted to their wives because their wives are no longer sexy. But as we all know, attraction is in the mind. So what the husbands really need to do is to recreate in their minds their initial attraction to their mates.

At the root of my book *Kosher Adultery* is the idea that the adulterous wife is the most written-about character in world history. Anna Karenina, Madame Bovary, Tess, and Lady Chatterley are sexy, fascinating, alluring, mysterious, and very desirable. There's something very compelling about someone who is unknowable, untamable, and unpredictable, someone who can be possessed by no man. Of course adultery is the ultimate sin in marriage, and the book's point is to show that the erotic principles behind an adulterous affair can be transported into marriage.

I have a secret for men who have come to see their wives simply as a mother or even just as a fixture across the breakfast table: No woman in the world, no matter how devoted, can ever be fully possessed. Women are much more sexual than men, and they respond to other men's attentions—even when they make a conscious effort not to. Every woman, I tell the men I counsel, can stray if you neglect her. You win her trustworthiness only when you pay attention to her needs. In other words, every wife has the potential to be an adulterous wife. So why not turn your wife into your mistress?

Paradoxically, trust can kill the sexual spark in a relationship. The husband thinks: When we were dating, I was on my very best behavior because you didn't trust me yet. I had to seduce you to earn your trust. But now that we're married and have kids together I'm not so worried about what you think. So I pick my earwax in front of you, belch, and never offer compliments. A terrible mistake! Everyone likes to be seduced—whether it's for the first time or the 4,000th. What's needed to replace some of the lost sexual tension in most marriages is to put a little *mis*trust back into the relationship.

We booked Tijen for a luxurious two-hour-long massage at a spa. We told her it was to encourage her to think of herself once more as a woman, not just as a mom. What mother of two couldn't use some strong hands and warmed oil on her tired shoulders, not to mention two hours completely dedicated to her pleasure?

But we had a double cross in mind: While handsome Nathan would meet Tijen at the reception area, handsome Ali would be the real masseur. Tijen would be blindfolded and would not know the real masseur's identity. Ali thought he knew Tijen too well to be attracted to her—I wanted to prove to him that he didn't know her at all. So I encouraged him, under the guise of being Nathan, to go further than any professional masseur would really go. I told him he'd be surprised—and probably pretty aroused—to discover that his wife didn't stop him. He laughed at me—but I was content to sit back and wait while our little experiment single-handedly destroyed the myth of marriage as a boring trap.

The ruse went off brilliantly—at the beginning. If her groans of delight and her relaxed posture were anything to go by, Tijen was having the time of her life. With every stroke of Ali's strong hands she seemed to be remembering what is was like to experience her body as an instrument of pleasure, not just as an extension of the arms she used to hold babies and the breasts she used to feed them. Nathan stayed in the room, talking to Tijen as though he was giving the massage. Everything went fine until Ali started massaging Tijen's legs while Nathan was speaking to her near her head. Tijen poked her head up, saw Ali, and started laughing. "I knew it was you," she said.

I fell over—but all was not lost. Although our party trick hadn't come off exactly the way I had planned, this couple had still taken a giant step forward. Ali had done what I had suggested, touching Tijen in places that were really off limits. As I predicted, she didn't immediately stop him. She was a devoted and loyal wife, but she was still a woman. And Ali experienced what every husband in a similar situation does: a mixture of immense excitement, coupled with immense pain. He had just discovered that his wife was a passionate woman who could be brought to a place where she loses control. It meant that he would never get bored of her, because she *was* the sultry seductress he'd read about in novels—but it also meant that he could never fully trust her. In fact the only way he could be sure that she was worthy of his trust would be by catering to her emotional and physical needs so that she wouldn't have to find another man to satisfy her.

By the end of the experiment Ali had seen Tijen in a totally different light. She was not just a mother but a woman relaxing under the warm glow of what she thought was another man's hands. On the other hand, Tijen had discovered that the guy whose touch had made her feel so incredibly great was none other than her own husband! This couple had fanned the smoldering embers of their erotic life and could now warm themselves by the flames; they had found out that married sex could be as hot—or hotter—than they had ever thought. We turned off the cameras and let the massage continue in private.

This was a very satisfying episode for me. The Wexlers are a beautiful family, and we made a significant difference in the household. We did a short appearance together on the *Today* show, and I was happy to note that their passion was back, the baby was in his crib, Ali was back in the marital bed, Dilara's relationship with her parents was greatly improved, and Ali again had a relationship with his father. It was time for us to move on.

Lessons for Life

Don't fight in front of your children. It is especially important not to idly raise the specter of divorce. The idea of the family breaking up is more terrifying for a child than any bogeyman; introducing it, especially as a threat, is an act of violence against the family.

Don't allow sexual intimacy and your time together as a couple to be a casualty of your growing family. Make certain that you always get at least an hour of "grown-up" time together a couple of times a week. And get the babies out of your bed!

Whenever possible, mend your relationships with your parents. Grudges prevent healing and are toxic to your relationships with your own kids. Also, try not to judge your parents; you cannot ever fully know the circumstances that led to them making the choices they did.

Husbands, attend your wives! Women are more sexual than men. A neglected wife may turn to other men for attention. Adultery is a terrible sin, but it is only one form such attention can take. Even harmless and platonic exchanges—if they replace, rather than complement a husband's attention—can weaken a marriage.

Changing for Our Children

According to the U.S. Centers for Disease Control and Prevention, a staggering 4.4 million children have been diagnosed with Attention Deficit/Hyperactivity Disorder (ADHD). Of those, approximately 2.2 million children are currently receiving treatment in the form of medication.

Those numbers practically knocked me off my chair when I discovered them. I had never even heard of ADHD when I was a child, and indeed the disorder was first diagnosed in the early 1980s. Even more disturbing to me was the news that those statistics are increasing by leaps and bounds every year. So I was very interested to meet with Paula DiJoseph; her fiancé, Gary; and her ex-husband, Robert, who were struggling to cope with Savannah, a beautiful 6-year-old girl who had recently been diagnosed and medicated for ADHD.

I would like to make it clear here, as I did with the DiJosephs, that I'm a rabbi, not a doctor. Our mission with this family wasn't to confirm or contest Savannah's diagnosis. But as I told the DiJosephs, I am not without bias in this area. As far as I'm concerned, too many healthy American children are being put on pills to treat behavioral problems—and, even more disturbing, for *behavior that is actually normal for a child,* if not for an adult. In an age where parents are overscheduled and have precious little time for their children, they often turn to pharmaceutical alternatives to make their children more controllable. So I have to confess a general skepticism and discomfort with the general ADHD diagnosis. Having said that, I am perfectly willing to accept that I may be hopelessly wrong. So I was curious to spend some time with this family and hoped that by the end of the week I'd have a better idea whether Savannah's behavior was really due to her biochemistry or was a symptom of what was going on in the house.

You'll discover quite a bit in this chapter that you didn't find out from the show. For a variety of reasons, the final cut of this episode of *Shalom in the Home* was the one I liked least of the original ten that we filmed. Production was difficult: We lost a crucial conversation with Paula due to technical problems, and although I spent more than four hours talking with and counseling Robert, due to time constraints, very little made it to the screen. So I welcome the opportunity to show you here a little more of what I saw when I showed up in Florida with the *Shalom* mobile studio.

Blended Family

Like many families in America, the DiJosephs aren't a nuclear family in the traditional sense. Paula and Robert had married and had two children together before a painful split in 2001. Since the divorce, Paula had met and become engaged to Gary, a Vietnam veteran and military hero who had spent the majority of his adulthood in the Marines before becoming a successful businessman.

Paula and Gary were doing most of the parenting; Robert saw the kids only twice a month on weekends and on some of the school holidays. Although it was his first time around children, Gary loved Paula's kids and took an active role in their lives. He quickly came to see them as his own children, and they related to him as a second father and called him "Dad."

But while Gary told me repeatedly how much he loved the

children—and I could see that he was sincere—his efforts at demonstrating that love too frequently fell short. For instance, we taped him telling 7-year-old Michael that he would be punished for crying; we taped him telling Michael that he was ashamed because the child couldn't find one of his toys. That's a pretty hard line to take—misplaced toys and occasional tears are pretty commonplace occurrences for a little kid.

Unfortunately Gary's child care inexperience showed, particularly in his emphasis on discipline that I considered to be more appropriate for older children. Please don't get me wrong: I am a big believer in discipline when it comes to kids, and I do my best to raise my children with clearly defined boundaries so that they understand what is acceptable and unacceptable behavior. But Gary's disciplining of the children often smacked of a lack of patience.

Gary didn't mean to be short-tempered. Later in the show he confided in me that he had been raised in a cold and uninviting home and shipped off to military boarding schools at a young age. This was his first extended exposure to children, and after spending the better part of his life in the military, he was used to barking out orders and seeing his commands followed to the letter. But little children need choices in order to learn, and most of all they need patience.

I didn't judge Gary; patience would not make a list of my foremost virtues either. On the contrary, I related to him as a hero, a man who had not only served his country valiantly but who had taken in two children who were not his own, treating them as his own flesh and blood. Gary had dedicated himself to this family and lovingly provided it with significant financial support, even though his efforts came with no medals or public acclaim. For him to be successful in his chosen role, he needed to be shown what it meant to be a firm and trusted influence in a child's life—*without* coming across like a drill sergeant.

Compounding this, Paula seemed to have limited patience herself. She absolutely adored her kids and would sacrifice anything for their welfare. But when I watched the footage that is prepared for me by our production crew in order to get to know the families, it struck me that Paula felt this was *her* time. After suffering through two broken, long-term relationships, both of which had produced children, she was tired and ready to take care of herself for a change. She wanted to enjoy her life with Gary, but her young children, with their incessant demands, were getting in the way.

I could understand the sentiment. It is not crime for a mother to want to have a life of her own and to enjoy some alone time—indeed it is healthy for parents to have their own needs and their own dreams apart from their deep desire to see their offspring flourish. But in the case of Paula, it seemed that her need to finally enjoy some rest and indulge some of her own needs after a life of constant sacrifice was directly in conflict with her young children's perfectly legitimate demands for attention. Paula was seeing her children, especially Savannah, as problems, when it seemed to me that they were just being normal kids.

Of even greater concern to me was the relationship between the children's two houses, which could only be characterized as hostile in the extreme. "The relationship between the children's father and us has been very strained and terrible," Gary told us. Gary and Robert did not exchange a single word, so drop-offs after Robert's weekends meant that the kids crossed dark parking lots by themselves to go from one vehicle to the other, like spies over the Berlin Wall at the height of the Cold War.

It's really hard for kids to be shuffled to and fro! I remember how much I hated getting all attached to my mother and my home in Miami, only to fly to L.A. to see my father, get attached to him and his home there, only to be ripped away from it as I returned to Florida. It was emotionally excruciating. Parents must do everything in their power to ease the transition.

Throughout my career as a counselor, parents who have been about to divorce have asked me what living arrangements would minimize the disruption to their kids. In response I always tell them about a friend of mine in London. When he and his wife decided that their marriage was irretrievable, he bought two small apartments—one for him and one for his ex-wife. The children stayed in the matrimonial home. While he lived with the children in the house for three days of the week, his ex-wife lived in her apartment. When his ex-wife returned to the family home, he returned to his own apartment. Now I realize that most of us don't have the financial resources to support three homes—indeed most of us struggle to afford one. But I think this story is a good example of the lengths to which we should go to minimize disruption to the kids after a divorce.

As for Paula and Robert, I believed that the extreme enmity between the two houses was very problematic. My parents' divorce was very bitter and, like Paula and Robert, they never communicated. I didn't need them to be best friends or to go to the movies together. In fact I preferred that they not be best buddies—if they could get along and be nice to each other, then why did they have to tear the family apart? But they weren't even cordial, and I had to constantly question whether it was even appropriate to say something nice about one in the other's presence. I couldn't be natural in my own home! And I believed that Paula and Gary were making the same mistake to the detriment of the kids.

A further and serious complication was Paula's encouragement of Gary to assume the role of father to her children, replacing the children's biological father, Robert. For me bells went off when I heard both Michael and Savannah say that they had "two dads." Gary was doing wonderful things for the children, but that did not make him the children's father, and so it was wrong for them to call him "Dad."

Michael and Savannah had a mother and father—even if they weren't under the same roof. It was imperative for the kids to *bond* with their father, not to replace him. And Gary didn't need the title "Dad" to be an active and important part of the children's everyday lives. You can nurture and mentor children without being their parent.

In any event I chose not to address this issue on the show because I felt it would close Gary's and Paula's hearts to me. I wanted to focus on healing the far more important issues in this home, the ones that were truly causing the children harm. This is the hardest part of filming a television show like *Shalom in the Home.* I only have a few days to try my best to bring healing and peace to these families. That often means triaging the family's problems and choosing my battles wisely. I stand by my conviction that children need to have a primary bond with their

real father and should not be confused by calling another man "Dad."
But there were far more destructive issues at stake that needed to be
addressed without raising the family's defenses.

Foremost among them was Paula's admission to us on camera that
she had gone so far as to explore legal avenues for cutting Robert out of
the children's lives. I believed that would be an absolutely devastating
mistake, and I saw it as my job to make sure that this family never got
to that point. Children need fathers as much as they need mothers, and
Robert loved his children and desperately wanted to remain part of the
children's lives. Now he was not seeing his kids enough: two weekends
a month. For a father who lives only ninety minutes away by car, that
is a poor commitment. In addition Paula argued that Robert was not
meeting his financial commitments to the children. But the solution to
all this had to be to inspire Robert to make a greater commitment to
his kids, not to remove him entirely from their lives.

Not surprisingly with all this going on there was an atmosphere
of nervous tension at all times in the DiJoseph house, and I couldn't
help but wonder if that tension didn't have more to do with Savannah's
ADHD than with some chemical imbalance.

Don't Let the Pressures of Life Choose for You

Ideally all three adults would have joined me in the trailer to talk about
the problem with Savannah, but Paula and Robert hadn't spoken a civil
word to one another in months. So as a first step, I invited Paula and
Gary down to the Airstream.

I had looked closely at the footage we had of Savannah. She did
indeed seem distracted—she had a hard time meeting another person's
eyes when they were speaking to her, and she fidgeted incessantly, but
her behavior was certainly not off the charts. To me it seemed more like
nerves than a serious medical problem, but I was willing to hear how
Paula and Gary viewed the situation.

I did notice one thing: The person who seemed to suffer most from
the lack of tranquility in the home wasn't Savannah but her mother,
Paula. Over and over we saw how Savannah's demands, no matter
how minor, sent Paula off the deep end. "I wanted to throttle her

*Turbulent parents
do not raise peaceful
children. We must heal
ourselves of the wounds
of our own childhoods
in order to raise strong,
secure, and healthy
children.*

today. I'm telling you, she's going to be the death of me. She was just *on me*—boom, boom, boom—just on me. She's just on me and on me." When talking about how Savannah's demands made her feel, Paula openly used phrases like "frustrated," "bent," and "pushed to my limit." She responded immediately when I used the phrase "black hole of affection" to describe how her daughter seemed, to Paula, absolutely insatiable when it came to her mother's attention. Paula could not escape Savannah's gravitational pull, and like a black hole, Savannah's demands felt like they weighed a million times the weight of the sun.

But there was a disconnect to me: The attention I saw Savannah asking for didn't seem excessive. As a father of eight, I can confidently vouch for the fact that little kids need attention—lots and lots of it. But Paula had little patience—her tolerance was pushed to its maximum by seemingly small demands made on her by the kids. And that meant that she treated them, especially the more dependent Savannah, like a nuisance, a burden too heavy to bear.

I was also struck, as I heard Paula talk about her daughter, by how perfectly normal, little-kid "pay attention to me" gambits were suddenly being treated as a condition requiring medical intervention. Savannah wasn't just clamoring to show off a new trick; she "had social issues." She didn't just want a hug or a piggyback ride; she had "no concept of personal space." Suddenly Savannah was "an ADHD child," an umbrella that conveniently encompassed any and all annoying, childlike behavior.

Maybe she was a little needy, a little unfocused. But was criticizing her and pushing her away the answer? Was yelling at her that she was too demanding not going to make her even more nervous and distracted? Who really had to change? Savannah—from being a kid? Or Paula—from the way she was experiencing motherhood? I was not judging Paula, but I did want to help her rediscover her patience as a parent, just as I often need to do myself.

In the next clip I showed, Paula's frustration—and her behavior—had escalated. In it she was actually threatening the kids with violence in a roundabout, joking kind of way. Now I don't believe in using any threats of violence or abandonment (which was also what this was) with a child (or anyone else, for that matter)—no matter how lighthearted they might be. And I have also said some pretty stupid things to my kids, which I've later regretted. But Paula was genuinely aggravated, and her threats, however theatrical and supposedly humorous, stemmed from genuine anger and frustration. That seemed like a real problem to me, and it was clear from the children's muted, confused reaction that they too detected a serious side to what Paula was passing off as a joke.

A few days into my visit with the DiJosephs, I discovered that Paula had grown up in a violent home with an abusive father. It had been a truly horrible relationship. Her father had tragically committed suicide, and Paula refused to attend the funeral or even visit the site where his ashes were kept. That tremendous anger had not found any resolution, and now the children were suffering with a well-intentioned, loving, but nervous mother who had never reconciled herself to the traumatic experiences of her own upbringing.

Paula was always on tenterhooks; everywhere you touched, it was raw. She was a woman in pain, in deep anxiety over unresolved emotional trauma that robbed her of her ability to enjoy her children; she loved them but sometimes didn't seem to like them. Much that they did, no matter how innocuous, seemed to upset a delicate equilibrium. Kids need a lot of patience, and patience is one thing in short supply when you're struggling with a tremendous amount of emotional turmoil. And the message Savannah and Michael were getting, little by little, was "everything you do is wrong."

Paula was not quite a volcano ready to burst, but lava was slowly oozing out in the direction of her children, and it was suffocating some of her most important relationships. I struggle with these issues myself, given the turbulence of my own upbringing. The fear that I will either consciously or subconsciously transmit my own inner turmoil to my kids is always before me. I recognize that I will never be able to really raise stable and sturdy children unless I simultaneously heal myself. This was a lesson I would have to communicate to Paula without raising her defenses.

When it comes to the issue of finding patience for children, I am not without compassion. The attention that small children demand, day after day, can be taxing. It doesn't help that they don't have the social skills of an adult. My wife, for instance, will usually wait until I finish typing a sentence to ask me a question. But I feel lucky if my children don't erase the entire hard drive by climbing into my lap in their hurry to be heard.

I struggle every day with my own frustration issues—issues that I regrettably sometimes take out on my children. Life can be difficult, and it is very tempting to take out our exasperation—with our colleagues, our financial woes, and our howling rage at not being able to find the ringing cell phone—on the people who are closest to us. After all, our kids won't fire us for shouting. They won't even stop loving us, and that's what makes our behavior especially cruel.

But their constitutions are too fragile to absorb the assault. Children are like fragile pieces of pottery. They break inside, in a very terrible and irreparable way, when you scream at them just because they ask you a question while you're standing in the hot sun looking for your missing keys. I will not sugarcoat this: *When you take your frustration at life's pressures out on your children, you cause irreparable damage to your children and to your relationship with them.*

I'm speaking to and about myself now as well. Many times I have yelled at my kids. In each case I had a choice and I made the wrong one. The idea that my inability at times to control my temper has damaged my children causes me endless pain and sorrow, even as I write this. We are not animals; there is always a split second of choice before we act. And those choices, more than anything else, define who we are as people. So we have to choose better. We have to control our moods so that our moods don't control us.

I have come to realize that it is one of my greatest responsibilities as a parent to rein in my frustrations so that they don't affect my interactions with my children. One of the great gifts of parenthood has been the opportunities it has presented me to learn the virtues of patience. It was this that I had to convey to Gary and Paula.

In an attempt to illuminate the possible consequences of allowing frustration and tension to infect their children, I told Gary and Paula a painful story from my own parenting experience. My daughter Chana is the most sensitive of all my children and the one who is most like me. She is complicated, brilliant, warm-hearted, and at times dark. (I make no claims on brilliance or warmheartedness, but can relate to the darkness.) A few years ago I noticed that Chana was avoiding me because she was afraid of my unpredictable temper. A distance had grown between us; to my horror she had turned into one of those children who gauge their parents' mood before approaching them. That assessment is the beginning of the alienation that takes place between parents and children.

Seeing this was devastating to me. There is nothing more important to me than being close to my kids, especially my daughters, whom I have raised as Daddy's girls. When they walk into the room they hug me and I hug them. When they leave the house they kiss me and I kiss them. So how could this distance possibly have sprung up? Well, I had no one to blame for my daughter's distance but myself. Kids need to know that when they come to Mom and Dad about something, they're going to find a soft, affectionate, and receptive parent. If they don't, they'll stop coming.

I was absolutely heartbroken that I had allowed such a barrier to come up between us. As I told my wife, "I cannot believe that I frighten my own child." So I sat down with Chana and apologized to her, speaking from my heart: "Before you were born I thought I knew what joy was—but I didn't. Without you in my life, I would know no joy and I would know no wonder. Without you as my daughter, every smile would be fake. *You* brought the light into my life. If I have ever frightened you or made you feel I wasn't overjoyed when you walked into the room, then I ask that you forgive me. I'm not perfect, but you are. I make a lot of mistakes, and I'm sorry that my flawed personality has hurt you." Chana was crying as I made my apology, and she hugged me warmly afterward.

The story touched a nerve; as I spoke, tears rolled down Paula's face.

The next big issue for Paula and Gary was the co-parenting issue. The silence between the two homes was bad enough, but the situation was threatening to escalate into out-and-out war.

It was up to me to inject a little reality back into the situation. As far as I could tell, both of the men in this not-so-blended family were operating under some very dangerous delusions. Robert didn't want to acknowledge Gary's existence at all, so he was unable to acknowledge the tremendous contributions that Gary was making on behalf of his children. Of course this made Gary feel invalidated. On the other hand, Gary, of course, got Robert's defenses up in the worst possible way by playing "dad," as if Robert didn't exist. And Robert had very real reasons to be concerned about the effect this was having on his children.

This was a tragic situation. Here were good people, both of them devoted to the welfare of the kids in question. But like two nations arguing over territory, they had become enemies as each protected his turf. Difficult as it might have been, there was a real need for Gary and Robert to put the interests of the children first. That meant they needed to learn to get along with each other and to appreciate the contribution each was making to the children.

Gary openly felt that Robert's presence in the children's lives was detrimental, not positive in any way, and he felt that many of Savannah's "problems" were largely the result of Robert's influence. He also supported the ADHD diagnosis and was a driver behind the decision to medicate Savannah. Robert not only contested the diagnosis, he felt that whatever symptoms Savannah exhibited had only increased since she'd started with the pills.

Robert had a right to be concerned. Gary had openly stated his wish to adopt the kids, to become their father legally. The move would for once and for all erase Robert from the picture. Conversely, Gary had some very legitimate complaints himself, including the fact that he provided for the lion's share of the children's financial needs, even though he was not their biological father. These were most noble acts, but they did not make him their father.

I had to make these two men see that there was more than enough room for both of them. Children have an unlimited capacity for love, and the more loving, patient adults they have in their lives—to do things with them, to show interest in them, and to love them—the better. Robert had to come to terms with the fact that Paula had moved on and had invited a new man to share her life. But Gary and Paula also needed to acknowledge the importance of Robert's role in the

We yell at our kids when we're nervous or frustrated for one reason: because we can. They'll take it when no one else will. But they are helpless and vulnerable, and yelling at them damages them. We must make a better choice, absorbing the pressures of life without transmitting and amplifying them.

children's lives and to understand that it would not help anyone to confuse the children about who their father really was.

Divorce is deeply traumatic for children, but there is much that the adults in that situation can—and *must*—do to mitigate the effects that a split will have on the kids. I have counseled a number of people about to become stepparents, and the following is the advice I give:

First of all, don't rush into an emotional connection. You are, effectively, a stranger to these children. Spend a lot of time with them, get to know them, and let them get to know you. The emotional connection will come, but it cannot be forced.

Second, be honest. Sit down and have a conversation, just you and the kids, addressing concerns right up front. Say, "I'm not your parent, and I won't ever be your parent. But just because you aren't my flesh and blood doesn't mean that I can't love you and be a parent figure in your life, and I hope that I will be. That means you can talk to me about anything and ask me about anything—it means that I will always be here for you. But it also means that I'm going to say something if I see you doing something that puts you in harm's way, whether physically or emotionally. Because I care, I'm going to speak up."

I'm a huge proponent of the air-clearing "family meeting" for all families and especially for blended families. Give the kids a chance to vent. Sharing Dad's or Mom's attention with a new person sucks—so does having to share a bedroom and toys with a step sibling you're just getting to know, as well as the many other emotional and practical adjustments a kid has to make when families come together. These are natural feelings, and they don't hurt anyone unless they're ignored and never allowed to see the light of day.

Most of all, children are not pawns to be used in a power play against a former partner. Adults must learn to overcome their own sense of hurt and not use the children to try to punish the other parent. Don't extend the trauma of divorce by trying to turn the children against their parent.

In fact if the love/marriage relationship is already dead, then there is nothing to be gained from continuing to hurt each other. If you don't want anything more than a cordial relationship with this person, why waste time and energy on strategizing to inflict pain? On the contrary, when there is no hope of reconciliation, the adults must act like adults, which means that *every single decision must be made on the basis of what will be best for the children*. I know this is hard—sometimes your interests and the interests of your children are not the same; but they must come first. And losing a loving parent who was ready and willing to participate could never be the best thing for the children.

I strongly believed that Gary and Robert and Paula had to find some kind of rapprochement or "it would get ugly," in Paula's words. For the next day or two, I wanted to focus on Savannah and on Paula's and Gary's parenting skills, but I didn't let them leave the trailer until I had planted the seed of reconciliation with Robert in their minds.

Welcome to the Monkey House

I wanted to see whether Savannah had fewer symptoms when she had lots of undivided adult attention. I felt quite sure that she would be much less distracted if she could have access to adults who were lovingly and patiently reinforcing her focus and attention. So we took the family to a beautiful nature park filled with primates. I grew up about an hour from Gary and Paula, and I had wonderful memories of visiting this park as a boy. Paula, to my surprise, offered to take Savannah off the ADHD medication for the day. I suspect that she volunteered to do so because she wanted to prove me wrong, but I'll confess that I jumped at the opportunity to assess my theory without chemical intervention.

Unfortunately the day got off to a rocky start. Paula and Gary had had an argument earlier in the morning, and the unresolved remnants of their disagreement loomed over our expedition like a thundercloud. We didn't even make it all the way to the nature park before a bitter quarrel broke out. I asked them, in the spirit of the day, to put their bad feelings toward each other on the back burner and to focus their full attention on the kids, especially on Savannah.

I knew prior to my arrival in the DiJoseph home that Gary and Paula had a bad relationship with Robert. But I was just now beginning to understand the depth of the problems between Paula and Gary and how those were adversely affecting the kids as well. I wanted to see if Paula and Gary could put their moods aside and rise to the occasion. They agreed, but I saw with some unease that the tension between them did not lift appreciably—and that the children felt it too.

Regardless, I gave them two points of focus. I wanted them to make Savannah understand that she was the best little girl in the whole wide world, *even when she did something wrong.* Savannah was too used to hearing how bad she was. She was nervous because she lived with the constant fear of being scolded. It was time for her to have realistic goals, positive reinforcement, and inspiration. Instead of telling her how bad she was, Gary and Paula were to tell her how good she could be.

I am sympathetic. My son Yosef was by far the most challenging of any of our kids when they were 5-year-olds. When he was 4 I found myself scolding him constantly for his behavior, telling him that he was a naughty boy. But I hated being that person—and I wasn't changing any of his behavior anyway. So I decided to tell him instead that he was the best boy in the whole world. If his fingers were in his spaghetti, I'd ask him, "Who is the best boy in the whole world?" and he would answer "Me!!!" with a big smile on his face. I'd follow up with, "Does the best boy in the whole world eat with his hands or with his fork?" He would say, still with a smile, "With a fork." And he would pick up his fork.

Savannah needed the same encouragement. Paula and Gary had to learn to correct her without breaking her spirit or making her feel like she was a bad kid. And I wanted to see if they could find creative, patient, loving ways to help her by reinforcing her concentration instead of criticizing and yelling at her.

The park had two very basic safety rules: no touching the monkeys (although they could—and would!—touch us), and no touching the electrified fence. Savannah did a better job than either Gary or Paula in listening to the ranger as he explained these. I encouraged the grown-ups to periodically and patiently remind Savannah of the two rules as they enjoyed the monkeys—and I was overjoyed to see that this extra consideration worked! When Paula and Gary were paying attention and supporting Savannah with tons of positive reinforcement, she was indeed the best girl in the world—just a

It is our job as parents to act as shock absorbers for our children, to absorb the stresses of life, whatever those may be, so that we don't pass them along to our children.

normal, beautiful kid, squealing in disbelief and joy as tiny monkeys clambered all over her for treats.

Paula and Gary were having a tougher time. The tension between them kept flaring in little spats. Individually they didn't seem committed to the experiment either. Gary quickly got bored and got on his cell phone to make business calls. How could he possibly teach a child focus and attention when he couldn't concentrate himself? What was so important that it took him away from seeing the joy on Savannah's face as exotic monkeys cavorted on her shoulders? What was he more likely to remember—the content of that phone call or the once-in-a-lifetime experience he was missing in order to make it?

The day wasn't safe from Paula's anger either. As we left to see the gorillas, Savannah drifted dangerously close to the electrified fence, and Paula screamed at her and yanked her back with greater force than was required for her safety.

To be fair, I could see why Paula was frustrated; Savannah had been told a number of times to stay away from the dangerous fence, and yet she couldn't seem to remember. But there were two goals to this exercise: for Savannah to learn to focus and for her parents to learn to curb their frustration. Another mother, mindful of Savannah's forgetfulness, might have gently positioned herself between her daughter and the dangerous fence or engaged her in conversation about how the fence worked in order to keep it present in her mind. But Paula seemed to be setting Savannah up to fail—a challenge that she duly met by putting her hand almost unconsciously on the fence post as they turned the corner, provoking yet another bout of yelling.

We all sat down together, and I tried to model a more patient, loving approach by asking Savannah to look me in the eyes when I was speaking to her and reminding her to keep her hands in her lap. I wanted to reinforce Paula's message—that you listen to your mommy because she loves you and doesn't want you to get hurt—but I used questions, rather than yelling, to get Savannah to interact in the lesson. Getting Savannah to listen didn't happen on the first try; I had to direct her eyes back to me several times. But eventually she was attentive.

And that conversation led to one of the most heartbreaking moments for me in any of the shows we filmed. As I was wrapping up, I wanted to leave Savannah with a positive message, so I said, "I've known you for one day, and already I can see that you are the best girl in the whole world." And Savannah responded, "Without the pill."

I had to ask her to repeat herself. No one from the show had mentioned drugs in her presence—she didn't have any reason to suspect that we were testing a theory in this area. But even this 6-year-old didn't want to be medicated unnecessarily. Savannah did have some special needs, but they weren't chemical. She needed love, patience, help, and attention. She fidgeted and couldn't look Paula and Gary in the eye *because she was afraid*. She was nervous, responding to a pressure that was too great for her to bear.

My visit with the DiJosephs was arguably the most striking example in the first season of *Shalom in the Home* of how an angry and highly chaotic domestic situation can negatively impact on kids. Here we were seeing it in the most self-evident way—raising this little girl in a loving but dysfunctional home was resulting in her own diagnosis as dysfunctional. Again I am not judging these people. In fact I have many times been guilty of bringing dysfunction into my own home. I can be as nervous as Paula, as angry as Gary, and as out of it as Robert. My faults are worse than theirs, so I have no right to judge. And indeed, long after I left their home, I remained in close touch with both Paula and Gary, and they joined my family at our Passover seder in Miami. I counseled them on the phone together over some of the problems of their relationship, and I have a deep affection for all of them. Gary is a special man, honest and courageous enough to attempt to bring solid change into his life. Likewise, Paula is a woman who has suffered much in life and through it all has remained as devoted to her children as a lioness. It was always clear to me that the most important thing for Paula in her relationship with Gary was his acceptance of her children. So it is not judgment that I am passing against this family, but rather a sharp diagnosis of a problem which, if not checked, would ruin two innocent kids. Savannah and Michael needed a different method of upbringing, and I knew that with the smallest bit of positive reinforcement, Savannah especially could be inspired to rise above her nervous behaviors. Her parents needed to give her what she was asking for—changing themselves, if need be, to make that happen.

Heal Thyselves

As the kids hung out with the gorilla, Gary and Paula and I found a cool place to sit down and talk, very candidly, about Savannah, and about their relationship with her.

I told them that what I saw in Savannah wasn't a problem to be solved but a challenge to be risen to. Paula and Gary had been given a tremendous opportunity, as all parents have: the opportunity to be inspired by and inspiring to the children in their lives. For Paula it was an opportunity for her to learn patience, to put the hurt of her childhood and the destruction of her earlier marriage behind her. For Gary it was an opportunity for him to play and show his softer side, a side that had been suppressed during his long years in the military and in business. I went so far as to say to Gary that God had brought these two children into his life as a gift in recompense for all his service to his country. In the military he was taught to be tough and strong. Now, God had given him these kids to let him express his softer side and rediscover his own inner child. He should not resist the opportunity but instead allow it to change him into a softer, gentler, more patient, more forgiving man.

For both of these people, child raising was an opportunity for them to show and receive love—an opportunity they had sadly been too rarely granted in their own childhoods.

Paula and Gary were good people, but they had misunderstood the role of a parent. It's not the job of the adult to make our children act like us. When we do, we break the spirit of the child—indeed the very spirit of childhood. It's our job to focus the energy, the freedom, and the natural creativity that bubbles from every child—and to reap the benefits ourselves from doing this job well.

The story I told them offscreen to illustrate this point was about Joseph Kennedy, the patriarch of the Kennedy clan. Kennedy's parenting style was to mold his children in his own image. Because he was hypercompetitive, his children had to be hypercompetitive. Mediocrity was to be avoided no matter what the cost.

Not many people know the story of Rosemarie Kennedy, Joseph Kennedy's eldest daughter. She, like Savannah, was distracted, a little different—a child who needed a little more attention, a little more love so that she could meaningfully share her unique gifts with the world. Current psychologists who have reviewed her case are now squarely convinced her symptoms were a reflection of a severe depression, probably the result of a lifetime of being treated as if she were "less than" the other children.

But for Joseph, Rosemarie was a failure, and when she was 23 years old, he had her lobotomized—what I consider to be the mid-20th-century treatment for ADHD. It was a disaster, and she spent the rest of her life as an invalid—incontinent and institutionalized. Her brokenhearted mother considered it to be the first Kennedy tragedy.

I think there's a tremendous lesson there for all parents. Too much of modern parenting is an attempt to pacify our children—to get them to stop being kids! And I'm not talking just about the pharmaceuticals, but even of the more pedestrian pacifiers that we all use with our kids like video games, television, and frivolous spending. These are parental conveniences to avoid using up our energy, and they carry a price that is nothing less than childhood itself. A child is not supposed to veg out on the couch for hours at a time; he's supposed to run around until he falls in his own tracks like a puppy. She's not supposed to respectfully approach her parents with a request for a meeting; she's supposed to spill over with excitement and news and joy as soon as she sees them. He's not supposed to be insatiable for the coolest, newest thing with a plug; he's supposed to drive his parents crazy by mucking about for 45 minutes with a stick, a rock, and a puddle! *That* is childhood. And we lose something terrible when we ask our children to trade their childhoods for a premature adulthood—especially when we do so for our own convenience.

Savannah needed a little more support than some children, but there wasn't anything wrong with her as long as she got that support. Like so many children, Savannah didn't need to relax or to chill out;

she needed a healthy focus for her ample energy. And she didn't need a pill, but someone to give her enough time in order to help her learn.

Our day with the monkeys had not been an unqualified success, but some of my questions were answered. Savannah did indeed respond appropriately when she was given more attention. Now Gary and Paula had to rise above their own limitations, and the limitations in their relationship, to give it to her. So I called a meeting for that evening in the *Shalom* trailer, the DiJosephs' home away from home.

I'm Done for the Day

That night I brought the conversation around to Gary and Paula's relationship. Once again we had been called in to "fix" a child—and the real patient on the table turned out to be an adult relationship.

I brought into that meeting an index card with a single word printed upon it. The word was "commitment." Paula and Gary were engaged to be married, and yet I saw no real commitment in their relationship. It wasn't that they fought all the time. Rather both Paula and Gary threatened to bolt over disagreements that could easily be resolved.

It's commonplace now for American marriages to fail and for people to get a divorce, so now this is what we threaten one another with, "If you don't act right, I'll walk on out of here." But that's not commitment! That's telling people that you're committed to them as long as they toe your line. Real commitment means that you'll stay even when they don't act the way you want them to!

These people loved each other deeply, but they were threatening to leave in order to preempt rejection. But what Gary and Paula didn't realize was how much damage they were doing to each other with these threats—and to the children in the home as well. Threatening to leave is really a very harmful way of intimidating someone. Deep down inside, every one of us has a real fear that we'll be abandoned by the people we love most, and we know that if it happens, it will leave a gaping hole in our lives. Incorporate that threat into the arsenal you pull out during an ordinary domestic argument and you run the risk of doing tremendous collateral damage, like using a howitzer to kill an ant.

When, for our own convenience, we ask our children to act less like children and more like adults, we violate the very spirit of childhood and parenthood.

This threat also obscures the real issues. Threatening to leave shifts the problem—and the reconciliation—to "You're not going to leave, are you?" "No, of course, I'll never leave you." How convenient! Now you never actually have to address the issue that precipitated the conflict, like why someone speaks abusively to you—and why you put up with it.

For this couple, threatening to leave had become the ultimate weapon in their relationship. In fact during our conversation about their relationship, a fed-up Gary threatened to leave both me and Paula by storming out of the trailer. "I'm done for the day," he said.

I was pleased that he eventually agreed to rejoin us. And in wrapping up I asked Paula and Gary simply to take small steps toward wholeness by eliminating this most inappropriate and unhealthy behavior. They didn't have to change overnight—they just had to cut out the worst stuff immediately and for good. For them that meant two things. First, between themselves it meant never again threatening to leave. Never. Ever. And second, with the children it meant eliminating tension and anxiety wherever possible by showing a little more patience and tolerance.

I may have had to beg Gary to get him to come back and hear me out, but I think he was glad that he did; he looked like he'd shed ten years of tension by the end of the session. "I guarantee that if I don't have to fear that we're going to break up all the time, I'll be a lot different," he confided. In a private moment with the cameras, he said that he believed he would be a better man for the insights we had given him.

Meeting Halfway

It was time for me to talk to Robert. Not much of our conversation, due to time constraints, made it to the screen, which is a great shame. My time with Robert was inspiring and productive, and it got to the core of what I felt troubled him. I saw that Robert *also* had a tremendous opportunity for change if he could only rise to the challenge presented to him by his children.

In some ways Paula was right; Robert wasn't stepping up to the plate—and not just as a parent. During our conversation I learned that he had been devastated by Paula's decision to leave him; her departure had knocked him flat. In his words he'd been "beat up pretty bad over the last few years," and he'd gotten mired in depression. He had gained a lot of weight, something that he confessed made him very uncomfortable, and he hadn't been going out or dating as much as he would have liked.

It was clear to me that Robert's biggest problem in life was that he was utterly lacking in inspiration. He was a spent force, a used-up person, a man who believed that his best days were behind him. I asked him how he felt about himself, and he said, "Well, not great. I don't like the way I look. I'm overweight. I don't go out. I don't date." I told him, "In other words, you're not motivated. You can't find the inspiration to be the man you want to be. Your depression results from feeling like you can't maximize your potential in your life."

Incidentally I believe that this is the source of all human depression: a feeling of helplessness, like our lives are careening out of control and there is nothing that can be done about it. Whenever a gap develops between the person we want to be and the person we are, depression comes along and fills in the gap.

The problem with people like Robert (and the rest of us, for that matter) is that in order to get out of a rut we wait for some great epiphany to come along. We keep waiting for something external to come along to inspire us. We think to ourselves, "If only I won the lottery, then I'd be happy." But if you depend on externals to motivate you, to make positive changes in your life, you're going to wait a long time!

I told Robert that I wanted to share with him a life-changing insight. I shared the theory with him, shared by the great Jewish scholar Maimonides and the great Greek philosopher Aristotle, that we all have two selves. One is our congenital self—what scientists today might call your genetic set point. These are the characteristics and traits that you're born with—whether you're hotheaded or patient, ambitious or easygoing. The other is our habitual self, the self that is the result of repeated behaviors. If you do something over and over, it becomes ingrained. With enough repetition your habitual self can actually change your congenital self. So you might naturally be a miserly and cheap person, but if you force yourself to give to charity enough times, however much it hurts initially, after awhile that behavior becomes intuitive. Your nature has changed.

For some people, there's nothing they'd rather do than run laps around the park like a cheetah at six in the morning; the rest of us have to force ourselves to do it. But we can—and if we make it a habit, we can fit into the same pants as the cheetah-people. Like Paula and Gary, Robert was allowing the pressures of life to make decisions for him; and like them, he could decide to transcend them.

I shared what I consider to be the secret of a happy life: Emotions don't create actions—actions create emotions. We may not—dare not!—wait for inspiration, some *deus ex machina,* or outside force, to inspire us to be a better person or to become the person we want to be.

I said to Robert, "You're in the dumps; you feel like garbage. The woman you loved and who bore your children is off with another man. Your kids are not that close to you. Your career path is blocked. Your physical appearance is not what you want it to be. In short, you feel like a loser, and you feel that you need some great emotional awakening to give you the wherewithal to pick yourself up. Well, it is not great awakenings that create action, but the other way around. Rather than waiting to find some amazing woman who will inspire you to begin exercising, force yourself to get up in the morning and go for a walk along the beach, even when it's the last thing in the world that you feel like doing. Initially you'll hate it—but by the third, fourth, and fifth morning you will *create* the inspiration.

"And don't believe the lie that you're a loser. You're a winner. You're a good man with a good heart who loves his children. You have a great mind and a bright soul. Now, all you need to do is translate your potential into the actual."

When you do something good and you push yourself to continue, the gap that develops between your will and your action is filled with inspiration. I told Robert that if he forced himself to be the man he knew he was capable of being, he would begin to feel really good about himself as he became that man.

We have to act to become better people and make more of our lives, whether we feel like it or not. Success isn't doing the right thing when you feel like it—*it's doing it when you don't feel like it*. Pushing himself a little to make something more of his life might start out as something Robert *did*, but it would end up as something he had *become*.

In his children Robert had the ultimate inspiration. What better reason to get off the couch than to play with, instruct, and inspire the two people in the world who mean the most to you? What better reason to hit the gym than to be able to join your children on the soccer field or on the sand at the beach?

I said two other things that I thought Robert really needed to hear. First, "You, *you*, are their father. They need a father just as much as they need a mother. They need you." Second, "Your kids will always want to be around you—no matter what challenges you might face—if you do two things: lift them up and elevate their moods and their self-esteem."

As a child of divorce I know that kids have long memories: They always remember who was there for them. If a parent does the right thing by a child, the child will remember and will always come back. You can't fool children for long. They know if you love them enough to always make time for them. Their BS detector is unfoolable.

I then asked Robert the toughest question of all: Could he choose to forget the bad history of the past few years and find it in his heart to meet with Paula and Gary, with an eye to forging some kind of rapprochement for the children's sake? It was a bold gambit: This was a collection of people who detested each other and who would not even communicate for the sake of the children. Suddenly, without any warning, I was asking them to meet. I knew it was the right thing to do, and truth be told, I had little to lose. The situation was so bad that it called for a radical solution.

Robert was a little startled to discover that I was asking to meet with them right now, but like a real gentleman he rose to the occasion and immediately agreed. But before we left the Airstream, I had one more thing to ask Robert. Could he manage to keep his own focus and attention on his own parenting skills instead of worrying about what others in the family were doing? He agreed to try that as well. And so we set off.

When I finally caught up with Paula and Gary, the situation with them was not good. They'd had a very difficult trip, which they partially attributed to bad directions given to them by a member of the *Shalom* crew, and they had found no place to park once they'd arrived. They were upset with us and were reluctant to go on camera—and they didn't even know yet that we wanted them to meet with Robert!

The crew got them some soft drinks, and I met up with them in an outdoor cafe. I sat down with them and let them vent for a little while. Eventually I told them that they were free to leave if they wanted to, but that their problems would go with them. "This is what it's all about," I told them. "I came to help you with your daughter, but in order to make a real impact, we're going to have to address the constant anger in your house. Savannah doesn't have ADHD or anything else—she just can't handle the constant nervous tension that surrounds her." I turned to Paula and said, from my heart, "Paula, this is your daughter. I know that you would never do anything deliberately to hurt her. But if you don't break this cycle, she will grow up to be just as angry as you are, and she will make her kids nervous in turn, and they will grow up to be angry, and it will go on forever unless you stop it now."

My words hit home. Paula had tears streaming down her face. In that one moment, all her humanity and kindness poured out. And her love for her daughter was exemplary. "Of course I don't want to hurt my precious baby," she cried. And she finally told me about her childhood. Her parents had a horrible relationship filled with acrimony. She hated and blamed her father, and when he died when she was just a little girl, she did not miss him and refused to go to his memorial service. All the pent-up rage she harbored toward her father (and all the guilt she had about feeling those feelings in the first place) was seeping out, poisoning her relationships. Now she was beginning to realize that if she didn't forgive her father—and herself for her ill feelings toward him—she would continue this circle of anger with her own daughter.

If you'd been able to see this scene, I believe the episode would have had much greater impact. Unfortunately, the camera crew was still with Robert, and the little audio we were able to get was so poor that we couldn't use it. It might not have made for great television, but it was a tremendous step forward for the DiJoseph family. I saw Paula in a heroic light, ready to battle her demons—and we all have them—for the sake of her daughter.

Meeting Halfway

Courageously, Paula and Gary agreed to meet with Robert. I brought these three adversaries together, and what transpired between them was very raw, very real, and very moving. Robert asked Paula to take off her glasses so that he could see into her eyes. She began weeping almost as soon as he started speaking. She apologized for hurting him and told him that she wanted him to have a relationship with their children. She even turned to him for reassurance, asking, "Is it going to be okay?"

Gary, for his part, was equally the gentleman. He not only acknowledged Robert and behaved very cordially toward him but told him that although he really loved Michael and Savannah, he recognized Robert's place in their lives: "You're their father and they need you. They're always going to need you."

After the adults had spoken, we brought the children onto the bridge. They couldn't remember the last time they had seen their parents in the same place. It's always glorious for kids to see parents who have been torn apart come together. When I was a child, I always dreamed of my divorced parents getting remarried to each other, but short of that, I at least wanted them to be cordial to each other. I enjoyed seeing them in the same places together on the rare occasions that miracle occurred.

Finally I brought the whole blended family together for a casual volleyball game on the beach—with Robert, Gary, and Michael on a team together against Paula, Savannah, and me. Wow. I felt really good, as if I'd played an important role in bringing this tattered family together. Volleyball on the beach? Who would have thought?

Of course there was still a huge amount of work to be done. Changes, particularly the kind of fundamental changes that were necessary here, don't come easily. But these people had the best motivation I could offer them to galvanize that change: the well-being of their children. If this family could come together, as they had on this beach, to overcome the pain and bitterness of their history, they had a chance.

After my departure from the DiJosephs' home, things started out well but didn't continue that way. I left the home feeling really connected to Paula and Gary, and the three of us had quite a few counseling sessions on the phone to try to advance the progress we had made, especially in their relationship.

Paula especially reported to me her desire to absorb the lessons she had learned and progress in her life. She said to me many times that her children were utterly innocent, and she reiterated a number of times how she did not want to transmit whatever pain she and Gary had experienced in their own lifetimes to their children. I'm very pleased to report that things with Savannah did improve tremendously.

But after awhile, things started to deteriorate between the two homes. Robert felt more and more alienated from his children, and Paula and Gary increasingly argued that Robert was destabilizing the children. They were convinced that whenever the children went to Robert's home, they came back exhibiting behavioral problems. I wasn't there to gauge the truth of any of these allegations, so I could only stand by my strong conviction that the kids needed more of Robert in their lives, not less. By the time our crew went to film the two-month follow-up, Paula was already contending that things had gotten worse with Robert since the show.

To be sure, I was very upset to hear that. But I am nothing if not realistic about what a show like this can do. We can try to show people the way, but they choose what path to follow. I felt truly terrible that we hadn't been able to do more for these special people for whom I had come to care a great deal, but I felt that we had marked the way, and it was up to them to follow the path we had marked.

I pray that God grants them the blessing of inner and outer peace.

Lessons for Life

After a divorce, no matter how painful, the right choice is always what's best for the kids—even if that conflicts with what's best for the adults.

Little kids need lots of patience and affection. If you feel overwhelmed by those needs, you need to get more help and support.

If your kids seem hyperactive and unable to focus, they may indeed have ADHD. But perhaps they are not getting the love, attention, and security they need to find stability within themselves. Before turning to medical treatment, try to minimize tension in your home and give your children much more attention, affection, and security, and see what happens.

If you marry someone with children, by all means try to be an inspirational adult role model for them. But don't try to supplant their biological parent, unless that parent is dead or categorically refuses to be involved in the child's life.

The hero is not a man who battles monsters and dragons that may harm his children but who fights his own inner demons for the sake of his children. The hero is a woman who heals herself so that she can raise stable and secure children.

The Parents Against the Kids

The video plea we got from the Herrons wasn't so unusual; the kids fought with each other all the time and ignored their parents. Their mother, Ruthi, reacted by nitpicking and nagging at them 24/7. Meanwhile their dad, Greg, took little enjoyment from his home life, complaining that he could find no peace.

None of this sounded like tranquility to me. So I went to Bethlehem, Pennsylvania, to see if I could smooth the tensions causing all the conflict in this home.

A Picture-Postcard Family

The Herrons and their four kids—14-year-old Nick, 13-year-old Forrest, 11-year-old Kira, and 9-year-old Noah—looked like a postcard advertising the American family. Ruthi, a yoga instructor, and Greg, a chiropractor, had been married for sixteen years. Clearly they were people who spent a lot of time bringing relaxation and peace to other people. I couldn't help but notice that these were qualities their own family life was sorely lacking.

There was no terrible issue in the Herron home, as there had been with some of the other families we visited. There was no cheating spouse, no child with ADHD, and no tragic death to recover from. But what I did see was a problem I have seen often in homes across the country: The parents and the children were drifting apart. There was no nucleus around which this family could revolve.

In the video plea the Herrons sent I was struck by the language that the parents used about their relationship with their children. It was rife with terms of conflict and war, as if Greg and Ruthi were stuck in a foxhole, doing anything they could to keep the enemy at bay. "They're beating us down to nothing," Ruthi said. Wow. What an uncomfortable feeling to have about your relationship with your own kids!

And the tension was beginning to show. Greg alternated between two states: He was either totally checked out, escaping to work, or sitting at the kitchen table with his face in his hands; or he was mad, yelling at one or the other of the kids. Ruthi felt ignored until she blew her top and became a shrieking harridan. I was moved when I first watched video of the family by how her foremost desire was to simply be an effective and inspiring parent. "I always wanted to be a mom, and I always wanted to be effective," Ruthi said, with tears streaming down her cheeks, "and I don't feel like I'm being effective."

"They don't respect each other, and they don't respect, particularly, their mom." Greg told me. Both parents were seeing the kids heading down a path of manipulation and dishonesty. The kids told a different version of the same story: "My mom nags way too much; she picks the littlest things and argues about them and complains." Attractive and well-spoken when we got them alone, the kids looked like prisoners in a work-release program when they were in the presence of their parents, as they sullenly hunkered down at the breakfast table, shoulders slumped, avoiding eye contact.

If you believe, as I do, that your home should be a place to unwind and recharge, then it wasn't difficult to see why Ruthi seemed so unsatisfied by her interactions with her kids and why Greg seemed so tightly wound.

Life is 10 percent what happens to you and 90 percent how you react. How you respond to things in your family's life directly determines the extent to which you will enjoy shalom in your home.

And it wasn't as if Ruthi and Greg couldn't see where this was going: "I don't want my kids to be, excuse my language, 'I just want to get the hell out of here, get the hell away from Mom and Dad.' I want something more than that." But that was precisely what was happening, particularly in the case of their eldest son, Nick, who was becoming increasingly estranged from the family.

In short, the Herrons were a good example of another major threat to the American family: its decentralization. The teen kids simply didn't want to be at home and found any excuse to get out. In many American homes it is the kids' friends who are the primary influence on the children. Parents can only keep their children at home through threats or bribery. They must find out details of their children's lives from external sources, like coaches and the parents of their children's friends. How terrible to feel rejected and unwanted by the very same children on whose behalf you have sacrificed so much!

The View from the Bunker

Once I had them in my trailer, I asked the Herrons to rate their marriage's happiness on a scale of one to 10. "If we could get rid of the kids," Ruthi laughed. We all laughed. But whoa! It was a telling first insight into this family. The Herron parents were seeking each other out, allies in the war against their children! Although Ruthi had always wanted to be a mother—now that she was surrounded by her kids, she wished she were alone. The kids did fight in pretty hurtful ways, both physically and verbally (and creatively—I'd never heard anyone called a "queer walrus" before). Greg, who characterized himself a peaceful man, was baffled by how all this chaos had found its way into his home.

But then we watched a clip of Greg chastising Forrest for carrying a dripping tray of blueberries across the kitchen—in a voice that drips with sarcasm: "Would a plate be a good idea? Yeah. Thanks. You know, for a smart guy, sometimes it seems like you're not thinking." Now I should interject here that, like Greg, I too often use sarcasm with my kids. But I do everything within my power not to;

I think it does considerable damage. Oddly, sarcasm is frequently used by people who would be horrified by the idea of raising their hand to their child.

Sarcasm is terribly damaging for two reasons. The first is that sarcasm *always* comes from anger. It's a way to vent rage, merely covering it under the invisibility cloak of "humor." Calling you a complete and total idiot must not count if I say it in this funny, jocular way. But of course it does count. And it violates a principle canon of parenting: We must always discipline our children out of love, not anger. The point of giving a kid a time-out or a stern talking-to isn't to get revenge for breaking your favorite bowl. It's to teach him, as gently and compassionately as you possibly can, the importance of listening when you ask him not to do something, because you know what is safe and what is not and need his compliance.

The other reason not to use sarcasm against a child is because it is humiliating, and humiliation is one weapon we should never use against a child. And if you can think back to the last time someone used sarcasm as a weapon against you, you can probably get back in touch with how truly horrible and embarrassing it is. Sarcasm tells its recipients that they're not in on the joke because the joke is on them. That alone makes it an inappropriate way for a parent to communicate with a child. As you can readily see, watching the cascade of emotions cross a child's face after such a cutting remark, it is a harrowing blow to self-esteem, one that will unquestionably leave a scar. Do it enough times and the scar tissue will build up, disfiguring an ego like the scars from cuts disfigure a boxer's face.

I don't know about you, but I don't want my children to toughen up, to develop the same kind of hardness and defensive posturing that I see in the adults around them. Their innocence, their purity of heart, is something that I want to preserve in them for as long as I possibly can. And when my children look at me, I want them to see someone who is on their team, every second of every minute of every day. Even when I discipline them, I want them to know that I am doing it for their sake. I'm not their enemy, and I don't punish them to get back at them or to make myself feel better. I do it to help them understand.

If we accept that sarcasm is a very dangerous tool to use against our children, then Greg was really playing with fire—especially because the whole kerfuffle was ostensibly about a few drops of water on the floor. Forrest had correctly diagnosed the problem, without our help, when he had told our cameras that Greg's anger had a "trickle-down effect." That was exactly what we were seeing here: Greg told Forrest exactly how deficient he thought he was—and then Forrest turned right around and passed the same sentiment along to his younger brother, Noah. After watching the clip, it was Greg's turn to be embarrassed—and it was no longer a mystery to him where the kids got their sassy mouths.

But the real problem with Greg was not too much passion but a lack of it. Greg suffered from the malady that affects tens of millions of American men and which I witness in so many families I counsel: He was a broken American male. Greg was pushing 40. When he looked at himself he saw a chiropractor with a medium-size practice and an okay income, and he thought that he was a failure in life. Other guys were rich and famous, but he was not. Other guys had that vacation home in the Hamptons, but he did not. Compounding Greg's feelings of worthlessness was the fact that as a very good-looking man he had moonlighted as a male model. That experience had given him a little taste of the spotlight, and compared with the spotlight his current life appeared a little bit dark.

Sure, he was a loving husband and a committed dad. But the world we live in doesn't value you for things like that. It was in the process of that subliminal calculation that Greg became what I call "a checked-out dad." Watching video of him in the *Shalom* trailer, I saw him telling his children things like "I'm going to work, so work out that argument for yourselves" or "I'm home for a brief lunch, so I can't focus on that stuff now." Even when he came home, he was not home; his thoughts were far away.

And his kids noticed. In fact the kids consistently told me that one of the biggest problems in the home was that Dad took little interest in the family and Mom was left to run the ship on her own. That's what happens with broken males. The home can't boost their ego, so they abandon it mentally. So getting Greg, who I could tell was a special and sensitive man, to reengage with the family was going to be a huge priority.

The next issue to tackle was the way Ruthi communicated—or failed to communicate—with her kids. The first step, as any good twelve-stepper knows, is to admit that there's a problem. Ruthi had all the right motivations. She simply wanted to be a good mom who raised good kids. Her greatest fear was that chaos would engulf her home and she would cease to be effective as a parent. But her fear drove her to badger her kids constantly. She nagged them to the point of distraction. Like many mothers who are just so overburdened with work that they feel crushed under the weight of their responsibilities, Ruthi had lost all sense of timing. Rather than choosing the correct moments to get her kids to do their household chores, she nagged them constantly to do what they were supposed to do. She could barely have an interaction with her kids that didn't involve this nagging.

The problem with being a nag is that not only is it counterproductive but profoundly alienating. Not only does the job not get done, but soon your children aren't going to even want to be around you. And as bad as a chaotic household filled with lazy kids who don't help is, a home where the children don't even want to be is even worse. And that is what was rapidly happening in the Herron household.

"I'm a nag," Ruthi said—and I made her say it again. But it wasn't that Ruthi didn't know what she was doing—she just thought it was the only way. "Typically, in order to get things done, I have to *freak out*," Ruthi told us. "I have to *melt down*." She talked a good game—"I don't want to nag you guys about this; it's your responsibility"—but she did it in the context of nagging the kids.

I would have to show her that there was a better way—a more inspirational approach, one that would not only earn her better results but also be less of a bitter pill for her kids to swallow. In the clip we chose to show the Herrons, Ruthi is issuing orders while cleaning out the fridge. Now, parents complain to me a lot that their kids don't listen. And when I watch how they interact with their children, I invariably see the same thing I did with Ruthi Herron: *They lead from behind.* They don't put any energy or concentration into giving the directives; of course their kids ignore them! Ruthi was telling her kids how important it was that they listen to her, but her behavior was telling them something completely different. How seriously were they supposed to take her when she couldn't even take a minute to stop what she was doing in order to make a personal connection with them, to look them in the eye, and tell them what to do? Call a two-minute family meeting and do the fridge later.

I am a great believer in family meetings because I am a great believer in having a plan. Most families have no plans for their lives; they are reactive rather than proactive. They stumble along rather than glide toward a predetermined destination. And in so doing they end up consuming triple the amount of energy to get the same things done as a family that has a plan that was mapped out at a family meeting.

Indeed most of the homes that I visit don't have a list of chores on the wall. Instead the mom and the dad have to constantly tell the kids their responsibilities. Ten minutes later the kids have forgotten, and the parent has to repeat it—and that's how you become a nag.

How much authority do you really expect to wield when there's no clear sequence of cause-and-effect? I see asking children to do chores as a four-step process:

You spell out to them exactly what it is that you would like them to do. Do so without any sarcasm, which already assumes that they'll fail you. Rather, help them succeed by ensuring that there is no confusion.

You make sure they understand it and repeat it back to you.

Set a deadline. Be sure the child knows that you will check to make sure the chore is done, properly and on time.

Make it crystal clear what the consequences will be if expectations are not met; e.g., if the kitchen floor is not cleaned by noon, the child will have to miss soccer practice.

Do all of these steps all of the time—and you will see a change, I guarantee it. And please don't forget that tone is important. Your kids aren't automatons; they need something more than a laundry list of orders. They need to be inspired. They need their parents to appeal to the noble part of their character, the part that wants to have something to be proud of, the part that wants to make you proud. Emphasize how much they're helping you, how much you rely on them. Give them incentives—not bribes, but motivation. Add praise when the chore does get done, and it'll happen again. *This* is how we assert our authority with our children. Constant nagging and empty threats not only won't get the kitchen floor clean, they will also start to get in the way of all aspects of your relationship.

What Ruthi was doing was passing along pressure. She felt frustrated and overwhelmed—and she inadvertently made sure that everyone around her suffered too. She complained that the kids were beating her and Greg down, but she was doing the same thing to them. That's why Ruthi's kids started rolling their eyes and ducking their heads when she approached—she was beating them down instead of lifting them up. Not surprisingly, her way wasn't working. The point of parenting this way isn't just to create a cadre of little soldiers who do your bidding and clean your kitchen floor. The best part about parenting with passion is that it puts the fun back into it. I want to have fun with my children! I want to have lots of time to enjoy their company, to shamelessly use them as an excuse to roll around on the lawn and eat ice cream in the middle of the day for no reason. I don't want to waste hours of our precious time together nagging about homework or chores or having some stupid fight about yard work. (But I will, and they know it.) Better to inspire them so that chores get done fast—and so that the doing of them lends a child a sense of purpose and accomplishment. I speak to my kids about these kinds of things all the time; indeed, I devoted an entire book to these talks, *Ten Conversations You Need to Have with Your Children.*

The last clip I showed the Herrons was a moving one: In it Greg confesses that he is going through a difficult time with his own parents, and he talks about his fear that he is similarly losing touch with his own children. He spoke very eloquently about his fear that the strife in the family was preventing him from passing along his values and the tremendous amount of love he felt for his kids. What came through very clearly was how much he wanted a better relationship with his children, how much he wanted to cultivate more tranquility and cooperation within his home.

Material goods will not bring your children happiness. Rather, the more purposeful we make our children feel and the more we can liberate them from the incarcerating cell of their own selfishness, the happier and more stable they will be.

When the clip was finished, I spoke to him from my heart. "You are not the thermometer in the home but the thermostat," I told him. "You are not reactive. You don't take the temperature; you *dictate* it." Indeed I believe what I said addressed the overall problems in the Herron household, from Greg's defeatism and rage to Ruthi's nagging. Greg was running away, and Ruthi was making the children run from her. Everyone was scattering in different directions.

In order to see things change, the Herrons would have to come together; to make that happen, Greg and Ruthi had to seize the reins. With their newfound control they had to reinvent the household, making it a place of joy, of excitement, of passion, and of fun. Only in that way could they finally achieve the relationship with their kids that they'd always dreamed of.

Back to Square One

I wasn't that heartened by what I saw the next morning. Seven o'clock on Sunday morning—breakfast at the Herron house: Greg reads the paper, Ruthi nags about book reports. The kids are sluggish and resistant, slumped in defeat against the inevitable onslaught before their mother even begins. When they answer, they speak so softly you can barely hear them. They offer up barely audible monosyllables. The scene ends when Ruthi gets up, leaving her kids with a parting salvo about cleaning up their dishes ("I'm not going to do it for you,"), and then *again* reminds them the kitchen floor needs to be cleaned.

If this was what the Herron kids were waking up to, no wonder they looked like zombies! And no wonder Ruthi wasn't getting the results she wanted! I felt exhausted just watching all this. It was time for an intervention; if they couldn't hear the truth from me, maybe they'd hear it if it came from the mouths of their own kids. So I asked the Herrons to sit in the Airstream, "eavesdropping" on the conversation I had with their kids.

There is a kabbalistic tradition that says hell is something called *kaf hakelah*; after you die, the heavenly angels throw your soul around the world endlessly—essentially showing you your life on an endless loop.

Why is it the worst form of hell to simply watch the life you lived over and over again for all eternity? Because when you see all the mistakes you made and all the opportunities you missed, the pain it causes you is indescribable. In effect we are in our own hell. And the sins of omission are even worse than the sins of commission. The bad things we do are never as bad as the good things we fail to do. As we watch our lives replay before our eyes, we are struck not by our mistakes but by all the missed opportunities to have used our lives for something noble and redemptive.

On our show, brave and courageous families, and especially parents, are put through that hell. We film their daily interactions and then show it back to them, highlighting their mistakes and omissions. It's a cathartic but incredibly painful experience. If that were not bad enough, showing parents what their own children have to say about them is a much more intense form of hell, only for the truly brave of heart. This is what we were about to put Greg and Ruthi through. But we decided that it was better for them to suffer through the momentary pain of being judged by their children than the permanent pain of being alienated from their children.

I sat down with the kids and tried to get them to speak candidly about the family. It was hard going. These were really good kids, but you've never seen a more morose lineup in your life. They looked like they'd been sedated; even Ruthi later said that they looked like they were on drugs. To get them going I lobbed questions at them that I already knew the answers to: "Do you look forward to waking up in this house? Do you feel alive here? Do you look forward to spending time away from the house?" The consensus seemed to be that Ruthi's way of communicating with her kids was alienating them instead of bringing them closer. No kidding! And Greg's grumpy mood when he got home and his checked-out demeanor the rest of the time bummed the whole family out.

I think we got to the real root of the problem when Nick told me that he'd gladly listen to advice, even orders, from the soccer coaches at his school than his own parents. Why, I wondered, would he listen to a soccer coach and not his own mother? "Respect," he and Forrest both answered. "What's the difference?" I pressed. And he gave me a really good answer; he said, "Fun. The coaches generate fun."

I returned to the sober Herrons in the studio-trailer. Ruthi was hurt and outraged to have learned that Nick would feel more comfortable talking to a soccer coach he'd known for two weeks—someone who persisted in calling him by the wrong last name—than to her. And Greg looked pretty depressed to hear his effect on the household. But I was sure within that outrage and hurt were the seeds of big change. And I was closer now to understanding the problem than I had been: The Herrons themselves were uninspired. They needed to get inspired themselves so that they could inspire their kids and give their whole home an inspirational makeover.

A Room of His Own

As the major project in this makeover, I asked Ruthi to make a sacrifice. Nick spent hours away from the home with his friends and even more time on the phone with them. Part of the problem, he claimed, was that he was still sharing a room—the smallest bedroom in the house—with Forrest. Although the two boys had a close relationship, Nick needed somewhere to go to get a little privacy. He was 14 years old. He was becoming a young adult. Yes, he absolutely had to be integrated into the family. But he also needed some personal space.

Since Ruthi used the house's spare bedroom for her office and art studio, I was hoping to encourage her to move her art to another part of the house so that Nick could have a room of his own. Ruthi's paintings were glorious with flowers and colors; I hoped that by getting Nick a little space of his own, we could take some of that exuberance and joy off the canvas and put it into her son's heart.

Greg thought it was a good idea and suggested a bright, sun-filled corner of the dining room (a room the family never used for its original purpose) as Ruthi's new art studio. But it was clear right from the start that Ruthi was having a hard time. Now, it was understandably difficult for her to imagine her life without this oasis of calm, but I felt that making the sacrifice would send a very important "truce" message to her children, especially to Nick. And of course the point of the experiment wasn't just to rob Ruthi of her inner sanctum or even just to give Nick a little space. The Herrons as a unit needed to learn what it meant to give something up for the greater good of the team. As parents, it was up to Greg and Ruthi to model this.

To be sure, I was conflicted about my own advice. So many American women feel that they lose their individuality as they become wives and mothers. It is almost always the mom who is called upon to make the big sacrifices for the sake of the family. Was I just going to reinforce this message by asking Ruthi to give her up passion so that Nick could have more privacy? But there was an alternative space, if not an ideal one, for Ruthi to move her art projects into, and so I felt that both family and mother could be accommodated.

Moving the studio out and Nick's stuff in was a big job, but I asked all of the Herrons to pitch in and gave them 24 hours to do it. The challenge would be for them to work together—without nagging or bickering—to do something for one of their own.

Over the headsets I encouraged the kids to give their mother a lot of support. It was clear how much it was costing Ruthi to move the seat of her artistic expression. At the same time I encouraged Ruthi to take the focus off what she was losing by focusing on what she hoped to gain by the move: a better relationship with her children. She didn't have to give up her painting altogether, just a designated room for it.

Nothing went smoothly. In fact midway through the move, Ruthi really melted down. She described her feelings as a "tug-of-war." Although she wanted to make sure that she did the right thing by Nick, she was also afraid that moving her art into another, nondesignated corner of the house would mean that she'd be losing touch with the part of her that expressed herself in this way. Ruthi felt, as so many mothers do, that she spent her life moving aside to accommodate the other people in the family. But that wasn't what we were asking her to do here.

What to do? I didn't have the right answer, but I could call a family meeting so that Ruthi could share her feelings about the move and the whole family could weigh in on what to do next. You see, it's not that good families don't have problems; they just have a constructive and productive way to deal with them. For me, seeing the Herrons sitting around that kitchen table, speaking respectfully to one another, represented an enormous step forward. Ruthi shared her concerns, and Greg and the kids heard them. Nick could see how attached his mother was to her art room, which made him appreciate what his mother was doing on his behalf.

And the rest of the Herrons were able to offer Ruthi comfort. In fact just seeing her family gathered around the table was the ultimate form of comfort: It showed her that the sacrifice she was making had already paid off by bringing the family closer together. Ultimately they decided to pull together and continue the move. *This* was what I wanted to see: discussion, conflict resolution, and unity of purpose. The family was moving forward. This is what loving families do.

Greg added a touch that I really liked: In celebration of their new, upgraded digs, he called the family together and asked Nick to carry Ruthi over the threshold into her new art studio. He himself then hefted his 14-year-old into his arms and carried (OK, dumped) him into his brand-new room. A small thing, perhaps—but to be honest it was precisely the kind of leadership I wanted to see coming from Greg. With good humor (and a strong back) he led his family into this new beginning—a far cry from the morose guy we'd seen so many times at the kitchen table.

Nice work, Herrons. The kids were calm and focused; Greg and Ruthi were inspiring them through leadership and example. The project was going well. But that didn't mean further roadblocks weren't going to emerge.

Noah had a meltdown—over his milk. Ruthi made a good effort at inspiring him to drink it by adding fun—she offered to make it a competition by chugging her big glass of water. "Cheers," Greg says to both of them, with a good-natured laugh. But Noah wasn't having it, "It doesn't taste right," he wailed—and nothing could convince him otherwise. Suddenly we were right back to where we started. "Noah, this has taken too much energy out of us," Ruthi yells. "Drink now!" Noah weeps, the rest of the children scatter—and I am roused from my *Shalom* trailer to see if an intervention is needed.

Amazing! A whole family was thrown into a tizzy by a kid refusing to drink his milk. But this was the problem. The Herrons, like many families, had lost a sense of perspective. They forgot the 90/10 rule: Life is 10 percent what happens to you and 90 percent how you react to what happens to you. Here Ruthi and Greg were letting their frustrations get to them and robbing their home of peace—and of enjoying a memorable moment—over something utterly ridiculous.

Good for Ruthi for trying to inspire Noah, for trying to turn this unpleasant little moment around and make it fun. But when you have four kids, you can't let one of them grind the whole family's activities to a halt over something as ridiculous as a glass of milk. As I told the Herrons, inspiration is a big part of it—but so is obedience. They had asked Noah to drink his milk, and now he had to drink the milk. I asked them to remember the four-step program of how to get your kids to do things, and they listened. There would be no negotiation, no more displaying willingness to argue or cajole or convince.

Again the Herrons handled it perfectly. Without anger they told Noah that he wasn't going to do anything else until he'd drunk his milk, and they put him at the kitchen table and left him there.

In Ruthi's new studio we hit another stumbling block. Greg was—sensibly, I thought—trying to get an idea of how the room would be set up. The family was running out of time; I think he knew how important it was to have the broad strokes planned, even if everything weren't set up perfectly. I believe he felt—as I did—that it would be psychologically important for Ruthi to be able to imagine where her easel and supplies would go, just so she really knew that it was going to happen, and that it was going to be okay. And maybe that's why Ruthi was so resistant—maybe she didn't want Greg to take care of her in this way, precisely so she could prove to everyone that it *wouldn't* be okay. But whatever was going on, the Herrons were beginning to fight. And it was important for the two generals of this army to hold fast and not to break ranks in front of their troops. Once again I stepped in to encourage the Herrons to pull together to get through a rough patch—instead of allowing it to crowbar them apart.

The elder Herrons aside, I could tell that the experiment was working, because in the kitchen, the kids *had* pulled together. Forrest and Kira had taken up the cause of getting Noah to drink his milk, with considerably more success than their parents. (The secret, for other parents who struggle with this problem, turned out to be copious amounts of hot sauce.) It was the most energized I'd seen the kids since we arrived.

Then it was Kira's turn to melt down. In this family, just as one member was getting it together another would lose it. But that's the way it is in most families. Kira's room had to accommodate some extra furniture and miscellaneous stuff as a result of the move, and she wasn't happy about the mess.

Once again instead of using this as an excuse to nag or whine, Ruthi did everything right. She brought Noah up to Kira's room and made him her "assistant," charged with helping Kira put her room back to rights. She gave her two children a sense of purposefulness and told them exactly what she expected of them. I was impressed to see Ruthi working on the two of them. She kneeled to be at eye level with them, encouraged them to work with one another, and modeled high positive energy herself—cajoling and teasing them into a better place. And by the time she left there were some grudging smiles. She was learning, all over again, what worked.

The whole family pitched in to help Nick paint his new room bright orange and fluorescent green. The Herrons had not only pulled together and made sacrifices for one of their own—but they had some fun in the process.

A Little Treat

I pulled the kids away from the painting project for a quick meeting. Although Ruthi, painting those garish colors onto the walls, looked happier than I'd seen her since I'd known her, I still thought she deserved a special treat. After all, she had made a big sacrifice.

I asked the kids what they could think of to do as a token of their appreciation. Forrest suggested a bath—and then got to work making it happen in a much more fully realized way than I could possibly have done myself. There were candles, incense, soft music, magazines—even flower petals floating in the water!

My favorite part was how Forrest got Ruthi up to the bathroom. "Mom, they need you upstairs," he wailed in a petulant, bored, "teen" tone that parents know and love so well. Nicely played, Forrest! Our cameras caught him grinning like a little kid in anticipation as she followed him upstairs—dreading the worst, I'm sure. I loved seeing that grin. It's great to be reminded every once in awhile how good it feels to do something nice for someone else. A week ago Forrest was barely speaking to his mother; now he was falling all over himself to surprise her with a relaxing, decadent treat.

Ruthi was indeed surprised and delighted to discover the spa-like paradise that awaited her. And before she closed the door on her private retreat I saw a vulnerability and hopefulness on her face that I had not seen before.

Every parent needs to know that even the most deadened teenagers can be brought to life. I meet parents all the time who tell me that their teenagers show no emotional response; they can't even get them to speak—much less smile and laugh with their parents. But deep down your teenagers want you to get through. They want to have a relationship with you. So I tell these parents that the secret is persistence, coupled with diplomacy and inspiration. Learn how to talk with your teen son or daughter. Show humility by admitting your mistakes as a parent. Show empathy by sharing your own experiences. And show inspiration by giving your children a vision of what they could be if they chose to make the effort.

In this case, Forrest, who had shown very little emotion throughout my first few days with the Herrons, displayed joy and enthusiasm because he felt inspired. He saw the change in his family, he felt like he was a part of it, and he felt closer to his parents.

A Family with a Mission

We ended our time with Herrons by taking them to one of New York City's greatest landmarks: the Bowery Mission, a sanctuary for the homeless that feeds more than a thousand men, women, and children every day. Instead of shopping or seeing the sights, the Herrons would be preparing a hot dinner and serving it to people much less fortunate than themselves.

Charity is one of the most important things we can model for our children—and I am always surprised to see how few parents make it a habit. It doesn't have to be a big deal, but it's important to me that the concept of doing something for others is part of my children's everyday existence. There are many ways that you can implement this. One of my friends asks her children to divert ten percent of their generous allowances into their personal "charity fund." At the end of the year they give the money to a charity of each child's choosing. It's not how much they give, or to which causes—last year her 5-year-old sent nine dollars to a shelter for *rabbits*—it's the concept of thinking about charity throughout the year. What we learn in childhood becomes part of us, and I'm willing to bet that her 5-year-old will give to people—and critters—in need for the rest of her life.

I also think it's important for us to give of ourselves—our time, our energy, our presence—not just of our pocketbooks. Doing something charitable together is a much more wholesome family activity than a trip to the mall. Fun is important; activities with a purpose are even more important. And doing good for others can be fun! One of my children's favorite times of year is Purim, a Jewish holiday where the kids dress up and give food parcels to others and two gifts of charity to the needy. The focus is on doing good things for others. The candy and cookies don't hurt the mood, but it's amazing that the happiest day of the Jewish year revolves entirely around doing things for others—and yet it never feels like a sacrifice.

Most of all, what our kids need is liberation from the incarcerating prison of their own selfishness. American children can be crushed under the weight of their own wants. We can allow them to live in a soulless, materialistic society where they can become bloated and self-absorbed, or we can help them nurture their natural traits of sympathy and empathy by focusing on other people's needs. We can kill our children's souls by not teaching them the joys of selflessness.

I also think that selfishness is a huge cause of childhood, and especially teen, depression. If our children are denied the liberating joys of doing something for others, they sink into a funk as they begin to question the purpose of their existence. The more purposeless they feel, the more depressed they become. Real joy comes from feeling that you matter: If you aren't making an impact on other people's lives, then you don't matter. Buying your kid a newer personal gadget will give momentary joy, but that joy will wear off as the novelty does. On the other hand, making your children feel that their lives matter is a gift that keeps on giving.

It warmed my heart to see the Herrons working together at the mission. There wasn't any of the complaining and griping that you might have expected during this "night out." And I think this family really got some perspective when they were behind the steam tables, dishing up the food they'd prepared to the streams of people in need of a hot meal. Indeed our final interviews with all the family members outside the shelter were heartening. Gone were the blank stares and faces of zombielike children. In their places were kids who exhibited the full vitality and joy of youth. Forrest felt proud; Kira felt she had gained a new understanding of all her blessings. And Greg and Ruthi seemed really energized—as parents will—when they feel sure that their family is once again on the right path.

Indeed several months later Ruthi took Forrest to Africa on a mission to work with destitute children. They lived in the most primitive conditions for two weeks and actually gave the clothes off their backs to impoverished children. Ruthi told me that at first Forrest had a hard time. "Why did you bring me here?" he asked, shocked by the absence of modern amenities and the indescribable hardship surrounding them. But when he returned home, he told his mother how happy he was to have gone; it was a truly unforgettable experience that will continue to enrich him throughout his life.

We cannot allow our family life to be another stressor in our lives. Our kids should inspire us rather than drain us. I am saddened to hear things like the study that reported that parents are generally happier to watch television or do housework than to interact with their children. That's crazy. And I can't help but worry that these parents are transmitting their lack of enthusiasm to their children. If we parent like our children are burdens, they're going to feel like burdens, and I don't think we can be surprised when they start to act like burdens.

But in order to make sure that our family life is fun and not a drag, *we have to make it that way.* Our children, even if they're teenagers, are kids. As parents it falls to us to be the leaders of the pack, the alpha dogs, the pied pipers—and we dare not lead from behind. Does it take work? Yes, of course it does. Does it take energy, and discipline, and patience—and sometimes faking all those things when the real things are in short supply? Yes. But soon enough, the inspiration kicks in, and even with all the work it entails, teaching our children how to be good family and community members doesn't feel like a chore.

My strategy with all of the parents who have appeared on the show has been the same: I want them to see what I see, their inner hero. In the case of the Herrons, Ruthi and Greg rose admirably to the challenge I set for them. In the service of a greater good, Ruthi was able to put aside her own anxieties about being displaced. And Greg was able to step up to take his place at the head of this family, whether that meant being the organizing principal, the head cheerleader, or a quiet guide.

Indeed the strategy I use on the show is actually some of the best parenting advice I can give. We will lead through inspiration, not exasperation. Nagging will never be as good—or as enjoyable—a solution as leading through positive motivation and encouragement and example.

Parenting isn't about creating automatons. So instead of going at your children with a chisel and hammer, chipping away at them until they come closer to your ideal vision, go for real change instead by encouraging them to find their own inner hero. If you can teach them to heed the quiet voice of their own conscience, and to meet the standards this quiet voice sets for them, you will have given them a gift that will serve them well throughout their lives.

The final shots of the Herron kids show them looking energized, engaged, and proud—and feeling good about themselves. They have become good friends of my family, sharing in many of our celebrations, like my son Mendy's bar mitzvah, where Greg stood out in the synagogue as the most handsome man there (with the exception of yours truly, of course).

One evening I was walking with my family when Greg reached me on my cell phone. He told me, with great emotion, that his mother had died earlier that day. I was one of the first people he had contacted. And then he said to me something that made *Shalom in the Home* very precious to me. "Shmuley, I was the one who told my father that his wife of more than fifty years had died. I was only able to do that because of the time you and I, Shmuley, spent together. You told me that I was a hero, and you made me feel like I was a hero to my kids. Without that I don't know if I would have felt worthy to tell my father this sad news. You made me realize that my own personal greatness comes from my devotion to my family." A few months later Greg's father also passed away, and Greg came with his whole family to my home for dinner a few nights later. There I endeavored to remind him that as long as he continued the commitment to family that his own parents had exhibited, they would live on eternally through him, his children, and his children's children.

Lessons for Life

Have fun with your kids! Make your home environment stimulating, and your kids will want to be in it.

—✳—

As parents we must be the thermostat in the home, controlling the temperature—not the thermometer, reporting it. If you want your kids to be happier, make them happier! If you want them to exhibit higher energy, whip them into a frenzy! If you want them to be more sensitive and generous, demonstrate those qualities yourself and reward them in others.

—✳—

If you have to nag your kids or your spouse to get things done, consider another way. Make a chore list, have a family meeting, use inspiration and encouragement. Nagging doesn't work—it's demoralizing for both the nagger and the naggees.

—✳—

Practice charity with your children. There's no better habit to instill them with—and no better way to put the family's own troubles into meaningful perspective—than helping others.

—✳—

Our parents and loved ones who have passed on live on through the meaningful commitments to goodness and righteousness that they have inspired within us. A man or a woman is not just a soul, and certainly not just a body, but the sum total of all the good deeds he or she did while on this earth. When we continue those deeds, especially in their name, we grant them eternal life.

Bringing Passion Back to the Home

April Warren was trapped between a rock and a hard place when she contacted me. The smart mouth and behavioral problems of her teenage daughter, Teaira, really rubbed her stepfather, Jack, the wrong way, while Teaira bridled under Jack's "my way or the highway" approach to parenting. After a particularly bad fight, the tension between the two of them had escalated to the point that they could barely speak a civil word to one another. It was breaking April's heart to see her husband and her daughter at odds in this way.

No parent in a blended family should have to choose between her children and her spouse, but unfortunately a great many are forced to make the choice. Not only was there no shalom in the Warren home as a result of the standoff, but April was concerned that Teaira was heading in a bad direction, staying out too late doing who-knows-what, and that the situation would only get worse without Jack's paternal hand.

As I parked the mobile studio outside the Warrens' apartment in Fort Lauderdale, I wondered, "Could I negotiate a détente between the two? Or would their tension explode into all-out warfare?"

Instant Family

Jack and April had been together nine years. A once-close friendship blossomed into a romance and eventually marriage. Jack took an active role in raising April's kids from her first marriage, Chris and Teaira. (The couple also has a child of their own: 6-month-old Jordan.) Jack is a computer programmer; April works in a doctor's office.

The Warrens were probably the most religious family I worked with in the first season of *Shalom in the Home,* and that created an instant bond between us. They were deeply steeped in the life of their church: April sang in the choir, and her uncle is a pastor. When I arrived at the home I saw that the license plate frame on April's car said, "Praised be the Glory of God," and it warmed my heart. I am a man of faith, and I have an instant affinity with any person of faith, no matter what religion.

April's first marriage was extremely troubled, and the children now have precious little interaction with their biological father. But for the last nine years, Jack has been there to fill that void. Guys like Jack are heroes. To raise someone else's children as your own, to give children a home and offer them love and emotional and financial support is one of the highest demonstrations of character. I gave Jack a tremendous amount of credit for the role he had played in their lives; he had really stepped up to raise them as if they were his own. As a result his relationship with the kids had always been close, and that closeness continued with his stepson Chris, who called him his "best friend."

Once the same had been true for Teaira: Jack told us that up until a few years before, she had been more likely to talk to him about something troubling than to her mother. But now his relationship with Teaira was something else entirely—and it had just taken a severe turn for the worse. After a big fight with Jack, Teaira had called her biological father to complain about the way Jack had spoken to her, and her biological father had jumped on the opportunity to call and castigate April. For Jack that phone call was the last straw.

I have seen this happen many times. A stepparent will enter the picture and try to discipline the spouse's children out of a sincere desire to do what's best for them. The child, bristling against the constraints, will call the biological parent to complain, and suddenly

The presence or absence of marital passion affects not only the parents but also the children. In a marriage where husband and wife experience joy and affection, the whole home becomes filled with light.

the biological parent, who may have had minimal to no involvement with the child, is up in arms: "How dare you discipline my child?"

Of course this is silly. A child needs guidance and discipline. And you would think that biological parents would welcome adult supervision, especially if they were living far away from their children, as Teaira's father was. But the dispute is not about the child but about ego. The biological father feels threatened and disrespected that some stranger dares to discipline *his* children. Fair enough. But you can't have it both ways. If you don't want someone else to raise your kids, raise them yourself. But if you live far away and you make little effort to see your kids, should they be left to raise themselves?

Parents—biological or not!—need to bury the hatchet for the sake of their children. So many parents end up fighting with their ex-spouses and their new spouses, behaving territorially over their kids. It puts the interests of the children way behind the interest of the parents.

Where's the Spark?

I welcomed the Warrens into the trailer. I should say right up front that I could very much relate to this couple. They were very down-to-earth, were not at all apprehensive to meet and speak with me, and had no airs.

The Warrens were both a little baffled to see the first clip I'd selected. In it April describes herself as "the Energizer bunny" and talks about how tired she is. And she looks tired—with good reason! In the highlight reel we put together we never see her sitting still or without the baby on her hip—and this after she comes home from looking after other people in her full-time job as a nurse. I didn't see Jack helping out as much as he could—or should—and I wanted to talk about that too. But the Warrens weren't sure why we were talking about their relationship at all; they thought I was there to talk about the fractured relationship between a troubled teenager and her stepfather. I was. But the strands of a family are not so easily divided: Pull on one, and others generally follow. There was method to my madness, but the Warrens would have to wait a little while for my meaning to reveal itself to them.

This happens all the time. Couples apply to be on *Shalom in the Home* because they're having troubles with their kids. They want me to come into their home and "fix" their children. When I then start speaking to the parents about *their* relationship, they are positively baffled: "What does our marriage have to do with this? What do *I* have to do with this? Shut up about me and my sex life and get out there and fix my kid!"

But—at my strong insistence—*Shalom in the Home* is not a parenting show. It's a family dynamics show. It has to be. There is no such thing as a bad kid. Children are utterly innocent. They are a *tabula rasa*—a blank slate. We as parents determine children's actions by the way we ourselves act; it is our characters that determine how their characters will develop.

And it is from the way we relate to our spouses—the most central relationship that they observe—that our children learn how to relate to their fellow human beings, both inside and outside the family. So our marriages—the level of intimacy and even passion that exists between mother and father—have a direct effect on a child's behavior. In a marriage where is there is constant fighting, especially when the fighting takes place in front of the children, the children internalize pugnaciousness and chaos. They become unsettled kids. And in a marriage where there is no passion, the children become sullen and withdrawn, sunk into themselves like their parents. They don't know how to express emotion because they haven't learned. But in a marriage where the parents not only get along but love each other deeply, the children drink from a nourishing fountain of affection.

I had my suspicions about the Warrens' marriage, simply from watching the video they'd sent. And those suspicions deepened during our conversation when it emerged that while the Warrens did share a marital bed, the majority of the fun happening there seemed to be taking place on Jack's video game player. April said that Jack stayed up very late every night playing video games with Chris, well after his wife went to bed. Nice father-son bonding, maybe, but not a great development for the Warrens' romantic life.

When I pushed the subject a little, Jack punted the problem back to April. "It takes two," he told me. "Not really," she retorted. I laughed and told the couple that in my religion, one of the big rules of sex is that the woman had to be awake; from their reaction, I told them humorously, it didn't seem like a condition that had always been satisfied in the Warren household. It was a frank and funny conversation, particularly for a group of religious people. And Jack and April—good, easygoing people— took the conversation in stride. But what had emerged was confirmation of what I already knew. These two people loved each other deeply, but their marriage was in the doldrums. The thing missing from the Warren home wasn't love, or discipline, or values, or some of the other essential qualities so often missing from American homes. The quality most absent—and most needed—in the Warren household was *passion*.

If I had a dollar for every husband who told me that his wife was uninterested in sex, I could pay off all Third World debt. But the reality is that women are much more sexual than men, but all too many men snuff out their wives' innate sexuality by not showing them desire and by not helping sufficiently in the home.

So many wives today are simply too tired and worn out to feel like women! And then instead of helping out, their husbands complain that their wives have no sexual desire. When one person in a couple is too tired to have sex, the couple *must* look at what is wearing that person out, and both must do something to change it. Even a little help can lighten someone's load—whether it's a redistribution of chores, getting a neighborhood teenager in to help in the afternoon a few times a week, or just making sure that someone has the opportunity to get an extra forty winks on the weekend. Life—work, kids, running a household—is hard work. It's our responsibility to help each other as much as we can.

A woman's lack of desire isn't, of course, only about sex. For a woman it's about feeling desirable and having her husband lust after her. Now the question of what a woman wants has stymied better men than I (including the esteemed Sigmund Freud), but during thousands of hours speaking to women during counseling, I have finally alighted upon what I believe to be the answer: What a woman wants is to be chosen. Why do women want to get married? Looked at logically, marriage is a seemingly bad proposition for a woman. It usually leads to childbearing, and up until the twentieth century, one in three women died in childbirth. She loses her freedom and gains

The goal of our disciplinary efforts must not be to suppress our children's passions but to develop them and channel them into healthy pursuits.

the obligation of making her husband a home; even in an egalitarian society where men are supposed to share the responsibilities, study after study shows that it is still the women who end up doing most of the work associated with child rearing and running the home. She even loses some of her identity as she takes her husband's last name.

And all this for what?

I believe that a woman wants to get married because marriage caters to her biggest desire: the desire to be chosen and to have her uniqueness established in the confines of a loving relationship. A woman is chosen whenever a man makes her the center of his world, when she becomes the sun around which he, the planet, revolves. That is what so many women search for in life.

Unfortunately, very few find it. In the Ten Commandments, when God chooses the Israelite nation as his "bride," as it were, the first two commandments He sets forth are these: "I am the Lord your God" and "You shall have no other Gods before me." These commandments establish the two primary aspects of being chosen: primacy and exclusivity. They say, "I must always come first, and you can have no one else." Primacy and exclusivity are what women seek in relationships as well. After all, aren't they what it means to be someone's one and only? But men today seem uniquely incapable of delivering these ingredients. Women have to compete for attention with work, sports, and video entertainments. And to be the exclusive center of her mate's attention, a woman has to compete with many sexualized images of women.

Increasingly I see the despair and loneliness of married women as their husbands continue to put career, sports, friends, Internet porn, and video games before them. A woman's core desire to be chosen by a man, to be placed at the center of his universe, eludes them—and its absence leads to much marital turmoil.

The absence of a physically intimate life between husband and wife was not an anomaly. Of the ten families I worked with in the first season of *Shalom in the Home*, four had not had sex in more than a year and another two averaged a sexual frequency rate of about six times a year. For all the stereotypes of us being an oversexed society, one thing's for sure: It ain't happening in the marital bedroom.

At night in bed, a husband has the opportunity to show his wife how much he wants her. But if he has not taken the time to assist her at home, he might just get what seems to him to be something akin to a corpse, a wife too tired to feel erotic or intimate. And that's a shame. He gets a tired, irritable "pod person" instead of the passionate, energized person he fell in love with in the first place!

Two Sides of the Same Coin

The fact that there was little excitement in the Warrens' marital relationship was the canary in the coal mine. Their intimate life (or lack thereof) was a symptom of an overall lack of excitement in the home. It alerted me to a danger. Could the lack of passion between the Warrens explain why Teaira rarely wanted to be at home? Did this high-energy 14-year-old feel that she had to get out of the house in order to feel alive?

A teenage girl is like an instrument precisely calculated to seek out excitement, a virtual Geiger counter for things that are passionately interesting and engaging. And if that isn't what she finds plentifully represented in her family life, she's going to go elsewhere to find it. A teenager's abundant natural curiosity and need for stimulation must be satisfied by channeling them into a positive outlet—or else she will keep looking, knocking on all the wrong doors until she finds something much less wholesome.

Even really good parents like April, who strongly believe in discipline, believe that discipline consists in telling your kids what *not* to do. That's a recipe for rebellion. We don't want to rob our children of their abundant energy, their curiosity, their passionate interest in everything around them. Indeed these are things we want to encourage. But we must help our children to manage their passions constructively by directing their curiosity to good things. When we only apply the "what not to do" approach, the result is a sullen child at home who does everything he or she can to get out.

This was what had already begun happening with Teaira. The Warrens were right: This girl was struggling with some real anger issues, but I could also see the other side of the coin. Jack often complained about her mouth—and she indeed did speak disrespectfully to her parents. But she was also very funny, and I saw something very courageous in her insistence on having the last word. Teaira, for all her shouting, behavior problems, and attitude, was incredibly *alive:* She was crackling with energy, emotion, and passion. And, craving something more charged and electric than the home that the exhausted April had created while Jack was working or playing with the baby and Chris, she was turning to her friends for stimulation and fun. To the dismay of her parents, she was finding what she was looking for—by staying out all night.

I told the Warrens what I believe about all children, whether they're misbehaving toddlers or teenage girls staying out until four o'clock in the morning: If you don't make your kids feel valued by giving them the attention they deserve, they're going to get your attention in the *wrong* way. When I watched Teaira's outbursts, a great many of them seemed designed to give her parents a shot in the arm, an effort to get something more than apathy out of them. I felt sure that if her environment changed, she would begin to change. If she were given a little more of what she was looking for in the first place, there would be a lessening of her dramatic overreactions.

This lack of passion is absolutely and without question one of the foremost problems I see in American homes. Parents are stressed and exhausted from long days at work—and distracted by the buzzing BlackBerries and work calls at all hours, even when they're home. They have nothing left to give their kids. All they want to do is shovel some food into their mouths, relax for an hour or so in front of the television, and get into bed. In fact that was the first thing I noticed when I visited the Warrens' home: The TV was always on.

Believe me, I can relate! When I get home after a long day, I also find that stimulating and disciplining the kids is very hard work; sometimes I too feel like just vegging out with a book or magazine. Even writing books, like this one, in the evening is a lot easier than making the kids do their chores and the like. But that is not why I became a parent—and I know that it's a disastrous strategy if, in the present and the future, I want to have more than the most cursory relationship with my children.

When the house is boring, a kid will go elsewhere for excitement—and before long, your parental role will be reduced to that of cop. Your authority over your children will be dictated by bribery and threats rather than by inspiration and affection.

Is that why you had kids? So you could spend your life sniffing out lies and enforcing curfews? Instead embrace your inner preschool teacher, your inner clown, your inner Baptist preacher, your inner cruise director—in short, make the home as fun, inspiring, exciting, and joyful as you possibly can. Then you'll be able to put the billy club and handcuffs down for good.

Instead I try to model myself on the great camp counselors I had when I was a child. They seemed to have boundless energy to devote to chasing and challenging us. Although they were probably just trying to wear us out so we wouldn't torture the campers in the cabin next door, they really inspired us. So even—or perhaps especially—if I feel like dragging my feet, I pack the kids into the car for an expedition, or give everyone five minutes to get into bathing suits and into the pool, or start a game of basketball in the backyard. I think of myself as the general leading his troops—or a coach right before a crucial final play.

How crucial it is for our children to see us modeling passion! I'm often a little surprised to hear how unsure parents are about activities they can do with their children. My advice is always the same: Start with what *you* love. Our enthusiasms are the sparks from which our children's kindling will be lit. And few things are as satisfying as watching your children embrace your passions. For instance, one of my great passions in life is history. So whenever I am in a new place, whether on a vacation or on a book tour, I try to find out where the historical sites are in order to pay a visit, and whenever possible I bring my children with me.

Sharing in my passions is a way for them to get to know me better—and I'm always conscientious about keeping my side of the bargain. I know that a Civil War burial ground may not be the most compelling place for an 8-year-old girl. So I do my very best to bring it to life for my kids, whether that's telling the most poignant and dramatic stories I know about the historical event or by acting out all the parts in a battle scene. (Boys are particularly fond of my "death by bayonet.") You'd be surprised how much, if you persevere, the kids will get into it. I don't know whether any of my kids will grow up to be history buffs like I am, but at least I've endeavored to model a passionate existence for them.

A friend of mine, a bibliophile, takes her daughter to used-book stores to search out old picture books. Mom gets to be in close proximity to her beloved books, and her daughter gets to look at old pictures of princesses and ponies. Everyone's happy.

Another friend delights in taking his 8-year-old son to Queens, New York, one of the most diverse areas in the world, where they sample

Our spouse and our kids deserve the very best we have, not what's left over after our boss and our hobbies have depleted us.

street foods from as many different cultures as you can count. Dad loves tasting authentic Salvadorean *pupusas* and Trinidadian *cassava pone*; his son loves hearing all the different languages, taking the elevated train, and seeing his dad excited.

Too often home is the place where we collapse in fatigue. That's gotta change.

Sometimes you have to fake it until you make it. Sometimes I'm expressing an enthusiasm and energy level I don't really feel. But midway through pretty much every expedition, just as my children are getting really excited, I find myself remembering how easy it would have been to just blow the whole thing off. And no matter how hot the sun, how irritable the baby, how sticky the kids, and how tired my feet, I'm always glad I didn't.

So if you feel, like the Warrens, that there's a lack of passion in your home, think about what you can do to add a bit of life-giving oxygen to the atmosphere. What's your passion? And how can you effectively convey what excites you about it to your children?

A Legacy of Abandonment

That passion was something we needed to put back into the Warren household. But we also needed to address Teaira's anger issues. I felt that Teaira, like all children who have been abandoned by a parent, was blaming herself for her biological father's lack of involvement in her life. A child who has been abandoned by a parent *should* wonder what is wrong with a parent who could do such a thing, but she very rarely does. In my experience, what the child is invariably asking is, "What's wrong with *me*? Why am *I* so unlovable that my parent left?"

Jack knew exactly what I was talking about: He too had been abandoned by a father who lived mere blocks away and yet made little effort to be part of his life. But without realizing it, he was repeating the pattern all over again. Maybe he hadn't left the house, but he was giving Teaira the impression that he'd washed his hands of her. What was that if not a form of abandonment? And yet Jack was a really good guy who loved Teaira very much. But he was stung by her rejection. I think Jack was right to be put off by Teaira's attitude—even I found it a hard pill to swallow. But he, of all people, could do better. These two people had a tremendous amount in common, more than anyone else in the family. As April said, "To me, they're both the same person." If Jack could use his own painful experience to relate to Teaira, he might find some redemption for himself there too.

I see a funny thing sometimes with parents and children; the similarities between us can often drive us apart. My beautiful daughter Chana, who everyone agrees is most like me in temperament, is the child whom I often have to work the hardest with in order to connect. We're not exceptional—it's often the kid who's most like us that we butt heads with most often.

More Than I Wanted to Know

So I was going to have to do some cheerleading of my own to get the juices flowing and the communication happening. My crew and I secretly went to each family member and asked them questions about their passions, likes, and dislikes. Then we staged a version of the television game *Family Feud*. Some questions were embarrassing: "Who wishes Chris would shower more often?" (Answer: The entire panel except Chris.) Some were more than I wanted to know: "Who wishes someone would use the bathroom with the door shut?" Some questions were intimate: "Who wishes he had a better relationship with Teaira?" (Answer: Dad.) "Yeah? I wish that too," Teaira said. It was a small step toward bridging the gap between them. The path to a better relationship is made up of such steps. In most cases all that is needed is willingness.

The game was simple but thrilling. It showed that a boring day with the family can be turned into an unforgettable adventure in just minutes with a bit of creativity. So many people don't make the effort to make family life exciting, thinking that excitement and adventure lie somewhere across the seas. But you don't have to fly off to Paris for the weekend to find excitement. It's right there in your backyard.

Raise Your Voices and Sing

But then Teaira missed her curfew, and all hell broke loose. Teaira and April locked heads: "You treat me like a little kid!" "You're 14 years old—you *are* a kid!" "No, I'm not!" It's a fight, I'm willing to bet, that happens at least once in every house occupied by a parent and a 14-year-old girl.

As parents it's not an argument that we can afford to lose. Unsupervised children face risk from alcohol and drugs, sexually transmitted diseases, pregnancy, and many other hazards. But they run a much greater risk when they *act* like adults before they *are* adults: the risk of missing their childhoods. And I believe that loss is something we must fight at all costs.

The most creative, successful, and happy adult is one with a germ of child at the center: Without a real childhood, one can never truly be a child. The innocence and curiosity and lack of cynicism that come so naturally to a child are like flames that must be sheltered and protected so that they will always burn brightly at the very center of our beings, warming us at our core for our whole life. Over our lifetime, winds will blow and rain will fall, threatening to put that fire out. And every time we see someone do something small-minded or cruel or unfair—or when we do something of that sort ourselves—that childlike fire dims. We become more cynical, more selfish, and more jaded. But those of us who have been given the chance to build a roaring blaze during childhood weather the elements much better than those who were forced to grow up before their time.

Of course April was right: A 14-year-old is not an adult and has no business staying out until four o'clock in the morning. Any parent who would allow that is irresponsible. But Teaira was right too. She was no longer a child, content with childish things. She was beginning to need something of her own: a creative outlet, a passion, a hobby to channel her own hopes and dreams and ambitions into. She needed a healthy conduit for her prodigious energies. But because she was still a child, her parents were responsible for helping her find that activity. April couldn't restrict Teaira from fun activities with her friends without providing something equally

The grass is not always greener on the other side of the fence. It's greener wherever you water and tend to it.

stimulating in their place. If she did, her daughter would consider her unjust and unfair. And Teaira would rebel! What was she supposed to do at home—watch Jack nap?

So I called the family together and announced their big project for the week. Teaira had a golden voice, just like her mom, and had nurtured a dream since childhood of singing in front of an audience. But she was also paralyzed by self-consciousness and doubt. I told the Warrens that they were going to hold a concert at their church, a concert starring Teaira and Mom. The whole family would pull together to make it happen: April would help Teaira with her skills and confidence, while Teaira's brother and stepdad would work on filling the church. And because I've found that anxiety only grows the more time you have to worry, they didn't have much time to make it happen—just 24 hours. They were going to have to hustle to get everything done.

Here, then, was a workable plan, one that addressed two birds with one stone. Give Teaira an outlet for her exuberant energy, a passion she could cultivate and develop. And have the whole family participate in and coalesce around the development of that passion. We'd help drag Teaira away from destructive pastimes and into a promised land of singing bliss, and we'd unite the family at the same time.

Later that day I accompanied Teaira, her best friend, and April to singing lessons. While Teaira was running through some scales, I stole a moment to talk to April. I wanted her to understand that the experiment was bigger than just this single event. This wasn't just about a gospel concert; it was about helping Teaira to find a positive outlet for all the energy and emotions that she was currently putting into her temper tantrums. It was about paying attention to her, and giving her lots of positive reinforcement when she did something right, so their whole relationship didn't consist of yelling and disappointment. We have to inspire our kids, not just criticize them. Most of all it was about showing Teaira that her family could and would pull together to support her in a constructive endeavor.

April's support was crucial. But so was Chris' and Jack's—and boy, did they ever drop the ball. The two were supposed to be burning up the phone lines inviting every friend and family member to see Teaira's debut performance. But the footage of the two of them bumbling around and slipping into a coma in front of the TV was downright comical. I couldn't believe how long it took both of them just to find Teaira's address book! Watching them felt more like watching the two of the Three Stooges than two people committed to helping out a family member. And why? Not because they didn't love Teaira but because they thought the whole idea was dumb. (They would later be gobsmacked at how successfully the whole project would turn out.) But for now, the television was a lot more compelling than becoming concert impresarios.

Their efforts, if you can even call them that, fizzled out early. I came back to find practically no calls made, Jack out cold in a chair with the baby on his chest, and Chris missing in action. This sucked. I'd asked these guys to pull together to help Teaira—and they hadn't even done the bare minimum required of them. I blamed myself; if I'd really communicated properly with them, made them imagine the church packed to the rafters with loving friends and relatives and the radiant look on Teaira's face when she saw how everyone had flocked to her event, would their efforts have been so lame?

It was too late for regrets, but if I didn't act fast, Teaira was going to receive a much less supportive message. I left Jack napping and went looking for Chris. I found Chris to be a genuinely good guy—a gentle soul and one who seemed very invested in making his family as strong and cohesive as it could possibly be. And the scene of me, a short, bearded, bespectacled guy hunting him down in the midst of hundreds of tall, mostly African-American basketball players, was one of the most memorable—and humorous—of the season. "Chris! Chris!" I yelled, at the top of my lungs, as the cameras trailed me. Within minutes, hundreds of "Chrises" responded, seeking out their moment of TV stardom. I'm not sure how he felt when I used our cameras to hunt him down on the basketball court—"You mean you didn't tell your friends you're *Jewish?*"—I asked in mock seriousness when I found him. But he agreed to go home and make flyers to announce the concert so we could hand them out together the next day.

Something to Wear

The Warrens seemed a little thready the next day when I came to pick Chris up. Chris was game to get out there and rustle up some strangers for his sister's concert—a change from his low-energy state the night before. But now Teaira seemed shaky and nervous. I sent her upstairs to rest, and Chris and I spent another memorable day walking around a giant flea market, telling people about the concert. We were yelling at the top of our lungs, "Gospel concert tonight! Come to our gospel concert!"

A whole bunch of Jewish vendors looked at me like I had lost my mind. What was a rabbi doing promoting a gospel concert? An Israeli guy came over to me and asked me angrily, "Are you Jews for Jesus?" I told him I wasn't; I was the host of a TV show that fixes broken families, and we were working with a Christian family, and their daughter was going to be putting on a gospel concert. He believed this answer as much as if I'd told him that I was from Mars. "Nah, you're from Jews for Jesus," he said again. Oh well—the show must go on. A few minutes later an Israeli vendor was singing to us in Hebrew, and his song made the show.

In the car on the way to hand out more flyers at a mall, I got a call from Teaira. She was in tears but wouldn't tell me directly what was bothering her. With some persistence I decoded her oblique references (remember, there are seven women in my house), and I was finally able to figure out what she was so upset about: "If you get your hair and clothes done, you're going to feel more confident at the concert tonight—is that right?"

I didn't think Teaira was a brat, or begging, as she was worried I would; in fact I know it took a lot for Teaira to make that call. After all, this was someone who felt that the adults in her life were fundamentally unreliable. Her father had left, her stepfather was withholding his affections, and her mother was exhausted. Teaira didn't like asking for anything from them because it hurt so much when they didn't come through. Indeed it told me that she felt more comfortable calling *me*, someone she'd only met a few days before, than her mother or stepdad.

But it was the right thing to do. As I told her, we must all lean on each other—nobody can handle the pressures and responsibilities of

Anger is a great isolator. No matter how satisfying it feels in the moment to vent rage or to hold a grudge, it is always a false satisfaction. Anger will always cut you off from other people—the person you're angry with and the people around you, who will eventually tire of hearing you fume. Anger will leave you alone and forlorn, as you occupy the center of a field of tattered relationships.

life alone. And it's completely natural to want to look and feel your best when you're getting up in front of an audience for the first time. Indeed I was sorry that I hadn't thought of it in the first place. So we made sure that Teaira had what she needed: I took her to the beauty parlor myself. I just hoped that someone besides me would show up to see her!

Clearing the Air

There was one more thing to do before the concert. Before Teaira got up on stage, I wanted to clear the air between Jack and Teaira. I knew that having his support would really give her a lot of confidence, and to do that I was going to have to break down some of the barriers that had sprung up between these two.

April wasn't wrong: The two of them were very similar. Because they were so alike in certain ways—independent and hardheaded—it was very easy for them to achieve the kind of standoff they'd come to. But they were also deeply emotional people and were capable of a very deep level of honesty and candor. It was that angle I hoped to bring out in our conversation.

I cannot overemphasize the importance of having conversations of real import with your children. In fact I wrote *10 Conversations You Need to Have with Your Children* to help parents survive this particular minefield. Too often we dodge the really difficult conversations with our kids. We avoid confrontation because we don't want to feel the discomfort of having a fight and sometimes because we can't bear to hear what our children have to say. But relationships break when we hold our negative emotions in. I set aside regular times to discuss family issues—and in fact twice a year, I let my kids tell me exactly what they think I'm doing wrong. It's a tremendous learning opportunity for me, and knowing that I hear what they're saying validates their sense of disappointment and anger. It can be very painful for me, no question about it; but I would rather be momentarily wounded than suffer the permanent injury of not being close to my kids, God forbid.

After a few minutes of conversation, it became clear that the big stumbling block between these two was their pride. Teaira was too proud to admit that she needed a father—or anyone else. She was a wounded child who had been effectively abandoned by her biological father, so she had tried to become self-reliant as a defense against the pain she felt. Now she didn't want her stepfather to know how much she needed him. But of course she did need people. We all do, especially young people. But Teaira was too stubborn—and too afraid—to admit it.

Jack also needed Teaira—he needed her to need him! And Jack was too proud to admit that sometimes he hadn't handled a situation well. Teenage girls, as I know all too well, sometimes need to be handled with a lot of diplomacy. Unfortunately Jack's style—like that of a lot of dads—was more bull-in-a-china-shop than Talleyrand. That didn't mean that he wasn't right, but he had to make the relationship between them better so that his words would penetrate instead of simply adding to her list of grievances against him.

All this pride was the reason for this particular impasse. These two people were too proud to admit their need for one another. Both abandoned, they had both built up extensive defenses. Out of fear that they'd be rejected, both had acted preemptively, rejecting the other person before the other person could reject them. But it was clear within five seconds that these weren't two people who meant nothing to one another, as their postures would have you believe. Indeed the precise opposite was true: These were two people who loved each other and needed each other so deeply that they'd cause themselves real pain just to avoid being rejected by the other.

Then I told Teaira what I really think: The idea that people won't understand you is no excuse for not talking to them—in fact it's a self-fulfilling prophecy. If you don't tell someone about your life, how can you possibly complain that he or she doesn't understand your life? Jack needed to approach Teaira in a more supportive and gentle way, but when he did, she had to let him in instead of shooting him down with her flamethrower words. All she was doing with these temper tantrums was isolating herself; you can't warm your hands by the fire of your anger. So the angrier she got, the lonelier she got.

It was a very moving conversation. These two stubborn people needed to be led to the conclusion that was obvious to me: They really loved and needed one another! I could tell we were making a great deal of progress, but even I was unprepared for the breakthrough that happened at the very end of this session.

When Teaira started to cry, I encouraged her to go over and not only give Jack a hug but to acknowledge that she needed him very deeply. And I asked her, "Why haven't you told Jack how much you love him and how much you need him in your life?" Between sobs she said, "Because I was afraid of getting hurt." Once in his arms she relaxed and started to cry for good, the kind of cathartic weeping that discharges a tremendous amount of pain. I had seen Jack many times with 6-month-old Jordan lying on his chest, and the similarities between those occasions and this one were unavoidable in my mind. As he comforted her, in a way that only a father can, I was reminded: For all of Teaira's attitude and years, she was as much a child as Jordan was. And that was a good thing. We dare never lose touch with our inner child.

So many of us avoid talking to our teenagers. We believe the tough exterior they present, when we—of all people!—should know the tenderness and uncertainty that lies beneath it. We wonder how they became so cold and uncaring, wondering what happened to the sweet kid of a couple of years ago. But we dare never fall into the trap of believing that they don't want our tenderness or affection—because it is only through our tenderness and affection that we can thaw their hearts, soothing the pain and hurt we have unwittingly inflicted upon them. In this goal we must always persevere.

Showtime!

Friends and family came out to see Teaira's debut. She looked gorgeous, and although she claimed to be terribly nervous, she looked calm, cool, and composed—as self-confident as I had ever seen her. In our last *Shalom* family meeting backstage, I reinforced the goal that I ultimately hoped to leave this family with. The point, I reminded all of them, wasn't to suppress Teaira's passions or to punish her for having them, but to harness them for good by channeling them productively.

Music is one of the most important arts. It matches the rhythms of our life; it pierces our emotions. Our response to it is spontaneous, uncalculated, and immediate. If you've ever watched people dance at a wedding, you know that music can be a physical manifestation of the joy we feel, just as the notes of a funeral dirge can articulate our grief better than words can. Music, I believe, is the sound of our souls.

And it is all-inclusive—colorful, yet color-blind. Just look at how Teaira's concert had brought together not only the members of her family but people of all colors and creeds—not to mention the Orthodox rabbi who introduced her! Music is an outlet for people with talent, like April and Teaira, and it brings a tremendous amount of joy to those people who have none at all. The ancient biblical prophecy of the end of days is that it will be a time when the nations of the world will join together to sing with one tongue. So in my introduction to April and Teaira's appearance, I reminded the congregation how important it is to sing—a message I fervently hope that all of the *Shalom* families have received. Yes, we have to work and empty the dishwasher and pay taxes. But when we're not doing those things (and perhaps even when we are), we should heartily embrace everything that is joyful in our lives. For me there is no purer expression of rich emotion than song. There is so much joy to be taken from music and so much to be given. It is so important in fact that God chose to have the Israelite monarchy stem from David rather than Moses: Moses prayed, but David *sang*. Moses gave us the incomparable Bible. But David wrote the Book of Psalms.

Introducing Teaira from the pulpit of an African-American place of worship reminded me of the very strong affinity between black communities and Jewish ones. I believe that one of the keys to this tremendous affinity is the strong faith that forms the central pillar of both of our communities.

The same chains of slavery that bound the Jews in ancient Egypt bound the blacks in the New World. While those chains may have imprisoned their bodies, they liberated their spirits. Those chains taught the Jews and blacks, above all else, to rely on God for their salvation rather than on any professed human liberator, be he as righteous as Moses or as determined as Lincoln. Both became nations to whom faith was endemic and sustaining. And I believe that people of faith—no matter what faith—share an unbreakable bond.

Now, I have preached in several black churches, including the Martin Luther King Jr. Chapel at Morehouse College in Atlanta—and when I did so, I did so in the presence of his widow, Coretta Scott King. I love the passion in black churches—many black preachers have an amazing, inspiring, passionate style, a style that *works*. Many people tell me that when I preach I remind them of the great black preachers. In the field of religious speaking, there is no greater compliment.

All too often congregants in white churches and synagogues sit silently watching the clock. But in black churches the congregations are responsive. It's a very active way to worship, with a tremendous amount of give and take between the audience and the pastor. Indeed even while I was preaching, the congregation was crying out, "Praise God!" I find the transfer of energy to be completely enervating.

And, as I had predicted, Teaira's performance elevated the audience. In one short week Teaira had gone from being a discipline problem to someone who could lift the spirits and wet the eyes of a congregation. There was a great deal of joy in the church that evening when April and Teaira sang in praise of God.

At the end of the episode, the hugs were warm, the thanks, genuine. I was amazed and thrilled to meet April's family, who were deeply religious people and who were pleased themselves that the Warrens had sought help from a religious source. Indeed I felt very good about the Warrens as I drove the *Shalom* trailer away. And I was even happier when we returned to check in after two months.

I have to say, the transformation we saw in the Warren home as a result of our stay with them was really pretty amazing and very satisfying for me. Everyone seemed happier and more relaxed, especially Teaira. The scowls were gone from both her and Jack's faces. And Jack had, of his own accord, instituted a new policy: He took them out on a family outing on one of the weekend days. When we visited, they were at a nearby beach. And I cannot tell you how happy I was to see Jack and Teaira walking up the beach together, her hand in his, like a proper little girl.

My relationship with the Warrens remains close. The family joined us for a Passover seder at my sister's house; as Christians, they were very interested in seeing what a Jewish seder looked like. And I was extremely flattered to be invited to Chris' high school graduation.

Sometimes you find exactly the right key to unlock the floodgates of family feeling; in this case it had everything to do with thawing the icy relationship between Jack and Teaira. She needed to realize—and then to show and tell her stepfather—how much she loved and needed him. Opening up to him in that way completely changed who she was to him. As he said, "She's like a whole different person." And Jack heard me when I told him that if he weren't prepared to be the strong male figure in Teaira's life, she'd find someone else to be that. And he stepped up admirably, as indeed he had done since she was small.

A miracle happened once these two were able to take off the heavy armor they'd been carrying around. Instead of colliding up against each other with matching scowls, the seeds of a real relationship—one based on mutual trust and love—could once again take root.

Lessons for Life

Make your home exciting! If it's not a fun, energetic place to be, then your kids will want to be somewhere else.

Your goal is not to kill your children's abundance of energy but to channel it into productive ends. Don't just tell them what they can't do; instead inspire them to find a hobby or to pursue a passion.

We need each other! To ask for help or affection or support is not a sign of weakness; it is a show of strength.

Music is the language of the soul, and song is the melody of the heart. We should not only be *listening* to music on the radio, but singing at constant celebrations with friends and family.

Broken relationships can always be mended as long as the participants are prepared to acknowledge their mistakes and apologize for them. Doing so allows the aggrieved parties to feel that their pain has been validated, giving them the power to move past their pain.

Sharing the Burden

We received a request for help from Roy Gordon that illuminated the problem in his house quite clearly. The video he sent showed his second wife, Ro, as she stormed through the house, yelling, albeit without malice, at her family about infractions both real and imagined. I felt exhausted just from watching and agreed with Roy: The Gordon house could use some shalom.

Here's the Story of a Lovely Lady ...

Ro and Roy were both recently divorced from other people when they met doing a community theater production of *The Best Little Whorehouse in Texas*. They fell head over heels for one another. Six months later Roy and his teenage daughter, Arielle, had moved in with Ro; her teenage daughter, Juliet; and her 9-year-old son, Peter. A few years later, the couple had a son, Aidan, together.

Ro was easily one of the most memorable characters in the first season of *Shalom in the Home*. I received scores of emails from her admirers as well as her detractors. Whether you were a fan or not, there was no arguing with the fact that Ro Gordon was a woman of phenomenal charisma and presence. (Indeed my crew and I were convinced that Ro would be discovered by Hollywood after the episode aired, such was her screen presence.)

A lot of people—okay, a lot of women—could really relate to Ro. The night the episode aired, my eldest sister, who is the mother of six children, called me and said, "I love this episode. This is your best one by far." "But why?" I asked her. "Because, Shmuley, I am Ro. This is exactly my life. I am forced into the same position of having to yell at my children to get them to do anything." Yes, Ro was a screamer. But the real question was: *Did she have a choice?* In this age when kids can be really selfish and lazy, do you have a choice but to yell to get your kids to do anything? In this age where the average mother is so stressed from nonstop work—both at a job during the day and with domestic chores at night—is there really any choice but to howl? That was the question at the heart of the episode: Was there a better way?

I was very disturbed when, in the wake of the airing of the episode, many people wrote to me saying that Ro was a witch who screamed like a lunatic, a really bad person. Now there's no doubt that Ro's yelling was unpleasant for the entire family. Roy, who did indeed have the patience of a priest, looked exhausted and depleted by his bouts with his wife; her yelling—much of it leveled at her husband—certainly wasn't good for their new marriage. It wasn't good for any of the kids to see their mother or stepmother roiling through the house like a tornado.

But I think a lot of American women, like Ro and my sister, find themselves pushed into a position where they simply can't handle what's on their plates. These women are heroes, but they have been pushed past their limits. They are the hearts and souls of their families. They are the ones who wake up early to make breakfast for the kids, dress the babies, tidy the house, do the laundry, make dinner, feed everybody, clean up—not to mention whatever they do to contribute to the household's income. In Ro's case she did all that for both her own children and her husband's children. If that isn't a hero then what is?

So I did not go into this particular episode ever questioning Ro and the kind of person she was. I admired her from the first moment

I met her. She was one of the warmest people I encountered in our entire season of filming. But the question remained: Could we inspire Ro to find a better way to run her household? Could we inspire Ro's family members to assist her a great deal more around the house so that she wasn't always so pressured? And could we influence all the other yellers out there by showing them just how unsettling all that screaming is?

Perhaps I related especially to Ro because, like her, I can be a screamer. I was raised in a loud household, and when under pressure, I can be pretty darn loud myself. And I know firsthand that yelling can become a vicious cycle because it seems to work better than gentle persuasion. Actually, as we all know, it's very counterproductive. After a while people become immune to it, and it robs the home of any vestige of peace. A better approach, of course, is to get our children to internalize the inner voice of inspiration, the one that asks them what they want to be and how they can act to achieve it.

So we had our work cut out for us. Blended families are always difficult to negotiate. It's hard enough to make a marriage work, and it gets harder the more personalities you add, which definitely contributes to the fact that two-thirds of all second marriages end in divorce. It was up to me to see what I could do to make sure the Gordons didn't become a part of that unfortunate statistic.

The State of Affairs

Complicating all the Gordons' issues was the staggering fact that (prior to Aiden) *every single one* of the Gordons—kids and parents alike—was a child of divorce. It was quite a legacy of pain to overcome.

Arielle's birth mother was still heavily involved with her, so the effects of the divorce and the blending of the families did not seem to wear on her too badly. I did wonder whether Roy and his daughter had a sufficiently intimate level of communication, but I would look more at that later. Ro's daughter, Juliet, also seemed to be adjusting okay.

On the other hand, Ro's son, Peter, was really starting to show the strain of his parents' divorce and his mother's remarriage. And not seeing his father often enough wasn't helping either. Ro's kids only

It is our actions—rather than our intentions or our motivations—that dictate our character. The great tragedy of life is that we so often get pushed off our intended trajectory and end up at a destination we never desired. We must never forget that we have the power to choose how we react and how we will behave; in that, we have control of our lives.

saw their father twice a month, and although Roy clearly loved Peter, he perhaps understandably favored his biological child with Ro, 2-year-old Aidan. I didn't blame Roy; Aidan was sweet as honey, truly one of the cutest kids you could ever meet, and he was attached to his father at the hip. As a result, Aidan was the very portrait of confident toddlerhood, while Peter seemed to vacillate between anger and despair.

When I met Peter, one of the first things I asked him to do was to write a letter to me about what could be improved in his family. It tugged at my heartstrings when the letter came: In it Peter talked about how lonely he was. He said that he wished that his sisters didn't kick him out of their bedroom as much and that they would play with him more often. And without meaning to, Roy's devotion to Aidan made Peter compete for his attention in a way that I felt wouldn't be good for either of them in the long run.

A Lifetime of Hurt

When Ro was 2, her mother left the house to buy a jar of mayonnaise and never came back. Obviously, Ro had spent her subsequent childhood and adult life struggling with a series of difficult emotions, including the misplaced guilt that she somehow was responsible for her mother's disappearance. And, as all children who have suffered serious trauma will do, Ro had come up with an elaborate series of coping mechanisms to keep these sad emotions in check.

Ro as an adult sought to soothe her internal chaos by turning instead to those things she did control—particularly in the way her house was cleaned and organized. Instead of coping with inner turmoil she was chasing an impossible perfection in the outside world—and screaming like a banshee when something got in the way of her impossible dream. Understandably she felt exasperated by the constant onslaught of work and by what she rightly perceived as the family's failure to support her efforts. But she got so angry when her family members failed to live up to her very high standards that it was nearly impossible for them to participate without disappointing her and incurring her rage. So in the video Roy sent, we watched Ro scrub, and tidy, and cook, and wipe, and sew, and sort, and fold—and scream.

So when I asked Ro and Roy down to the studio-trailer, I started out with guns blazing because I felt that the message I had for Ro was too important to be sugarcoated or muttered into my beard.

"The first thing you have to know," I told her, "is that your mother was wrong. There was nothing unlovable about you then, and there is nothing unlovable about you today. Your mother left because she wasn't a good enough mother. *It had nothing to do with you.*" It's difficult to give love if you don't feel loved, and it's difficult to feel loved after something as traumatic as abandonment by a parent.

Ro needed, for once and for all, to feel absolved of the terrible burden she had been carrying around since she was old enough to walk: the idea that she had been the force that drove her mother from the house. I'm not sure that anyone had ever addressed this with her before; certainly I saw a softer, more vulnerable side of her than I had seen up to this point. I could only hope that my words would penetrate her heart, but it can take more than an insight to combat a childhood trauma—not to mention years and years of destructive thinking.

We watched more video—this time of Roy attempting to defuse an argument even as Ro escalates it. Perhaps most poignant is the way the camera catches Peter anxiously tapping his screaming mother's shoulder in a frantic attempt to distract her or to capture her attention for himself. Again it was very stressful to watch her; even Ro looked chagrined. After I'd stopped the tape I asked the couple point-blank: Is the way Ro speaks to Roy helpful or conducive to an intimate marriage? Both of them agreed that of course it was not.

But Ro claimed that she "didn't know any other way." I argued that she did—she was, after all, engaged in a perfectly civilized conversation with me at that very moment. I wanted her to understand that she was *choosing* to relate to Roy and her children by screaming, even though she knew it to be destructive. Roy clearly believed that there was a quieter, calmer way to motivate the family. But when confronted with this, Ro naturally became defensive. Roy backed off, and I did too—but not before letting her know that she could choose to communicate differently simply by deciding to do so.

The conventional belief is that external events motivate our response to situations. It's called cause and effect. If people feel really pressured, if they're hit with a situation that they can't control, they freak out: If someone hits you in the face, you hit back. But we cheat ourselves when we see ourselves this way. That's why the Bible's doctrine of freedom of choice is the single most empowering idea in history. It maintains that in any conceivable situation, a person still retains the power to *choose* how he will respond. Our lives are not scripted. There is no fate. Our destiny is not written in the stars. Nor is our life controlled by uncontrollable external events, no matter how overbearing or powerful.

Holocaust survivor Victor Frankl, the celebrated author of *Man's Search for Meaning* and the founder of Logotherapy, illustrated the phenomenal force behind this idea, and its application, even in the most horrific of scenarios. Frankl relates that while he was in Auschwitz, the Nazis were able to rob him of his freedom by incarcerating him. They robbed him of his hope by murdering his family, and of his dignity by forcing him to defecate into a bucket in public. But there was one freedom that even those barbaric monsters could never take from him: his ability to respond to what they were doing to him. Frankl explains that human choice upends the whole concept of cause and effect—instead there is cause, *choice*, and effect. There is always a split second, an infinitesimal period, where the human being chooses his reaction. Though the Nazis could destroy Frankl's body, and while they could exert the full pressure of all their monstrous "causes," they could not ultimately control the "effect." They could not destroy Frankl's spirit, and within that spirit lay a spiritual power to rise above any situation by choosing his response.

I wanted to convey to Ro that she too possessed, at every time and in every place, the power to choose how she would act and that she would determine—by that simple act of choosing—the kind of person she would be. What Ro needed to ask herself, as she watched herself screaming on the monitors, was this: Is this the person I want to be?

In the next clip we looked at together, Ro is doing the dishes and calling for help while Roy, Juliet, and Peter sit playing a video game together. Ro repeatedly calls for help, but no one moves; Roy playfully nudges Juliet on the shoulder, but she doesn't go to help her mother, even with the prompt, and Roy doesn't force the issue. I turned off the tape again. What we'd just seen gave credence to Ro's complaint that she was laboring endlessly in obscurity without any help or support from her family.

And I believe that when Ro asked, "What would happen if I didn't do any of this stuff?" she had a good point. She was indeed the engine that drove the house, as many American women are. (More men are assuming this role, but the vast majority of the domestic responsibilities are still shouldered by women—even, I have learned, in households where dads stay home with the kids.)

As women have been saying for years, all that "invisible" work—the cooking, the cleaning, the child care, the scheduling, and the chauffeuring—is both essential and largely unheralded. Kids thrive on order—they just don't want to help create it! It really is very selfish, and it is something that I see over and over in American homes.

Ro's family expected her to carry the entire burden and then blamed her for freaking out. And I felt that sometimes they even used her yelling and perfectionism as an excuse not to help so that they didn't have to be active partners in the home.

But I also thought that Roy had a point when he told me that he sometimes suggested that Ro cut one thing or another from her prodigious "to do" list in order to give herself a little breathing room. Nobody was suggesting that the Gordons take a backward slide into squalor. I could completely relate to Ro's need for order—it was a response to her inner turmoil and the chaos of her early life. And even if that hadn't been true, there is absolutely nothing wrong with wanting an orderly home. But I think Roy's point was that sometimes even that noble goal needed to be subordinated to the preservation of peace in the home. (Expecting to keep a house spotlessly clean when it is inhabited by six busy people living their lives is just setting yourself up for failure.)

What, after all, is the point of keeping an orderly home? Efficiency and ease. If the basketball is always in its special place on the shelf in the garage, the kids will easily be able to put their hands on it when they want to play instead of spending valuable playtime (and disrupting the other members of the household) looking for it. The point of all of Ro's cleaning and organizing was supposed to be to create order and tranquility. But trying to reach that goal resulted in anything but tranquility. Instead of unifying her family, her orderliness was sending them running for the hills.

So I suggested that she consider letting some of the more minor stuff slide, sacrificing some of the more superficial vestiges of order for some real shalom. A plate in the sink is a worthy tradeoff for some peace and relaxation. As I knew she would, Ro looked scared and threatened by the suggestion. To her it wasn't a pile of unfolded laundry or an improperly wiped counter—it was a direct assault on her precariously constructed fortress. She thought that if she gave an inch, everything would come tumbling to the ground.

But I thought we could get both Ro and Roy what they wanted—her an orderly home, him a peaceful one, if the family could be inspired to help more.

A Kind Word

Next I showed the Gordons a clip of something that happened every night: Roy returning home from work. In the clip the first thing Roy does, still wearing his suit, is to go find Aidan in his room. The affection between the two of them is obvious and heartwarming. But our cameras also captured footage of Peter sitting in his room alone, listening to Roy greet Aidan with teasing and hugs. Peter goes to the kitchen, where Roy is, to get a snack from the cabinet—a replacement, perhaps, for the affection he feels he's not getting—and Roy scolds him, reminding him that it's almost dinnertime. Peter protests, Roy holds his ground, and Peter slams the cupboard door and runs into his room, slamming the door behind him.

It was an interesting clip because I sensed that what we were seeing here was a pattern: Aidan got the warm, affectionate side of Roy's love while Peter got the discipline and the limitations. I took no issue with Roy laying down the law: Of course there shouldn't be snacking while dinner is being prepared. But given that this was their first interaction of the evening, might there not have been a gentler—perhaps humorous—way to handle it?

Kids need tons of positive affirmation. They need endless amounts of support and encouragement and pats on the back. They need to feel—even if you have eight of them, as I do, thank God—that they are number one in your life every single day. I'm as firm a believer in discipline as you'll find out there, but I don't think you should greet *any* child with a scolding, especially a kid like Peter. This was a child who was already struggling to cope with the circumstances of his life, including too-infrequent visits with his biological father and living with a whole new stepfamily. He needed to warm himself under a little extra love and interest and attention—certainly more than he needed to be scolded for snacking.

I'm always interested to see how people greet one another. I overheard one of my friends answering her cell phone; from the warmth and enthusiasm in her voice I thought she was hearing from a long-lost friend. Who was actually on the other end of the line? Her not-so-long-lost husband. How warmed he must have felt by how happy she was to hear from him! I was very impressed by this and have made a practice of implementing it in my own life. Just because we see and talk to our spouse and children all the time doesn't mean that we shouldn't greet them as warmly as we would a friend. And certainly there should be no scolding before hugs and kisses and hellos!

Now that Roy had seen the pattern, I knew he was more than capable of showing this attention-starved little boy the love and positive affirmation that the child needed. We simply have to accept that children of divorce are more broken and more angry than kids from happy homes. In a culture that has become so blasé about divorce, it bears repeating. Peter was not merely some 9-year-old child with normal problems; he was a child who traveled like a boomerang between two homes, seeing his biological father only twice a month. That's a really heavy load for a little boy!

Stepfathers have difficult roles to fill. They are, at best, *second* best. What a child really wants is an actual parent. And because stepdads know and feel this, they often refrain from extending themselves fully in connecting with their stepkids. They preempt rejection by holding themselves back. This is especially true when it comes to talking with their stepkids. But conversations that help a vulnerable young child deal with the hurt and pain of his parents' divorce and the subsequent unavailability of one of the parents are absolutely fundamental. Very often a stepparent can talk to a child about issues that even a parent can't address because the parent is too emotionally involved, and perhaps in too much personal pain, to be of much help. I wanted to encourage Roy to build a stronger relationship with Peter.

Walking the Boards—or Is It the Plank?

Ro and Roy had met in the theatre, so I thought it would be the perfect place to begin the process of getting their family back on track. I arranged to have the noted acting coach Alan Gordon (no relation to our couple) join us at a local theatre to help this family act out their current roles—and to try some new ones on for size.

It was pretty fascinating to watch. Ro's a terrific actress—or maybe she just found it very easy to get in touch with the tremendous feelings of exasperation and frustration that characterize her daily life. In the tableau we set up, true to form she barked orders loaded with specific instructions. Also true to form the kids sullenly executed her orders, ducking their heads as if trying to physically shield themselves from her aggression. It was really quite realistic; Alan was impressed.

As far as I was concerned, that was a good thing. We human beings are capable of a very high level of denial about our own behaviors, so that often in a counseling situation I spend a lot of time just showing people what they're really doing as opposed to what they *think* they're doing. You see it over and over as couples watch themselves in the footage I show them in the *Shalom* studio-trailer. Family members can be genuinely surprised at what they see. That wasn't the case here. In fact, all involved seemed to have a really good idea of how they acted in their everyday lives and even knew the effects those behaviors had on the people around them.

But Ro was also powerfully defensive and was committed to the position that she knew only one way to communicate: "If you did what I said, I wouldn't be acting this way." But Roy claimed to have a better way. So although Ro bristled at the mere suggestion that Roy could run the house better than she could, I asked Ro and Roy to switch positions in order to see if we couldn't find another way of achieving a well-ordered household without so much volume and drama.

I'm no Olivier, but even I had to admit that Roy hammed it up a little while demonstrating his quieter, more respectful strategy for getting the toys cleaned up and the table set. And Ro, it goes without saying, was practically squirming out of her chair, alternating expressions of disbelief and exasperation with hysterical laughter. But the kids were responding, and although I wasn't putting him up for any Oscars, I still thought Roy was on the right track. He asked, he didn't tell, and he definitely didn't yell. And when the kids did what he had asked them to do, he went heavy on the praise and gratitude. It was clear that his goal really was a calmer, more harmonious home.

As I told these two, words that come from the heart penetrate the heart. Words spoken out of pressure or anger bounce right off their intended recipient like an echo. The best reason not to nag our kids isn't just that it creates an unpleasant atmosphere in the home, although it does: The best reason not to nag our kids is that *it doesn't work*. Eventually they will tune us out, retreating into a private world of their own. And the real pain comes when we realize that we can't penetrate that private world *at all*, even when we want to talk about something of more substance than the right way to take out the trash.

"This is the best laugh she's had in a long time," Alan Gordon said to me, and Ro watched her family easily gathering at the prop table for "dinner." Although it was nice to see an expression on her face that wasn't rage, I felt that Ro's laughter meant that she wasn't easily going to give up the position she'd taken that Roy's way wouldn't work. In fact as soon as Ro playing "Roy" sat down at the table, tempers flared. "This is bulls**t! It would never work, and you know it!" Ro yelled.

I quickly stepped in. Was our fictional exercise just that—fiction? Or could it become reality?

Well, Ro was right about one thing: It would take two—or in this case six—to tango. Roy and the kids *did* have to get off their butts to support her efforts. And she was probably right that she sometimes needed what I called "the sledgehammer"—the yelling and the threats. There probably isn't a parent alive who hasn't had to resort to such tactics at least once or twice. But I know from my experience and from watching others that the best way to get people to do something is to *inspire* them to do it. Motivating people with positive words beats haranguing every time, and I suspected there was a grain of truth in it when the kids said that they would respond to a kinder, gentler approach. The exercise ended very positively when Ro proposed a bargain: "I'll change a little bit, if they'll change a little bit."

Taking the Taco Test

The Gordons' next challenge was "The Taco Test." The plan was that Roy and the kids would make dinner while Ro stepped back a little and relaxed. I would be watching what happened from my trailer.

A night like this might be a mini vacation for many moms, but I suspected that it would be a difficult task for Ro. And right from the outset, it was clear that Ro had no real intention of loosening the reins. The good news was that the volume was lower, but there was still a high level of control—and nervousness—in how Ro dealt with her family.

In the trailer it was my turn to squirm off my chair in exasperation. We were talking about tacos, for crying out loud—who cares if they're not served off the finest china or if someone steals a chip! But of course the issue at hand was more than just Tex-Mex, and I don't for a minute mean to minimize what Ro was going through. This was a person who had made her way back from considerable trauma to create a functional household and family life—even if there was room for improvement in the way she made it happen. I wasn't watching a woman fixate on flatware; I was watching her soothe and manage her anxieties. Seeing how hard it was for Ro to relinquish even the slightest control over how things were done made me realize exactly how tightly wound she was; she really felt that her grip on the wheel was the only thing keeping the car on the road. Clearly Ro sometimes felt that her sanity literally depended on the perfection she achieved in the outside world. If she kept anything less than a constant pressure, the patient would bleed out, the center wouldn't hold, and the walls would come crashing down. So they weren't just tacos. She was treating setting this table like it were a matter of life and death because for her, it was.

The evening was, to put it mildly, not a success. (I consider any social event that ends with a teenager stalking off while miming a bullet to the brain to be a failure—maybe my standards are too high?) It was time to take more serious measures.

Enjoy Your Stay

I sat with the Gordon kids, with Roy in the background, to hear their side of the story. Unsurprisingly it was different from the one Ro told.

I had seen for myself, over the week I'd spent with them, that they were fundamentally good kids. But they were beaten down from being constantly criticized and yelled at and nagged at. They *did* help around the house, they told me. They *did* respect Ro. The things they *didn't* do—like cooking—they didn't dare to try because they knew that Ro wouldn't or couldn't tolerate anything that wasn't done her way—the perfect way.

I told them my plan for the next two days: In order to break Ro cold turkey of her stranglehold on the household, I was putting the kids in charge of the whole show. We'd divvy up chores and household responsibilities, and they'd do them as well as they possibly could. This would give their mother a much-needed break— all while showing her that they were not only capable but also willing to share the burden of the responsibilities. I would, in turn, secure a pledge of noninterference from Ro—a promise that the kids met with some skepticism.

The great philosophers Aristotle and Maimonides both maintained that the best way to live was to embrace the golden middle path, defined as the perfect medium between two extremes. But what happened when someone veered from the golden middle and ended up at an extreme? How do you reachieve balance? Maimonides argued passionately that often the best way to come back to the healthy middle is to go to the exact opposite extreme of where you are.

I told the children that I knew they must be asking themselves: What's in it for me? Well, there normally were two answers to that question. As every mother who has ever gone on strike knows, kids really do thrive when they're surrounded by order, and they do tend to freak out when it falls apart. A great deal of good parenting is simply keeping kids clean, well fed, well rested—and yes, knowing exactly where the basketball is in the garage. But for the Gordon kids I had only one answer, the same one I'd had when I arrived at the beginning of the week, and that was shalom. Only by stepping up and participating could they show their mother that her tremendous anxiety was misplaced, and only by quelling that anxiety would the Gordon family achieve the domestic tranquility they sought.

So we welcomed Ro back into her house—this time as a guest, as if she were spending the weekend in a small, family-owned bed-and-breakfast hotel. The only rule? No interference. No complaining, no criticism, no suggesting—or insisting on—a better way. It would be a hard row to hoe for the kids, but I knew that it would be even harder for Ro. She appeared to be on the verge of a panic attack when I left her with Roy, and when he asked her how she was feeling, she responded with a question of her own: "What am I going to do?" Except that it sounded less that she was asking "How am I going to fill all this free time?" than a deeper question, "What will become of me?" I could only hope that Ro's day off was a challenge she would accept.

A Brand-New Day

Roy and the kids were up at the crack of dawn. And, as Roy had predicted, the kids did wonderfully well with a gentler, more inspirational style of leadership. Breakfast was prepared and eaten, and the atmosphere was considerably lighter than we had previously seen in the Gordon household. I was really pleased to see that they all went out of their way to do what needed to be done. There was only one exception: Peter, who sat sullenly in front of a video game with his joystick. I counseled Roy to be gentle and patient with him, and Peter eventually joined in the project.

Roy's challenge over the next few hours—and the next few months— would not just be to get Peter up and participating with the rest of the family, but to make him feel that his contribution was a vital and essential one. In truth the dynamics of this family had made this little boy feel that he was left out of the mix. The girls had each other, and Aidan was Roy and Ro's biological child. Peter was stuck in the middle and, like so many children, his primary way of securing some parental attention was to misbehave. Ro and Roy had to give him enough positive attention so he could stop feeling that he needed to check out—or act out—to get noticed.

Implementing this—even in a minor way—on this busy morning really paid off. Roy was patient but persistent and quick with a compliment when it was due. So although he rolled his eyes, Peter eventually did allow Roy to draw him into the project and ended up doing his share.

What children want—indeed what everyone wants—is to matter. They want to be noticed; they want to feel that they are special. And God has given parents a unique role and a unique capacity: to make the most vulnerable creatures of all, children, feel that they matter. Even though Peter was not Roy's biological child, the moment that Roy began to take a greater interest in Peter, the child's behavior changed for the better. It was validation rather than freedom that he craved.

The morning was a banner success. The house was spotless, and it had all been done without any shouting or criticism. Roy had been right about the effectiveness of his style. Under his supervision the kids worked well, and even Peter (with some extra attention and praise) had gotten into the swing of things. I really liked seeing Roy and his daughter sitting together on the couch folding Aidan's tiny pajamas; it was proof that even the most banal of household chores can bring a family together if it's handled correctly.

But I couldn't quite relax. Ro was still sleeping—and it was her reaction, not mine, that would determine the success of the experiment.

And when she did wake up, my glorious experiment went straight to hell. Ro came out swinging, without even a token attempt at gratitude for all the hard work or a compliment on the results. According to her, everything was wrong. The house was a disaster. Arielle made too much noise while rinsing the pan she had used to make her stepmother's special breakfast. In fact Ro not only failed to be complimentary, she seemed hell-bent on finding fault with the job her kids had done. She made a big production out of finding an eggshell in the scrambled eggs Arielle had volunteered to prepare.

I couldn't believe it! If your stepdaughter makes you a special scrambled egg breakfast, it's probably a good idea to smile and tell her it's one of the best things you've ever eaten, even if you're crunching on gravel. And the same thing goes for the rest of the family's efforts. The house was pretty darn clean, and Ro's kids had made it that way. If your kids have pulled together and spent a weekend morning doing a week's worth of chores, you ought to consider breaking out into a tap dance of gratitude. How can you possibly expect people to continue to make an effort if you don't reward them when they do? Children especially put so much stock in a kind word.

Instead Ro went on the warpath, nitpicking the tiniest details and expressing dissatisfaction with Roy and the kids and the job they had done: "I'm going to have to spend the whole day redoing everything," she yelled. If the question was "Could Ro let go and let the other household members do the work so she could rest and have a break?" the answer was a resounding no. Ro *was* pressured from too much work, but she also needed to be busy to feel alive. Not having anything to do drove her positively crazy.

Needless to say, the mood in the house, at first so hopeful and positive and cooperative, collapsed.

Shalom—Inside and Out

As the morning's work fell apart around the Gordons, I felt like an opportunity was lost. Ro was a great woman, a great wife, and a great mother. But her control issues were so fundamentally tied up in the fragile structure she had built around herself to protect herself from the painful chaos of her emotions that anything that even *touched* on them caused a major fault line to rupture. The idea that the house could run without her and that Roy's way might be more effective than her own when it came to motivating the kids acted like a major earthquake. She reacted by allowing her terrible fear to bubble up into anger.

Ro, like many people, needed work in order to feel fulfilled. The quiet moments she had to herself frightened her. She felt she only existed when she was *doing* something. Not that this was a fault unique to her; in fact I'd argue that it's a defining fault of our time. We are a generation with little understanding of the importance of rest. Instead we've become workaholics, for whom "doing" has superseded "being" as one of our major goals. Our whole being, our whole sense of self-worth, is thoroughly embroiled in a culture of frenzied activity. There are a million ways to relax, and yet nobody has any peace. When Pharaoh enslaved the Israelites in Egypt we learn that he made them work "dispiriting labor." By this the Bible doesn't mean that he made them carry backbreaking stones or had them whipped, although certainly there was much of that as well. Those jobs, no matter how painful, would break the body but not necessarily the soul. Rather, the meaning is that the work had no end. Pharaoh trained the Israelites to feel that they were born for nothing but work. The meaning of dispiriting labor is that it quashed the Israelites' spirits and robbed them of all hope because it convinced them that they were born for nothing but labor, like oxen to the yoke. And this is what happens to us when we live to work instead of work to live.

The Talmud explains that Pharaoh gave them work without end. The Hebrew slaves would often be awoken unexpectedly in the middle of the night and forced to perform heavy labor. Without a clear and definite delineation between times designated for working and times designated for resting, the Hebrews were always preoccupied with their labors, even when at rest. They could never relax. They slowly developed a slave mentality.

Sound familiar? Our work lives occupy so much time and energy that we're working even when we're not working. But when we live this way we lose sight of our humanity and our own physiological and psychological needs.

Ro needed to understand that she was a woman, not a machine. She had to not just find peace but to be comfortable with peace. She had to master her insecurities so that she didn't feel she was always treading water, one desperate paddle away from sinking into the abyss. So when I went into the house to interrupt Ro's tirade and to see if I could get her to tell me what exactly had set her off, I didn't go in to yell at her. I simply wanted to get through to her.

By the time I got there, she was into another rant—this one a slightly more lighthearted one about a miscommunication regarding a clogged toilet (brought about courtesy of one very embarrassed member of our crew), but she was the only one laughing. She was still committed to her position. "I'm just a loud person," she told me, laughing. "I don't mean to be loud." Well, that might have been an easy way to discount the rage I'd witnessed when she woke up that morning, but I wasn't going to let her get away with it. In a calmer moment she could dismiss the heavy-duty emotions roiling under the surface that had caused the ranting and raving, but we all knew they were there. And those emotions were what I wanted to discuss.

I told her that I thought she felt better about herself when she was being "productive"—bringing order to her world, which was why she felt so uncomfortable with any kind of leisure time. Usually in my experience that's the result of someone who doesn't want to spend too much downtime examining her internal life. When I told her that she just had to accept that the world hadn't treated her fairly, the look on her face changed entirely; instead of the defensive posturing, suddenly she looked like a woman who was forced to fend for herself.

"The show is called *Shalom in the Home.* There's an inner home and an outer one. We're here to bring you a little peace to the inner one," I told her. As we talked, she said gently that she felt criticized by our presence—she felt that Roy had called us in to "fix" her. No, I told her firmly. That's not what happened. Roy knows that you are the soul of the family, the engine of this house, the hearthstone, the thing that warms it from within and makes it run. And he sees that you're working at cross-purposes, exhausting yourself, and asking for help in a way that virtually guarantees you don't get any.

He just wants to help. "We support you, we love you," Roy told her. I believed it. Did Ro?

Your standards, I told her as an objective observer, are just a little high. You want to fix what is broken, but you can fix a thing too much. When you scream and yell, even when literally provoked, it's not a peaceful home, even if the pillows are perfectly aligned. When you tell your kids that nothing they do is good enough, they will stop trying. Worse, they will start believing it about themselves and in other arenas beside the domestic.

I had one thought to leave her with. One day a week just enjoy the world—don't try to exert your mastery over it. Be one with the universe. That's the biblical concept of the Sabbath, which is central to nearly all cultures and civilizations. Jews practice it on Saturday, Christians on Sunday, and Muslims on Friday. You don't have to *do anything*. In fact you're not *supposed* to do anything. It's good advice for all of us. Our culture drives us to maximize every spare moment, to capitalize on everything we come into contact with. But all that meaningless activity just obscures the still, small voice at the center of us—our own personal shalom.

On the Road Again

I don't flatter myself that we completely transformed this family in the week we spent with them. But I was very pleased to see that two months later when we came back, they had put some real changes into place. The kids were more considerate and more participatory than they had been—and Ro was encouraging that participation. Roy had stepped up to help her manage the children instead of hiding from her with them. The family's support had made a big difference: Ro did seem more relaxed. She told us that she yelled less, although she hadn't entirely given up "supervising." Even more encouraging, Roy was sharing his time, attention, and affection a little more evenly between the two boys. Today the Gordons remain dear friends of mine, and I continue to admire and respect Ro especially. She may be a little loud, but she is a remarkable woman.

If there's anything I've learned from doing the show it's that there's rarely a single culprit. When things start going wrong in a family, it's usually because of a much more complicated cascade of events and behaviors that begin to interfere with the dynamic. What can we learn from this? Simply that it takes more than just a single person making changes to get a family back on track. If a family is going to achieve real change, as the Gordons did, *everyone* has to do his or her part.

Lessons for Life

In a blended family everyone has to work a little harder. The parents have to work harder on their marriage and to not to show favoritism toward their biological children over their stepchildren.

—※—

Homes—and families—work better when things are neat, and clean, and organized. With that in mind, everyone needs to pitch in and help. Keep a chore list so that everyone knows what he has to do without being nagged.

—※—

Reward effort! All of us—especially children—need praise and encouragement when we do something right (even if it is not as right as you'd like it to be). As the old saying goes, catch them doing something *right*—even if it's only one sock in the hamper. With enough encouragement soon it will be two.

—※—

Yelling at your children may bring about an immediate result, but the change is always temporary. Rousing your children with the still, small voice of inspiration, while taking a bit longer to achieve your ends, will bring about permanent transformation.

—※—

When we are innocent young children and our parents ignore us, it does not mean that we are unlovable. Rather it means that their parenting skills are sorely lacking. The defect lies with them rather than us, and we must always remind ourselves of our essential virtue, even if our parents were not able to see it.

Achieving Self-Worth Through Our Children

The Sterlings were, by far, the most controversial family we counseled on the show. With homosexuality and gay relationships arguably the most consistently contentious political and religious issues in our country, we knew that some viewers would commend and some would condemn our choice to highlight a lesbian couple with biological children. But our show is about helping people; these were two real women, with two real children, and we weren't about to withhold our caring because we might be condemned.

I do not intend in this book to get deeply into the issues of homosexuality. Because I have a gay brother, also an Orthodox Jew, whom I love with all my heart, you can imagine that it is an issue that has occupied a great deal of my thought. I have written several lengthy papers on the subject. But whatever any of you thinks about homosexuality, I believe that it is utterly immaterial when it comes to children in crisis, and that is the approach we took.

Melissa and Ilene have been together for fifteen years, and they are very devoted to each other. As Melissa herself told our cameras, "We have so many things that we do well together; we're a good team."

Several years into their relationship they decided to have children through artificial insemination, with Melissa serving as the biological mother. Their daughters, 7-year-old Sierra and 12-year-old Alexi, are pretty special kids—smart, funny, and polite.

Loving parents, great kids, an intact home—there seemed to be a lot of shalom in the Sterling home already, even without our intervention! In addition they were living in a neighborhood that accepted them completely. They sent their children to a school where they were treated like any other couple. Both daughters said they were completely comfortable with having two mothers. So what were we doing here, and why did the Sterlings invite us in?

There was one big problem: Alexi's obsession with her homework. "Doing well academically is very important to me," she told us; important enough to spend six or seven hours a night on her homework. Apparently her sessions would begin as soon as the girls got home from school and last late into the night. This undermined any sense of family harmony—the Sterlings couldn't do anything as a family because Alexi's homework was all-consuming.

Her parents were concerned that this massive outlay of time was interfering with Alexi's recreational time—including time she might have been spending doing fun stuff with the rest of her family. And Melissa and Ilene were concerned that all the fighting about the homework issue was going to start to act as a wedge between them and their daughter, fraying their relationship so that Alexi no longer felt comfortable talking to them about anything. "Once she starts being more on her own, if we don't have a line in to her, we're sunk," Ilene told me.

So although most parents in America would have loved to have the Sterlings' problem—imagine, a kid who takes too much time and care with her homework—they (correctly) were worried about a much bigger trend and ultimately about the possibility of losing their daughter. And Alexi seemed pretty unhappy to me. So I drove the *Shalom* studio-trailer to leafy Park Slope, Brooklyn, to see if I could help.

Meet the Sterlings

Melissa had always known that she wanted children, so she and Ilene used a sperm donor—the same one twice, to have Alexi and Sierra. The girls look like the sisters they are, but their personalities are tremendously different. Sierra is sweet and silly—a completely lovely goofball who endears herself to you instantly. Alexi, on the other hand, has a much more thoughtful, serious temperament, and she has shown a real talent for what she describes as "figurative, opaque" poetry.

When I met Alexi I found both her mannerisms and her poetry to be sophisticated beyond her years. She struck me instantly as a child protégé. But I also noticed what seemed to be a broad streak of melancholy, troubling in someone so young. And she seemed to have little interest in anything childlike. Most of the 12-year-olds I know take a great deal of pride in acting like adults, but they betray their interest in childlike things when someone reads an adventure story aloud or when they find themselves in front of an enormous ice cream sundae. In other words they may talk a good game, but they still have at least one foot squarely planted in childhood. Not the serious Alexi. I agreed with her parents' assessment that there was something wrong, but suspected that the problem was deeper than how to get Alexi to do her homework faster.

"Look, Pa, Perfect Children!"

As a lesbian couple Melissa and Ilene had come up against more than their share of rejection, not the least from the people who should have been closest to them: their own families. Melissa's family in particular condemned her homosexuality as well as her relationship. Her father— ironically, a judge who had a distinguished career as a prominent civil rights attorney battling for justice on behalf of the oppressed— considered her relationship to be morally wrong. I never met the man, so I can't speak with any authority, but I will say that he did not sound like a bad man, but one without a choice. A devout Catholic, he took seriously his religion's teachings on homosexuality and rejected his daughter's lifestyle as an abomination.

Moreover, Melissa's family positively abhorred her choice to have children and tried to talk her out of it. They called her selfish and said that any resulting child would spend its whole life struggling under the weight of a stigma. One can imagine how much it hurt Melissa not only to be an outcast to her family, but also to have her parents view her own children as the product of a deeply sinful union.

This I believed was the root of the problem. Faced by the most painful of all rejections—to feel hated by those you most love—Melissa set about proving her parents wrong. She was going to be the exemplary woman with the exemplary children. First, she was going to become the best damn prosecutor ever, to prove herself to her father, the civil rights lawyer. And so she became a distinguished assistant district attorney. Then she was going to raise children who were geniuses, to prove to her parents that not only were her children *not* abominations but were instead the best children in the world.

Individually and together the Sterlings had thrown themselves into proving that they weren't less than other parents, and they had indeed proven themselves admirably. Both moms could claim significant professional success. Melissa left the attorney general's office and entered education in order to spend more time with her children; she subsequently became a wildly popular first grade teacher.

Ilene proved herself as a high-end graphic designer. Their historic brownstone was beautifully restored and filled with plants and books. Their parenting had produced two terrific kids—the contemplative Alexi and the charismatic and charming Sierra.

It seemed that the pressure from the outside had even served to bond this family together, as soldiers will bond in the field. But I suspected that some of the problems the Sterlings were seeing in their home were indirect, negative consequences of all that outside pressure. Because although they seemed uncomfortable with the amount of time that Alexi spent on her academic work, they also seemed to put a pretty high level of importance on it.

For instance, in the footage we took of their family we saw the moms—Melissa in particular—raise the issue of Alexi's homework over and over again. And we saw Melissa proofreading an essay that Alexi had written. To this rabbi the essay looked superb, something a college student would be proud to submit, and certainly an extraordinary piece of work for a 12-year-old. Melissa, however, was nitpicking the smallest turn of phrase, despite Alexi's clear frustration with the process.

Now I could only applaud Melissa's level of involvement. As far as I'm concerned, the world would be a much better place if more parents would take an hour or two every night to help their children with homework. But Melissa was *too* involved—and too controlling. Although Melissa had brought us into the home to help Alexi gain control of her perceived homework problem, we saw endless footage of Melissa asking Alexi—even on Sunday—whether she had done her homework and offering to sit with her to get it done. So who had the obsession with homework—the daughter or the mother?

The point of helping your kids with their homework isn't to make sure that they turn in a press-ready essay with nary a split infinitive in sight. Homework (and helping with it) is to help students coax out their own inner voice, to help them identify and pursue their passions. Of course we need to be there for our kids when they need help, but it's not our job to copyedit their papers and vet their science experiments. Perfection isn't the point of homework; *learning* is.

As I always tell my own kids, "As far as school is concerned, all *I* want to know is that *you* want to know." I have long told my children that I couldn't care less about their grades; at most, grades for me are nothing more than a barometer of their level of intellectual curiosity. I don't want children who are circus monkeys, trained to perform for their teachers and parents by bringing home A's. Rather I want kids who can overcome boredom— life's biggest disease—by always finding life, people, and facts fascinating.

And, as too many parents who mistake "telling" with "helping" discover, taking too much of a professorial approach just alienates the kid. The Sterlings often complained that Alexi didn't always respond when spoken to and that she was uncommunicative in general. I suspected that she was sometimes ducking a lecture about how something she'd done could be better! More important, children need a great deal of privacy for their thoughts, just as adults do, and I didn't see Alexi getting a lot of that time.

Now Melissa is at heart an ambitious woman. In fact she told us that she'd had presidential hopes in high school. So she had taken the challenge seriously: Through her kids, she was going to prove that a lesbian couple could not only raise kids but raise the best kids in Brooklyn. And Melissa's ambition, let us remember, was not selfish; she wasn't looking to become rich or powerful. She simply wanted to overcome the unjust rejection of both her parents and society and prove that she didn't deserve to be rejected or judged.

But we cannot live through our children. They're not our possessions, totemic symbols of our success to show the world. They're kids! And, as you probably noticed, they have their own personalities, their own likes and dislikes, their own strengths and weaknesses, right from the moment they are born. They come into the world as people, not as clay to be molded into the image that will best complement us. Without their even realizing or intending it, the Sterlings—especially Melissa—were walking around the house with hammer and chisel in hand, constantly sculpting Alexi into the image of a perfect child prodigy. The Sterlings meant no harm—to the contrary they were sweet and sensitive women who were simply unaware of how destructive their efforts to elevate their children might be.

When I spoke to Melissa and Ilene I asked them if they were perhaps overcompensating, creating "perfect" children and the "perfect" family as a living rebuttal to the argument that they weren't fit to parent at all. This idea certainly resonated with the couple.

"I feel like I'm not good enough, so I have to do more and more things to be good enough. My parents can't accept me for who I am, so I must not be good enough," Melissa said.

Of course she felt this way. This is precisely the legacy we are left with when we do not receive the unconditional love we should from our parents. Indeed our parents are supposed to be the people to whom we *don't* have to prove ourselves. The pride they take in us is supposed to be the organic and natural outcome of *who we are* rather than *what we do*. When such unconditional acceptance is withheld, it results in incalculable damage for children.

I believe that giving unconditional love is one of the most important aspects of parenting. Unlike our friends, our parents don't love us just because we're good listeners or because we're quick to buy a round at the pub. Unlike professional colleagues, our parents don't like us because we run a tight meeting or because we do what we say we're going to do. The kind of love we get from our friends and at work is *conditional* love. It too is essential to a feeling of well-being—we need to feel chosen, the way a boss or a friend chooses us. But if one group doesn't like us, we can find another group that does. Parents are not replaceable. To be as strong and confident and secure as we can be, we need to know that there are two people out there who love us *no matter what.* We need to know that our parents think we're beautiful no matter what blemishes mark our skin; we need to know that they think we're smart no matter how ridiculous a thing we've just said; we need to know that they think we're special, and unique, and perfect no matter how ordinary we seem in the eyes of the world.

Melissa's parents, as so many parents sadly do, had allowed their personal feelings, religious beliefs, and politics to get in the way of that unconditional love. They had told her, essentially, that they loved her less because she was gay. That had left a wound that even after all these years was indescribably painful.

Here I will address my religious readers for just a moment. People often ask me how I, as an Orthodox rabbi, relate to my gay brother. I tell them calmly that I love my brother to the very end of the earth, as much as I love myself. He is a good man, a wonderful and loving brother, a generous and committed Jew. If every aspect of his life is not lived in accordance with God's dictates, well, that is regrettable. But it in no way subtracts from the outstanding human being he is. I would do absolutely anything for him, and the fact that he is gay will never, and could never, come between us.

When my wife was in labor with our eighth child, she asked me what sex I hoped the child was. (We chose not to find out during the pregnancy.) I told her the truth: I would be ecstatic with whatever God gave us. But I added that I wanted a boy—for one reason. The person who holds a baby at his circumcision is called a *sandak*, and it is considered to be the highest honor in the Jewish faith. My father had served as *sandak* for my first son; my older brother, Bar Kochva, had served as the *sandak* for my second son. I wanted a third son, if only to give my brother the honor of holding his nephew as he entered the covenant of Abraham. And a few hours after the baby was born, I called my brother and asked him to be the *sandak* at the circumcision eight days later. He did, and his presence there and the honor we accorded him brought me endless delight.

Melissa's father, unfortunately, had drawn a completely different conclusion from his religious convictions. He believed that his religion prompted him to love his daughter *less* or to treat her as if she were a lesser person. *That*, my friends, is an abomination before God.

Once Melissa revealed that she was called to a different lifestyle, her father's message to her should have been, "Melissa, you tell us you're gay and in a committed relationship with another woman. To be honest, your mother and I don't really approve; you know that we're devout Catholics, and this goes against what we believe. But even so, heaven and earth could never come between us: Our love for you is infinite. And no matter how much we reject your lifestyle and wish you would choose differently, this could never affect how much we love you and adore you. You will always be our daughter; our home is always your home. So please know that amid our objections to some of your choices in life you will always be loved and accepted."

Now Melissa wasn't putting pressure on Alexi out of personal ambition, as many parents do. She was responding to the pressure of a culture that told her, over and over in myriad ways, that she was less than other people.

But in an effort to prove her father—and the rest of the world—wrong, Melissa was actually falling into the same trap that her own parents had fallen into. Her father had essentially told her that his love was conditional: "To earn my love you have to fall in love and have a family with a man." Now Melissa was creating children whose virtue and accomplishments, rather than whose essential being, would earn them love.

It's a terrible thing to tell someone, especially your own child, that her intrinsic self is not good enough to warrant your love. But it's even worse to cause that child to pass it on inadvertently to her own child. Although Melissa clearly felt tremendous love for Alexi and would do anything to protect her from the same pain she felt herself, the message she was actually sending through her behavior was very similar: "I love you—as long as you excel by making this essay perfect." By putting so much emphasis on performance, Melissa was unwittingly telling Alexi what her father had told her: I love you more for what you *do* than for who you *are*.

I want to make it clear that there was no malice here; in fact the opposite was true. Melissa thought she was doing the best possible thing for Alexi by pushing her. Certainly one of the most insidious aspects of bigotry is how it promotes self-hatred. Melissa, like every parent, wanted to do the right thing for her kids; she wanted to know, as every parent does, that she had made the right choices on her behalf. But how could she feel completely sure when one of the major influences in her life believed she'd made a terrible mistake? I think that at some level Melissa was really concerned that she *had* done something terrible to Alexi and Sierra simply by bringing them up within a lesbian relationship. She couldn't silence the niggling little voice at the back of her head that asked, "What if your parents were right? What if you had started these children off behind the eight ball by bringing them into a world filled with prejudice, judgment, and hate?" Well, then she'd better arm them with the best of everything: the best education, the best skills, and the best work ethic she could—because they'd need every weapon in a prodigious arsenal to fight back.

But that was a tremendous burden to carry—and it was proving too much for this sensitive 12- year-old. This pressure was what was driving her to put in seven hours of homework a night, and it was why Alexi's poetry sometimes felt so very dark.

So at the end of my first conversation with the couple I told them what I saw to be the truth. Their home was not deficient, thank God, in love. And it wasn't lacking in good intentions either. I knew that once I got the Sterlings on the right track they'd be fine. But there was something missing, something integral to the health of every family: joy.

Fun: Mission Impossible?

In search of some levity—a way to inject some fun and playfulness into the Sterling family life—I took them to take clowning lessons from Kendall the Clown.

The day turned out to be a disaster, and I could tell it was heading in that direction during the very first exercise. Kendall started the session off with some warm-up exercises—just goofy ways of moving and dancing to warm up the body and mind for the silliness to come. Sierra, of course, fit right in. In fact she looked pretty much the way she usually did. Melissa got into the fun, donning a red nose and executing very professional-looking pratfalls. Ilene and Alexi, on the other hand, were stiff as boards and about as happy. They were gamely going along with the program, but I felt more that I was torturing them than helping.

We moved into the next exercise, choosing costume pieces from Kendall's giant collection of silly accessories. I looked quite dashing in a long, blonde ponytail, chef's hat, clown nose, and a flowered housedress. I had nothing on Melissa's clowny old bag lady or on Sierra's hodgepodge. Alexi, on the other hand, chose a long, blue sheet that she fashioned into a chador, with a red wrap for her head. In other words, she found the most somber items in a grab bag of ridiculous choices and literally hid herself in them—because nothing says "teenager having fun" like dressing up as a self-proclaimed Muslim nun! In my opinion, it was a pretty striking statement.

Ilene didn't want to dress up at all. When I confronted her, she fessed up to her extreme discomfort, claiming a hatred of clowns. Fair enough—but it seemed more like self-consciousness to me. I talked to Alexi next. She too told me that clowning wasn't the kind of thing she found funny. Okay, fine—clowning is not for everyone; I know perfectly well that wearing a red nose and an apron is pretty broad humor. But I'd be willing to bet that Melissa didn't sit around watching Bozo for kicks in her spare time either—why could she and Sierra get into it when Ilene and Alexi couldn't?

I asked Alexi a perfectly logical follow-up question: "If you don't like clowns then what *do* you find funny? Monty Python? Old episodes of *M*A*S*H*? *The Daily Show* with John Stewart? Surrealist poetry from the late '20s?" I didn't care what she said; I just wanted this kid to tell me what in the world could get a genuine belly laugh out of her. Sadly, my question gave way to what I considered to be the most disturbing moment on the show. Alexi didn't answer me for a long time. She tucked her floor-length blue sheet even more closely around her body and ducked her head at a funny angle, breaking eye contact with me. After what felt like an eternity, she formally apologized to me for the extended silence: "I'm sorry; my parents hate it when I don't respond." And I never got an answer to what should be the easiest question in the world for a 12-year-old to answer: What's funny?

I felt—and not for the last time during the filming of this episode—like a complete jerk. I was supposed to be helping, but I just seemed to be causing this kid more pain. Here I was, a supposed relationship expert, and I couldn't even get a 12-year-old girl to lighten up a bit. The day was a serious setback—clown class had gone over like a lead balloon, and I felt that both Alexi and her mother Ilene were a little alienated from me and from the *Shalom in the Home* project as a result.

The activity was a misjudgment on my part for sure. This teenager was way too self-conscious for something like this. But one of the advantages of being a rabbi who has always pushed the envelope and done things a bit differently is that I have gotten used to criticism, and I know how to bounce back. So I was going to make up for my bad call with sheer persistence. Children always want someone to get through to them, and Alexi was no different. I knew that I could unlock her natural, childish aptitude for fun—I just had to find the key.

Strike Two

The next day I asked Ilene and Melissa to sit down with Alexi to share the insights we'd gleaned from our first meeting. I wanted Alexi to understand some of the reasons behind the pressure she felt from them. "Sometimes Mommy and I push you for reasons that aren't really good ones, and we don't want you to feel pressure because of that," Ilene told her. Wow, we were getting through!

But Alexi wasn't having it. "I need you to push me to do well at school because I can't self-motivate, which is what we're working on." I sat there at the table staring at Alexi in disbelief. Had I just heard a 12-year-old bitterly complain that she could not self-motivate, even though she did about six hours of homework a night?

It was a horrible evening, and my heart went out to Alexi and her parents. This had become a tragic household, not because of an external tragedy but because of a self-inflicted wound. Melissa and Ilene had been spurned by people they loved, and without ever meaning to, they were passing on the dysfunction, making one of their daughters feel that unless *she* was the very best, she wasn't good enough.

I tried to break through to Alexi with the same thing I tell my own children: "You are special and loved, no matter how you do in school. Your happiness is more important than any grade and shouldn't be dependent on what some teacher thinks about your schoolwork." Alexi wasn't having any of that, either. "My happiness lies with school—yes, it does," she rebutted when I protested. "You don't know where my happiness lies."

This was another rebuff, even more hurtful than the last. I felt useless. This girl clearly saw me as a silly interloper, and maybe I was. Here we were, three adults sitting with a troubled 12-year-old girl, who was sobbing uncontrollably as she lamented her inability to push herself even harder at school. This child wasn't really a child but someone who had already entered the adult world; someone who experienced adult disappointments, adult frustrations, and the adult propensity to feel that despite all our gifts we are still not good enough.

Now Alexi was saying that I didn't know what made her happy. But neither did she—and that was, in my eyes, the problem. What was evident was the tremendous pressure that Alexi was putting herself under. Instead of alleviating some of that pressure, our conversation seemed to have intensified it. By the end of the meeting Alexi was having a terrifying physical reaction to the stress; her face was a grimace of pain while her body shuddered with sobs.

This girl was in a darker place than I had even imagined, and I was going to have to reevaluate my role. Once again my attempt to break through to her had fallen flat. I wasn't convinced that her parents really understood how serious the situation was or what they were doing to contribute to it.

I went home that night as despondent as I had ever been on *Shalom in the Home*. I called my producer and director and had an impromptu conference call. Should we continue? They weren't sure either. We decided to revisit in the morning, and I stayed up much of the night feeling like absolute crap. I did not know how to help Alexi, and I started to hate myself for my own deficiencies.

Guess Who's Coming to Dinner?

I woke up still feeling very concerned about Alexi, who appeared to be under a great deal more pressure than I had even suspected. Her resistance to my efforts to help seemed fairly well entrenched. Should I quit or could I really help this girl? This was no longer about the television show. I felt intensely connected to this child who was in the same age range as three of my daughters. She was such a brilliant, sparkling soul that it seemed doubly tragic for that luminescence to be masked by such a thick layer of darkness.

The solution suddenly came to me: I knew how I would help her. I would get through to the joyous child under the dark adult within Alexi by *not* trying. I was not going to try to cure her, to help her, or to heal her—indeed that was the problem. I had correctly seen that all these adults were trying to make her into what they wanted her to be, but hadn't there been a chisel in my hands as well? Wasn't I doing the exact same thing, trying to turn Alexi into the perfect image of the content and happy adolescent I so prized? It was time to let this girl just *be*.

As you can probably imagine, it's highly unorthodox for a television host—or indeed a counselor—to bring the families he is counseling to his home. I do it all the time. I may be a counselor, but I am a rabbi first. I don't shy away from close, personal relationships with families I am trying to help; indeed I welcome them. Every Friday night at our home we have a big Sabbath dinner, and every week we invite people to join our family for this celebratory meal. Many of the *Shalom in the Home* families have been our guests, and my family and I love having them. Indeed I have remained in close contact with many of our families, and they have joined us for our family celebrations, including the bris of one son and the bar mitzvah of another.

I loved the idea of inviting the Sterlings to my home to eat and to get to know my family. I thought it would give Alexi an opportunity to get to know me as a person and as a father. Instead of trying to shape her I would give her an opportunity to let her hair down to just play and let loose.

I also think that the members of my family, for all of our failings, manage a pretty good balance between work and play, a balance that I see out of whack in many American homes, including the Sterlings'. Of course like every parent I want my own children to do well in school, and I nag them about doing their homework just like every other dad in America. But I try not to lose sight of the fact that their happiness and our family time come first. In our home, schoolwork doesn't take precedence over everything else. We don't live to work—we work to live.

I have the highest respect for scholarship, but I want my children to be motivated in their schoolwork by the desire to learn. I want them to be bitten by the same bug that bit me: the love of knowledge. I want them to know the deep fulfillment that comes from satisfying healthy intellectual curiosity. I want them to love reading, to learn how to research things they're interested in, and how to read critically and with care. But I don't want my children to be beholden to other people for their good opinions of themselves—even if those external opinions are those of their teachers. And I never, ever want them to think that they have to do something to *earn* my love.

In fact I have told my children over and over that I will always love them unconditionally and equally—whether they're awarded a MacArthur grant for their brilliance or if they fail algebra three years in a row. Of course homework is important, but it is more important to me that my children spend time with their parents, that they do good works, and that they interact positively with their brothers and sisters. So play is important in our house, and I love making my children laugh. I thought the Sterlings could benefit from seeing this in action.

There are no "buts" when it comes to the parent-child relationship. Personal feelings, politics, even religious beliefs cannot interfere with that bond. A parent's love must be unconditional.

I had another agenda for the evening: I needed to break through to Alexi, and I hoped that my own passel of kids might be able to succeed with her where clown school and a conversation with her mothers had failed. Never underestimate the power of your children's peers. Kids talk to each other with an openness and candor that they do not feel with adults. We often think of this in negative terms, as peer pressure, but I have seen many times how positive it can be when the influences are benevolent. All I wanted was for Alexi to feel safe enough and comfortable enough to relax and laugh a little. I hoped that she would find that more easily with my kids than she did with me.

It worked! My kids, particularly the girls close to Alexi in age, felt an instant connection to her, and I could see Alexi warm under the glow of their attention and interest. They all had lots to talk about, and in the way of teenage girls, they lost no time in getting down to it.

Another reason I wanted to make the Sterlings the first family to be invited to my home on the show was to counter the rejection they had experienced throughout their lives. Yes, I am a religious man and an Orthodox Jew. I take the teachings of the Bible seriously and am well aware of its prohibitions against gay relationships. But I also know that there is no higher religious truth than the fact that we are God's children and that every human being is of infinite value. I wanted to extend a most personal welcome to Melissa and Ilene so they would truly know that whatever precedent other religious individuals had set in making them feel like outcasts, *this* religious individual was proud to invite them into his home and treat them like the beloved children of God that they were. I wanted to make that statement publicly, to strike a blow against the increasing, irrational, and abominable hatred of homosexuals that is too often harbored in the name of religion. We may not all live lives that are in accordance with God's dictates in every way, but we are all God's children. And religious individuals, however much they may oppose homosexuality, should be at the forefront of demonstrating unconditional love to all of God's children.

The dinner broke the ice with the entire family. Melissa and Ilene and the girls were very excited to be with us and were clearly appreciative of the invitation. We loved having them, and all of us gelled. It was just as well because I was prepping myself for what I knew was going to be a difficult and painful, but highly necessary, conversation with the two parents.

After dinner I invited Ilene and Melissa into my office. I started off by telling them how admirable I thought they were as parents. But this time I didn't pull any punches in terms of what I thought was on the horizon if we weren't successful in making a turnaround with Alexi sometime soon. I wanted to be forceful without being alarmist.

I told them that I was concerned that she would burn out academically, and I shared my belief that she was ultimately heading for a serious depression unless something changed. "I want Alexi to be a much happier child," I told them. I have counseled many depressed teens, including some who cut themselves, and others who have attempted suicide. While I did not believe that Alexi was capable of any of those things, God forbid, she did seem to be living in a very morbid place, a place that no 12-year-old should be in.

I also told the Sterlings again that I believed they were unwittingly the source of much of the pressure. Although I think they agreed with the underlying premise, they resisted the characterization that they were concerned with what other people thought. Of course they were concerned about what other people thought! I reminded Ilene that just a day before, when I had asked her why she hated clowning around, she said that she was self-conscious. "Is that not the essence of being concerned with other people's opinions?" I asked her. She responded, "Touché!"

To some extent we all are concerned with what people think, and not many of us are under the same pressure to be model citizens and parents that the Sterling family was. I never worry that someone is going to draw terrible conclusions about all Jewish people if one of my kids screws up in school. But the entire society surrounding the Sterlings said right from the word "go" that these parents were fundamentally unfit to bring children into this world. Everything the couple had done since then was an indirect response to the criticism.

But Alexi needed help. So I set out a radical set of strategies for the Sterlings. First of all Alexi needed some space. No more interrupting her thoughts or editing her papers. As much as they loved her, it was time for these moms to back away a little bit.

Second, Alexi had to learn to put family life—happy family life—above all of her academic responsibilities, and the Sterlings would have to enforce this, just as they previously had enforced attention to schoolwork. Under the new Shmuley Edict, Alexi was to do no more than two hours of homework per night, and no homework at all on weekends except for a limited period on Sunday night. There was to be no talking about schoolwork in the home, and I asked the Sterlings not to put pressure on Alexi to be perfect. It was time for everyone to lighten up and get a little crazy. Aristotle and Maimonides both argued that when someone is too involved at one extreme, that person must temporarily go to the other extreme in order to finally find balance. The only cure for Alexi's intense preoccupation with her homework was to do the minimum amount for a time. She had to learn that life was not about work; she had to learn to feel comfortable in her own skin and just *be*. Besides, a bright girl like that could get a huge amount of homework done in two uninterrupted hours; I really believed it would suffice.

Both of the women were on board with my plan, and I felt greatly relieved as the three of us went back to join the party. I also was pleased to see that while the Sterlings and I had been talking, Alexi had really warmed up—enough that she even gave me a big hug at the door. Finally I was seeing a chink in the armor.

I have to give Melissa and Ilene a tremendous compliment. Nearly every parent who brings me in to heal their children problems uses the same approach: "My child doesn't listen; can you make her listen?" "My child yells; can you make him stop?" "My child wants nothing to do with me; can you change her?" Of course most of the time I quickly discovered that the real problem lies with the family dynamic, not with the child. In fact, let me be more blunt. Nearly always the problem lies with the parents rather than the children. So why don't parents own up to it? Because it is indescribably painful to accept that you have harmed what you love most in the entire world. So cognitive dissonance sets in and you can't see the truth. When Ilene and Melissa left me that night, they said something extraordinary that I will never forget. They said that when they first brought me in to meet their daughter, they feared there was something wrong with her. So they were absolutely delighted to discover that their daughter was fine and it was they who were the problem!

"Depression Girl"

When I arrived at the Sterlings' the next day, I was told that my producer and my director were inside the house trying to stop the Sterlings from pulling out of the episode. Needless to say, I was shocked. I felt that I had made an enormous breakthrough with them the night before. What had changed?

I rushed inside and joined the conversation. It turned out that Melissa and Ilene were concerned—even as they were grateful that we had exposed the depth of the problem with Alexi—that my prediction of depression for Alexi would fan the flames of critics who say that gay and lesbian people can't be good parents. They were also concerned that Alexi would struggle further once the show aired—this time not under the rubric of "the girl with two moms" but as "depression girl."

Once again I was reminded of the tremendous pressure these women felt to be role models, to present an impossible perfection. Even in their most intimate moments, as they reached out to get help for a strained child, these women were seeing themselves as standard-bearers, as representatives. Even as they struggled with the price that their insistence on perfection was taking on one of their children, they had to be apprehensive about the message sent to the world about gay and lesbian parents if their child were diagnosed as suffering from depression.

I was committed to finding a way for this family to stay with the project, and I felt comfortable addressing their concerns. It wasn't in order to salvage the TV episode—we already had an episode. And this is not my life. But I felt strongly that the Sterlings should stay with the program because we had not yet helped them to translate their commitment to have fun and be more relaxed into a practical program of change.

I wasn't at all concerned about the message that the show would send about gay and lesbian parents. This wasn't a theoretical debate as to whether lesbians should have or adopt children. This was a real family, with real kids. Let all those be damned who had no respect for or sympathy for the need for these children to be left alone to live their lives. The message I wanted to send was "Look at how kids respond to pressure—even when you do *everything else* right!" The problems the Sterlings were facing were problems that many American families face.

Let's face it: American kids are spending more and more time on schoolwork and less time being kids. As I write this there is an article in *The New York Times* ("In Kindergarten Playtime, a New Meaning for 'Play.'" Clara Hemphill, July 26, 2006) on a trend toward a more formal academic curriculum, even in kindergarten! Instead of playing in the sandbox and pushing cars around on the floor, even the nation's youngest children are now confronted with math and grammar drills.

This is happening despite the fact that education experts strongly recommend a more play-based approach. After all, children learn all kinds of important skills, both social and academic, from play. They're not just playing ice cream shop; they're really learning how to use their imaginations to acquire language skills and how to communicate, to make up and tell stories, how to share, how to solve interpersonal problems—even some math basics. I'm all for the best possible education, and I truly believe in study and learning. But the drive for measurable achievement is driving essentials like the dress-up corner out of our preschools, even though we know it's the wrong thing to do. In the article, Hemphill describes the children falling asleep, sucking their thumbs, and showing other classic signs of anxiety. And that's just the beginning.

It broke my heart to think that the Sterlings were worried that our show would harm them as parents. I made it very clear to them that we would be nothing but respectful of them and of their beautiful, talented daughter. I did want to use the show to show the effects of bigotry, and prejudice, and hatred on its victims, and I did want to show the effects—for all parents, whether gay or straight—on allowing outside pressures, including cultural pressures, to filter through to their children.

Indeed I told them the truth: If anyone suffered condemnation from the episode it would be me. I have a strong following among religious people of all persuasions who read my books and articles and listen to my broadcasts on family, spirituality, traditional values, and respect for women. I am invited to speak in synagogues and churches the world over. I knew that many of my religious admirers would clobber me for working with a lesbian couple to help their children on a national show. But I knew that helping the Sterlings was absolutely the right thing to do, and if I didn't care, surely they shouldn't either.

(Subsequent to the show I received hundreds of emails of complaint from religious people throughout the United States and Canada who felt I had betrayed my values by highlighting a lesbian couple. Some were polite; many were not. Then there was a movement among a particular group of religious Jews to have me publicly reprimanded, but it did not pan out. Did all this bother me? I guess so. I take a lot of criticism, and I confess that I am hurt by it. I'd like to be admired as much as anyone else. But I would do it again. All children are innocent, precious, and special, and deserving of whatever help I can offer. Period.)

It was good to clear the air. Thankfully we were able to make the Sterlings feel comfortable enough to continue with the show, but the conversation served as a further reminder of the kind of pain these women had lived with throughout their lives.

Sierra in Charge

Our final task for the Sterlings was simply to cook dinner together. After all, even regular family activities can be joyous and liberating. Instead of the usual six or seven hours of homework, Alexi would spend only one, and then it would be time to make and eat dinner together. Fittingly, the Sterling most qualified for the task took the helm, and I'm pleased to report that the rest of them snapped to attention and rose to the occasion as Sierra kneeled on a kitchen stool and ordered her family to have fun.

I could communicate with all of them through earpieces and gave them ideas of silly things they could do as they cooked dinner and baked cookies. We soon had Ilene lobbing chocolate chips at Alexi's open mouth. Alexi might not have embraced the experiment as openly as her younger sister, but I did see her crack a couple of smiles. Dinner and cookie baking segued into face painting—including a Rabbi Shmuley beard on Melissa. For once I could see this family enjoying the moment, not trying to get something done.

The Sterlings were, like many of the families we worked with, surprised by the direction the show took. They thought they needed help in getting Alexi to focus on her homework in order to get it done; in fact her procrastination was the symptom of a much deeper problem.

Over the course of the week with the Sterlings, it became clear to me: This wasn't a show about gay and lesbian parenting but a show about the pressures we all put on our children to sometimes cater to life's less-than-legitimate expectations. In this case the fact that these parents felt condemned by many in the outside world made them feel that they had to create the perfect kid. They simply needed to remember what so many of us need to be reminded of, and what all of us know in our hearts: Our kids are perfect just because they *are*. We dare never create human *doings*, but human beings. Yes, we have to educate and discipline our kids; we have to shape and mold their characters. But we also have to just let them be themselves.

Melissa and Ilene aren't alone in allowing cultural pressures to seep through and distort their parenting. A few years ago, I met a mother who was tacitly condoning her daughter's life-threatening eating disorder because she too felt a few extra pounds would be fatal. I see kids every day whose lives are so packed with the kind of "enriching" extracurricular activities so appealing to colleges that they haven't enjoyed an unscheduled hour in years. I counseled a man once who had broken with his son because of the son's decision to attend art school instead of his father's (and grandfather's, and so on) illustrious alma mater. All I am saying is that *all* of us, without exception, feel the pressure of the outside world bearing down. None of us is immune from a culture that values surface attributes like our physicality and how much money we make over what really matters. And too many of us pass those pressures through to our kids, allowing those pressures to warp and distort our relationships with our children.

But our job as parents is to filter that pressure. Our job is to shelter our children from the storm so that they have the opportunity to grow strong, not twisted by the cultural winds that blow through. We can never forget that our children are important and deserving of our love, simply because of who they *are,* not because of what they *do.* And the same is true, whether we like to admit it or not, about ourselves.

Lessons for Life

Everyone is a child of God. We may not make choices in accordance with every one of His dictates, but that does not make us any less His children.

Family life should be invigorating and *fun.* If it's not, something's wrong—and you owe it to yourself to spend the same kind of time and energy on addressing that problem as you would spend on any other problem.

Our children aren't clay to be molded or stone that needs to be chipped away to expose the beauty beneath. Put down your chisel in order to appreciate and encourage what's already there. Help your children discern and reveal their own inner voices.

Put school in its place! If you make the love, affection, and approval you show your children conditional on how they do in school (or athletics or anything else), you're telling them that they're valuable because of what they *do,* not because of who they *are.* Teach your children that intellectual curiosity is what matters, not grades.

Some religions may consider certain relationships illicit, but every child is absolutely perfect.

"Peace is the climax of all blessings."

Rabbi Eliezer Hakappar

Conclusion

As you no doubt know by now, shalom means peace, and it is the blessing that I want most for every American family. But I know too that it continues to elude us, both collectively and personally.

Life is a hurricane, and we are blown hither and thither by fierce winds. Our jobs are stressful. Technology makes it nearly impossible for us to escape the demands made upon us. Our "must-see" culture makes us feel like bumpkins if we're not in the loop.

That's why it's so important to have somewhere to go that offers us some respite. Because modern life routinely demands so much from us, it is especially important for our home to be a sanctuary from that hurricane, a place of calm and tranquility at the center of the storm. When our center is strong, we can withstand any amount of buffeting; no wind can move us, shake us, or tear us down. When there is shalom in our homes, they become the places they were intended to be: places for us to catch our breath, rest, and rejuvenate ourselves; places to celebrate our lives and inspire our children. There can be no greater priority.

Too many of the parents I meet, both in person and through email, feel that their homes aren't places of peace—and they feel that they don't have the ability to make them that way. They are overwhelmed and feel confused by all the conflicting advice from experts and are worried about making mistakes that could scar their children for the rest of their lives.

This is the primary reason behind my hosting *Shalom in the Home* and for writing this book. I know what it's like to live with parents who fight. I know what it's like to come home from school to a home with little peace. I know what it's like to be a child of divorce, and I know that few things are more horrible. As a society we have trivialized the effects of divorce on children. Divorce is so ubiquitous that we treat it like it is no big deal. Well, it *is* a big deal—a really big deal. And I want no child to have to grow up the way I did, a boomerang traveling between households, a diplomat at 8. The child of divorce is placed into the unnatural position of having to serve as a caregiver to two lonely parents. But a child is too unformed to form others; too weak to make others strong; too vulnerable to make others resilient.

When I was a boy, I came across the famous expression in the Mishna of how much God loves those who bring peace in the world, especially those who bring peace between a husband and a wife. I have forever since wanted to be one of those special people. This show has given me that opportunity. When I started hosting *Shalom in the Home,* I told myself that the greatest marker of my success would not be high ratings or great reviews, even though I wished for both those markers of popular success. Rather my principal marker of success would be if I could make a significant dent in the ludicrously high rate of divorce, and if I could strike a significant blow to the increasing gulf that was growing between parents and children. To do both those things would be to increase shalom in the home and shalom in the world.

In order to heal the American family, I feel an urgent need to do what I can to empower the nation's parents, to help you regain your confidence and your authority. You may not control the wind that batters you; neither do you control the vagaries of the economy, the loud cell-phone talker next to you on the commuter train, or the dry cleaner who inexplicably cannot find your trousers. But you *do* control what goes on in your home—and in this I mean what I say. *You are in charge,* and if you don't like what's going on in your home, it falls to you to make a change.

It is my belief that one of the corruptions at the root of modern family life is a lack of accountability. "I can't do anything with my kids," parents tell me. "They're out of control." But this I do not accept. It is the parents' job to assert and maintain control. When one of my children does poorly in school, mistreats siblings, or speaks disrespectfully to me or my wife, I don't look elsewhere for reasons; I step up squarely and take responsibility. If my children yell, it's because I yell. I formed them in my image, and I take responsibility for the image they assume.

Each one of us has a quiet, still voice at the very center of our being. When we can hear the voice speaking, we always know what to do. Parenting isn't really mysterious: We know that we are doing the wrong thing when we allow our children to date in their early teens or to watch television shows of which we don't approve. An essential part of us winces in shame when we lose our tempers and raise our voices, or use sarcasm against our children, or break a promise. It's very painful for us to be out of sync with that voice and what we know to be right. Only by following that voice can we find shalom, and when we have *shalom* in our homes and in our hearts, we can always hear it.

Now shalom does not mean that there will never be problems or conflicts. I can pretty much guarantee you that those will never go away completely. But shalom does mean that you and your family can deal as a team with whatever issues you may have so that everyone learns from the experience and the family draws closer as a result. The successful parent is not the one who does everything right but rather the one who never disengages from the battle. For righteousness as a parent is not found in fording the river and getting to the other side but by teaching your children to swim so they will not be pulled by the current. The mountain of life has no summit—and your daughter messing up in algebra is just another opportunity to spend more time with her.

Shalom also doesn't absolve you of work. Everything that is worthwhile in this life requires work; we come by nothing of value instantly and without effort. Our homes need work to keep them safe and attractive. Our bodies need exercise and wholesome food to keep them healthy. Our marriages need attention to keep them passionate and alive. And our relationships with our children require time, effort, energy, and forethought. But with shalom in our homes, doing that work becomes a pleasure, not a burden.

To treat someone as a member of your family means acting selflessly, loving that person as you love yourself. Isn't that when you truly knew you were a parent? When you stopped casting longing glances at the new roller coaster, contented to stand and watch your children enjoy the bumper cars for hours? But so many of us today feel that our selflessness is for naught. It might be the most natural thing in the world to want to see your children be happy, but it gets to be hard when your children treat you like live-in housecleaners and ATM machines. If your children are selfish, lazy, and unmotivated and they treat you like dirt, you made them that way, and you can reform them.

I do not, by any stretch of the imagination, mean for this to feel like an unsupportable burden. In fact the majority of the people I have worked with report that their newfound accountability has given them a whole new lease on life. It is ultimately very reassuring to know what we do can make a difference, especially because the remedies I am prescribing are so very simple to implement, and they produce immediate results and wonderful rewards.

I would also like to encourage you to enrich your marriages whenever possible, even when—or maybe, *especially* when—you and your spouse are taking a lot of time to address issues with your kids. As you may have noticed, something interesting happened in almost every family we visited: The problem we were called in to address almost always turned out to be a symptom of something else. In most cases the families were surprised by the direction the show took; in some cases even my director and producer were.

A couple's sex life (or lack of it) turned out to be the canary in the coal mine, telling us everything we needed to know about why their teenage daughter was so rebellious. A clash of cultures turned out to be two people who had let the fire of their romance die. Indeed the most common occurrence was that we were called in to fix a kid and ended up talking about a parents' marriage instead. This wasn't a coincidence. I don't believe that anything that happens in a family happens in a vacuum, and I believe that a strong marriage is the foundation upon which a strong family must be built.

I married a woman whom I know to be a better person than I. She is more feeling, wiser, less judgmental, and much more humble. One of the blessings of marrying someone who is a better person than you is that whenever you have an argument, you automatically know who is in the wrong. So it has been easy for me to apologize for my character flaws, even as it has been difficult to change them. Our spouses are not our dorm mates but our soul mates, and we must endeavor to bring intimacy to this primary relationship. The spark of connection so characteristic of the American marital union must be rediscovered. Only then will our children bear witness to a living example of love that is both intimate and passionate, inspiring them to bring those same qualities to their own marriages.

One final thought: I've been blessed to work with terrific people on the show, thank God. But if there's one conflict I had with my producers on almost every show, it was resisting their impulse to tie up all the loose ends into a perfect package finished off with a pretty bow. I have been invited into the homes of these families, and I have been as candid with them as I can be. I have made suggestions as to how the families might improve things, and in most cases they have attempted to implement those suggestions. Most of all I have sought to inspire them so they would continue to put their highest creativity, energy, and imagination first and foremost into their families. I feel that we have helped them to make significant strides toward greater fulfillment and happiness. But I do not flatter myself that I have left perfect families in my wake.

I think we spend too much time—no doubt because of the way we're conditioned by Hollywood—searching for an unrealistic perfection. We want the made-for-TV version of our spouses—ab-mastered and bleached of tooth. We want the burnished granite countertops of the house we see on the decorating shows. We want the wacky and nonthreatening kids from a prime-time sitcom. More than anything we want a happy ending.

But always-happy endings aren't real—and I would argue that they're not just unrealistic but undesirable. I'd rather have the deep, complex, passionate, and humorous woman I married than a one-dimensional "desperate housewife." I'd rather have crumbs and crayon marks on the counter—evidence of a meal that my family has prepared and enjoyed together—than the most sterile expanse of gleaming stainless steel. I'd rather have my brood—with their orthodontia, their poor grades in math, easy laughter, and their generosity of spirit—than a fake perfect family. We are all works in progress, and life is messy—gloriously and infinitely so. Because life is imperfect, it requires each of our contributions in order to make it better. It is specifically in the imperfections of life that our existence becomes necessary.

I hope the *Shalom in the Home* television show and this book have helped you to bring more shalom into your own home. And I hope that you remember that it is your family—with all its imperfections—that is your first joy and greatest blessing.

May God bless each and every one of you, and may He grant you peace.

Acknowledgments

Shalom in the Home *is, I trust,* to the viewer watching it on the screen an utterly absorbing, emotionally excruciating, thoroughly entertaining, and ultimately inspiring program that makes family life twinkle and sparkle. But behind the scenes, putting the show together is a herculean task that today still shocks me. Many dedicated professionals do the groundwork that allows me to saunter into a broken family's life and attempt to glue it back together. Mentioning all the contributors to this project might be a book in itself, but here are some of the notable names. David Abraham, head of TLC who—amid a 24/7 lineup of programming that he has to oversee—has been incredibly supportive of our show. Debbie Myers, the head of Daytime, Lifestyle, and Fringe programming, also serves as the matriarch of our show and its muse. Debbie is not only our executive producer but my dear friend. She breathed life into this project from its inception.

Ronnie Krensel, our show runner for our first season, was the life force behind the show. Without him it would not have come into being. Ronnie is like a brother to me, and although we now work on different projects, he graces our home regularly on the Jewish Sabbath, when my kids are positively thrilled to see him walk through the door. It was Ronnie's warmth, profundity, and sincere ability to connect with our families that allowed me to sparkle on the show, and any positive change I brought to our guest families is as much his doing as my own.

Our director for season one, Marcus Boyle, brought us great panache as the best-dressed and most charismatic Liverpudlian lad since the Beatles. Marcus made me laugh and made me think. Coti Villanueva, our field producer, really bonded with our families and, through their trust in her, opened their hearts. Roy Ackerman, Paul Sowerbutts, and Andy Harrison from our production company, Diverse, overcame myriad roadblocks to keep our show running smoothly and successfully. Our cameraman for our first season, Dominic Azoto, was the man we all called "hero," because he showed so much skill and bravery with the camera that at times we didn't think he was going to make it to the next episode. Our sound man, Rafael Sienkiewicz, pulled off daily miracles. Raf is also the sweetest guy you could ever want to work with. And then there is Dan Kelly, a dead ringer for Johnny Depp, who proved the most dexterous man ever to wear a cross, long hair, and leather armbands at the same time. There are so many other crew members who made the show possible, but I have been told by the publisher that I can't have fifty pages to mention all of them. I hope they will forgive me, as I am deeply in their debt.

My editors at Meredith had the idea of transforming the show into a book, especially the marvelous Lisa Berkowitz, whose constant confidence in and pursuit of me was both inspiring and humbling, and Alrica Goldstein, who did an outstanding job of editing the manuscript. As with much of my writing, Laura Tucker, my friend and editor of more than five years, took the jungle of ideas and amorphous mass of what my writing usually consists of as I shove it down into a word processor and helped organize it into a coherent whole. Laura's talent and insight are limitless. And as an amazing mother and wife, she is an extraordinary example of a successful and brilliant career woman who always puts her family first.

But the people who deserve the greatest thanks for this book are the families. And by families I mean both the families brave enough to come on *Shalom in the Home* and whom you have met in this book and my own family, without whom I would know next to nothing about family life.

Very often I receive emails criticizing the behavior of some of the families on our show: "Did you see how that mother screamed at her children?" "How could that husband shout that way at his wife?" Invariably I answer that I am surprised at their judgment. These are, after all, families who so love each other that they are prepared to risk public ridicule and censure in order to better their ways and grow closer to one another. Who has ever witnessed such courage? In short they are heroes from whom the rest of us have a great deal to learn.

As far as my own family is concerned, my thank-you is simple. I love being a father, I love watching my children grow up, and I thank my children for their love and for giving me the role of a lifetime. Yes, I love hosting a TV show. The glamorous side—to the extent that it exists—serves as salve to my fragile ego. But it doesn't come close to how excited I am at being a father. If you aren't a parent yet, consider marrying and becoming one: There's nothing like it in the world.

And then there is my wife, Debbie, to whom I have now been married, thank God, for 18 years. We were both basically grown children when we first married. I was 21, and she was 19. We have since matured together into an inseparable, indivisible oneness. Life without her is inconceivable. More than any person in the world, my wife is my inspiration.

To my mother, and father, I love you and thank you for all you have been to me. Mom, you are my greatest hero. I hope one day to be as good and as kind a person as you. Abba, I hope to be as determined and as wise as you. To my brothers and sisters, Sara, Bar Kochva, Ateret, Chiam, and Iris, you are my best friends and every moment I spend with you is sheer bliss and delight.

Most important, God Almighty is He who invented the family, and it is to Him that our greatest love and thanks must be directed. And it is from Him that we must seek the blessings that families must have if they are to endure. For God's name is peace.

Rabbi Shmuley Boteach
Autumn 2006